BEYOND H

BEYOND FOSSIL LAW

Climate, Courts, and the Fight for the Future

TED HAMILTON

O/R

OR Books

New York · London

© 2021 Ted Hamilton

Published by OR Books, New York and London
Visit our website at www.orbooks.com

All rights information: rights@orbooks.com

All rights reserved. No part of this book may be reproduced or transmitted in any form or by any means, electronic or mechanical, including photocopy, recording, or any information storage retrieval system, without permission in writing from the publisher, except brief passages for review purposes.

First printing 2021

Library of Congress Cataloging-in-Publication Data: A catalog record for this book is available from the Library of Congress.
British Library Cataloging in Publication Data: A catalog record for this book is available from the British Library.

Typeset by Lapiz Digital. Printed by CPI in the United Kingdom.

paperback ISBN TKTK • ebook ISBN TKTK

Contents

To Mom and Dad

Introduction

In the fall of 2016, a group of climate activists from the Pacific Northwest sent a letter to President Obama urging action on the global warming crisis. This was the autumn of the Indigenous mobilization against the Dakota Access Pipeline at Standing Rock, of the Trump ascendancy, of the lowest sea ice ever recorded in the Arctic.[1] Climate emergency met mostly with official inertia and prevarication. The activists wrote that the lack of action to address warming "raises the practical question of what a concerned citizen should do when our governments and economic systems are committed to a course of global suicide and are willing and able to bend the political system and civic discourse to their will."

The members of the letter-writing group—Michael Foster, Leonard Higgins, Emily Johnston, Annette Klapstein, and Ken Ward—had been involved in environmental organizing for years. Their study of climate science and political change led them to believe that it was possible for society to transition away from fossil

---

1   "Unprecedented Arctic warmth in 2016 triggers massive decline in sea ice, snow," *National Ocean and Atmospheric Administration* (Dec. 13, 2016), https://www.noaa.gov/media-release/unprecedented-arctic-warmth-in-2016-triggers-massive-decline-in-sea-ice-snow.

fuels and the ecological damage they cause. "It is not that we lack the traditions and values from which a practical and moral course of action might spring," they wrote to the president. "We need only to act with thought for generations to come, respect the earth which nourishes us, cherish wild things and wild places, and value people over things, happiness over wealth, and other people over one's self."

The activists posted their letter online on the morning of October 11. Shortly afterward, they traveled separately to remote locations in Minnesota, North Dakota, Montana, and Washington. They had come prepared with bolt cutters and flowers, and they carried a message of support for the Water Protectors at Standing Rock.

"We have tried every avenue by which engaged citizens might advance such concerns—in this case, ecological—in public policy, and nothing has worked," they wrote. "There is no plausible means or mechanism by which the extraction and burning of coal and tar sands oil from existing mines and fields can be halted on the timeline now required by any ordinary, legal means."

After their friends placed warning calls to oil companies, the five activists cut padlocks and entered pipeline control sites that lay in the middle of empty fields and alongside deserted county roads. They approached valves controlling pipelines that stretched hundreds of miles in either direction. As their actions were livestreamed to the world, they turned the valves and shut the pipelines down.

"The only option available to us is to engage in climate direct action, which is why we are acting today to shut down the five pipelines used to transport tar sands oil from Alberta, CA into the US."

Pipes creaked and the ground trembled and, within minutes, fifteen percent of the country's crude oil imports was taken off-line. After they placed flowers on the valves, the activists—the "Valve Turners," as they would come to be called—waited for the police to come and arrest them.

This book is an attempt to understand the Valve Turners' action. Why did five relatively comfortable Americans take it upon themselves to break the law in the name of climate justice? Why did they argue that it was necessary—not useful or strategic, but *necessary*—to take matters into their own hands? And why was tar sands oil flowing into the United States in the first place, when every government in the world has acknowledged that such fuels must be eliminated as quickly as possible?

These questions can't be answered with citations to scientific reports or with ruminations on the intricacies of supply and demand. Instead, they require a reckoning with "fossil law": the rules and regulations that legalize the disruption of the world's climate system while prohibiting the sort of intervention undertaken by the Valve Turners. This reckoning requires not only understanding the legal system's contribution to rising carbon emissions and the suffering and injustice that these emissions produce; it also demands grabbing hold of the incipient opportunities the law offers to reverse this state of affairs.

Law is too important to leave to lawyers. All of us are subjects of fossil law, and attorneys, regulators, and judges have proven far too tardy in their confrontation with the greatest crisis of our times. To build a legal system that promotes climate justice,[2] we need a law that is both more aggressive in its protection of the environment and more equitable in its allocation of rights. The Valve Turners are a good example of democratic legal activism. They did what the state refuses to do—stop the flow of tar sands oil—and, after arrest and prosecution, they brought their campaign into county courthouses, asking jurors to find that their action was justified.

One part of this book follows the legal saga of the Valve Turners. As an effort to both expose the injustices of fossil law and to craft a more moral alternative, the Valve Turners' defense against criminal prosecution is a case study in how legal activism complements the broader political project of climate justice. The activists used a strategy called the "climate necessity defense," which seeks acquittal based on the political and ethical justification for direct action against the fossil fuel system. In a series of cases in four states, the Valve Turners earned everything from imprisonment to the first judicial recognitions of the climate necessity defense, setting crucial precedents for activists going forward. Their narrative places these cases alongside other climate necessity campaigns and shows

---

2   For a definition of climate justice, *see* the Bali Principles of Climate Justice (Aug. 29, 2002), available at https://www.iicat.org/wp-content/uploads/2012/03/Bali-Princioples-of-Climate-Justice.pdf ("Climate Justice insists that communities have the right to be free from climate change, its related impacts and other forms of ecological destruction ... Climate Justice demands that communities, particularly affected communities play a leading role in national and international processes to address climate change ... Climate Justice affirms the need for socio-economic models that safeguard the fundamental rights to clean air, land, water, food and healthy ecosystems ..."). For a definition of "just transition," also discussed in this book, *see* "Just Transition: A Framework for Change," *Climate Justice Alliance* (2020), https://climatejusticealliance.org/just-transition/ ("Just Transition is a vision-led, unifying and place-based set of principles, processes, and practices that build economic and political power to shift from an extractive economy to a regenerative economy.")

how the principled action of a small group of individuals can have a profound influence on the state's encounter with global warming.

This book's other portion explains the legal context of such activism. Four analytical chapters explore the state of the law of the climate change, with a particular focus on the United States. The existing laws and regulations on greenhouse gases, such as the Clean Air Act and the Paris Agreement, are examined in Chapter 1, alongside the potential liability of fossil fuel producers for selling products they know cause serious damage to Earth systems and human health. The focus is on litigation rather than policy, as law's particular contribution to climate change resides in the doctrines and concepts employed in court cases more than in the prescriptions of legislation.

Because the legal system's treatment of climate change has clearly been inadequate—emissions continue to rise—Chapter 2 examines the history and structure of fossil law, looking to both the way that the law has contributed to the rise of our fossil-based global economy and to the inherent limits of currently existing environmental law as it deals with the issue.

But fossil law doesn't exist only in agency regulations and court opinions. It's alive on the streets and in places like the Standing Rock Sioux Reservation, where the owners and operators of the fossil fuel system—corporations and their government backers— enforce the use of their products and the growth of their physical infrastructure. Chapter 3 looks at fossil law's police phase, show- ing how governments are building new apparatuses of legal con- trol and how Indigenous communities in particular are bearing the brunt of state violence. At the same time, opposition to oil, gas,

and coal, particularly in the form of courtroom advocacy, demonstrates that the law can at times serve as a means of institutional
subversion, with fossil fuel resisters often able to take advantage
of the legal system's shaky commitments to procedural rights and
rational argumentation to hold governments and corporations
accountable for their role in the crisis.

Fossil law grew up alongside capitalism, providing a means
for the global expansion of property rights and private enterprise
while shifting the burden of environmental destruction to the
poor and the colonized. But law is not trapped in this role of accom-
plice. Concepts of environmental rights and stewardship, too long
dormant or underdeveloped, hold the promise of abolishing fossil
law, just as the liberal legal values that today contribute to ecological catastrophe once helped to overthrow the regimes of feudal-
ism and imperialism. Chapter 4 engages with promising strands
of climate legal activism—environmental rights, the public trust
doctrine, and the rights of nature—to offer a glimpse of how the
climate law of the future is already being assembled in courts and
constitutions across the world.

Why study fossil law and climate legal activism?

In addition to its role as regulator of social conflict and environmental well-being, the law serves a cultural and interpretive
function that is crucial for understanding the climate emergency.
The law espouses the dominant view of how we should treat the
economy and the environment: in court, for example, the property interests of corporations generally trump the health concerns
of future generations. The law's historical development also sheds
light on how our irrational ordering of society is rooted in a series

of often contradictory commitments to economic growth and individual liberty. By picking apart these strands, we can identify those aspects of social self-understanding we wish to keep and amplify—respect for personal autonomy, for example—and those we wish to discard, such as the instrumental view of nature. This exercise, at once theoretical and practical, can provide a limited platform for dissident perspectives, because the law allows itself to be interrogated on its own terms. The constitutional right to equal protection under the law, for example, can be used to impugn government support for the fossil fuel industry, using the state's law to change the state's practices.

This is not to promote a legalistic view of history or social justice. The law never suffices as a singular explanation of, or strategy for, progressive change. But the law is always there. In the present moment, as our ostensibly stable political and economic orders undergo foundational transformations and as these transformations manifest in the law, the lessons of Earth systems science and decolonial politics have been particularly important in underscoring the imbrication of humanity and its planet, and of the need to attend to the vast differences of position and power within each. Law deals with such differences of position and power. We cannot move into a future of climate justice without a law that responds to this new reality, one in which our recognition and rights expand beyond the narrow confines of an anti-ecological worldview.

This book is about that expansion. The movement from fossil law to a world free from the dominance of harmful fuels represents one of the law's most pressing tasks. Because our social and natural realities are inextricable from our use of energy, this is a project concerned not only with pipelines and permits but with the basic principles of how we should live together on the Earth.

We've identified the injuries of climate change. We've decided to seek a remedy by dismantling the systems of power responsible and by replacing them with a more just order.

It's time to build our case.

CHAPTER 1

Legal Warming

On October 30, 2019, Rex Tillerson, the former CEO of ExxonMobil, sat on the stand in a Manhattan courthouse. He was answering questions from a lawyer with the New York Attorney General's office, which accused his erstwhile company of defrauding investors. Years of investigative reporting had revealed that Exxon knew about the link between fossil fuels and climate change since at least the 1960s, and that, under Tillerson's watch, the company had funded P.R. campaigns to debunk climate science and to smear anyone who linked Exxon's activities to global warming. Now the company was charged with lying to its stockholders about the value of its oil and gas reserves, which would be worthless if the global economy shifted to renewable energy.

On the stand, Tillerson—sharp suit, bouncing jowls, Texas drawl—depicted his time at Exxon as a master class in responsibility and long-term planning, and said that the company's climate strategy had favored facts over short-term financial rewards.

"What we're really trying to do is be the most realistic, present our best view of how this is going to turn out," he said.[3] "You don't fool yourself."[4]

Tillerson was right: Exxon hadn't fooled itself. It had received remarkably accurate warming predictions in the 1960s,[5] and a 1978 internal report warned that "man has a time window of five to ten years before the need for hard decisions regarding changes in energy strategies might become critical."[6] The company had even implemented a plan to price its assets that took into account the risk of climate regulations, which would make oil and gas less valuable.

The issue, though, which Tillerson seemed to want to avoid, was that ExxonMobil had been telling a different story in public. Since 1988, company strategy had been to "emphasize the uncertainty in scientific conclusions regarding the potential enhanced greenhouse effect."[7]

3   Brendan Pierson, "Former Exxon CEO Tillerson denies misleading investors in climate case," *Reuters* (Oct. 30, 2019), https://www.reuters.com/article/us-exxon-mobil-lawsuit/former-exxon-ceo-tillerson-denies-misleading-investors-in-climate-case-idUSKBN1X912M.

4   Erik Larson, "Exxon Climate Plan Wasn't Fake, Tillerson Says In N.Y. Trial," *Bloomberg* (Oct. 30, 2019), https://www.bloomberg.com/news/articles/2019-10-30/tillerson-rejects-n-y-claim-that-exxon-s-climate-plan-was-fake.

5   E. Robinson and R.C. Robbins, *Sources, Abundance, and Fate of Gaseous Atmospheric Pollutants* (Menlo Park, CA: Stanford Research Institute, 1968), https://www.smokeandfumes.org/documents/document16.

6   Neela Banerjee, Lisa Song and David Hasemyer, "Exxon's Own Research Confirmed Fossil Fuels' Role in Global Warming Decades Ago," *Inside Climate News* (Sep. 16, 2015), https://insideclimatenews.org/news/15092015/Exxons-own-research-confirmed-fossil-fuels-role-in-global-warming.

7   Katie Jennings, Dino Grandoni, and Susanne Rust, "How Exxon went from leader to sceptic on climate change research," *Los Angeles Times* (Oct. 23, 2015), https://graphics.latimes.com/exxon-research/.

"I feel bad for men and women at ExxonMobil Corp.," Tillerson told the company's lawyer during cross-examination, "because they are accused of a fraud as well. They are professionals, diligent, operate at high levels of integrity. Sometimes I wish I could step back in time and should not have put a plan in place. Maybe we should have stuck our heads in the sand."[8]

It's an apt image. Contrary to Tillerson's fanciful history, institutions like ExxonMobil have indeed done their best to enforce inaction on climate change.[9] And the legal system has not proved much of an obstacle. In the case in which Tillerson testified, for example, Judge Barry Ostrager of New York Supreme Court (an intermediate state court) found Exxon not guilty of fraud. Although he acknowledged the company's culpability in the warming crisis—"Nothing in this opinion is intended to absolve ExxonMobil from responsibility for contribution to climate change through the emission of greenhouse gases in the production of its fossil fuel products"—the judge concluded that this malfeasance was irrelevant to the narrow question of whether it had lied to investors. "ExxonMobil does not dispute that its operations produce greenhouses gases or that greenhouse gases contribute to climate change. But ExxonMobil is in the business of producing energy, and this is a securities fraud case, not a climate change case."[10]

8 Pippa Stevens, Rahel Solomon, and Patrick Manning, "Rex Tillerson says Exxon had no incentive to downplay costs, testifying in climate change fraud trial," *CNBC* (Oct. 30, 2019), https://www.cnbc.com/2019/10/30/former-exxon-chief-says-company-had-no-incentive-to-downplay-costs.html.

9 Naomi Oreskes and Eric M. Conway's *Merchants of Doubt* (New York: Bloomsbury, 2010) is the authoritative account of the fossil fuel industry's misinformation campaigns.

10 *New York v. Exxon Mobil Corporation*, No. 452044/2018 at 3 (N.Y. Sup. Ct., Dec. 10, 2019).

Much hinges on that "but." The law is a field of constraints. Judicial action to address climate change is limited by precedent, which sets rules based on past court opinions; by process, which imposes standards for the framing and filing of cases; and by politics, which restrains policy-shaping ambition. Through a combination of accident and avarice—no one intended global warming to spiral out of control, but people like Tillerson are actively abetting it—the law finds itself severely ill-equipped to deal with climate catastrophe. The sale of carbon-intensive fuels for profit is legal, few laws have been passed to deal with global warming, and old forms of legal action are a poor fit for the massively distributed problems of guilt and harm that the crisis poses. I'll call this system "fossil law": the rules and institutions that perpetuate climate change.

How did we get stuck with fossil law? How is it possible that the legal system favors the demonstrably destructive activities of ExxonMobil while at the same time persecuting those who stand in its way? And what can we do about it?

This chapter is a first step in a constructive critique of the law's encounter with climate change. Before we can understand what the law might do in addressing the climate crisis, we have to understand what it's already done—or, more accurately, what it hasn't. This requires an inquiry into precedent, process, and politics, with a mind toward not just what the law is—how a lawyer might build a case to address climate change—but towards its blind spots and failings—why the lawyer is so severely restricted in her options.

The place to start, then, is with a brief history of climate law and a survey of the existing rules and regulations that govern greenhouse gas emissions. This discussion is focused primarily on the United States, but it will also consider some examples from other countries and efforts at global climate regulation. In addition to attending to the letter of the law—the devilish details that define how courts treat global warming—this study will also consider its spirit: how the political assumptions and ideological structures that define our legal system—its heavy emphasis on individualism and private property rights, for example—rig the game in favor of the fossil fuel industry while raising serious obstacles to reform. At the same time, certain countervailing interests within the law offer the potential for moving past fossil law and toward something more liberatory and ecologically sound.

The Law of Clean Air

Congress has never passed a major law on climate change. The Supreme Court hasn't said much about it since 2007. Regulatory agencies like the Environmental Protection Agency (EPA) have either been slow to act or have had their policies thwarted by political inconstancy. The U.S. has no national standard for atmospheric carbon dioxide concentration, and caps on greenhouse gas emissions are piecemeal and weak.

That's the short version. The law of global warming in 2021 is severely underdeveloped, largely as a result of the most severe restraint on climate regulation: politics.

But that's only part of the story. The long version explains these shortcomings within the context of the precedent and process of U.S. environmental law, a relatively recent and disorganized field.

Though it didn't have a name until about fifty years ago, environmental law has always existed in some form. From the days of the first legal codes, there have been rules about what happens when someone's cattle damages someone else's land, or how to divide up access to water sources. In the United States, such questions were traditionally part of the *common law*, the judge-made set of principles and precedents inherited from England. Other matters, such as leasing schemes for mines and ranchland, usually belong to *statutory* or *constitutional law*, which is written by legislatures at the municipal, state, and federal levels. Over time, statutory law has increasingly displaced the common law as a source of environmental regulation.

The bulk of what we consider environmental law today—think the Endangered Species Act and the Clean Water Act—stems from a flurry of legislation passed by the U.S. Congress in the early seventies in response to public outrage over incidents like the Santa Barbara Oil Spill and the burning of Cleveland's Cuyahoga River. At the time, there was bipartisan, even unanimous congressional support for improving air and water quality, protecting wildlife, and curtailing industry abuse. Republican Richard Nixon advocated for and signed laws like the National Environmental Policy Act, which was designed to "encourage productive and enjoyable harmony between man and his environment."[11] The Environmental Protection Agency began administering a new scheme of monitoring and regulation in 1970, and the federal government set itself ambitious goals like eliminating all pollution into navigable waters by 1985.[12]

---

11   42 U.S.C. § 4321.

12   33 U.S.C. § 1251(a)(1).

Since 1980, however, Congress has approved no major environmental legislation, with the exception of the 1990 Clean Air Act Amendments. In 1987, Congress passed the Global Climate Protection Act, which mandated "a coordinated national policy on global climate change," but the law required no actual government action and soon became a dead letter.[13] Resistance by industry, political conservatives, and the judiciary has hampered any efforts to expand, or even fully to enforce, the promises of environment law's golden age.

Compounding this lack of congressional initiative are structural impediments to broad environmental reform. Any legislation approved by Congress—and thus any regulations based on that legislation—must be based on the powers granted by Article I of the Constitution. Article I, Section 8 allows Congress to regulate interstate commerce. This seemingly minor provision has formed the basis of huge areas of law, including federal drug prohibitions and the Civil Rights Act of 1964. It's also the basis for almost every federal environmental statute: without it, setting atmospheric lead levels and prohibiting the hunting of Florida panthers would likely be unconstitutional. This means that, under our eighteenth-century constitution—which says nothing about protecting the natural world—the U.S. government can deal with environmental issues only insofar as they relate to commerce. This restriction—a constraint of precedent—not only limits the possibilities for effective regulation, which cannot be explicitly oriented toward non-economic concerns, but also serves as a

---

13   Pub. Law No. 100-204, 101 Stat. 1331 (1987), codified at 15 U.S.C. § 2901 note.

philosophical bias toward economic interest over environmental well-being.

So it's a daunting task to regulate the use of fossil fuels with existing laws. But there are options.

The obvious place to start is the Clean Air Act (CAA). First passed in 1970 and revised in 1977 and 1990, the CAA prescribes mechanisms for the EPA to reduce the level of atmospheric pollutants such as lead and ozone. Like most statutory environmental law, it's mind-numbingly complex, and it's worth getting just a sample of the acronyms that define the field: methods for reducing pollution range from requiring the best available control technology (BACT) or the lowest achievable emission rate (LAER) to defining new source performance standards (NSPS) and national ambient air quality standards (NAAQS). The act divides the country into attainment and non-attainment zones for some pollutants, which determines what sort of state implementation plans (SIPs) are required and whether the rules of the Prevention of Significant Deterioration Program (PSD) apply. There are entirely different regimes for regulating motor vehicles versus stationary sources such as power plants.

At its most basic, and behind this flurry of administrative distinctions, the CAA requires industry to meet certain pollution targets and to secure permits for emissions. The job of implementing these complicated schemes is delegated to the EPA, which drafts regulations that carry the force of law, while state governments handle much of the permitting and enforcement.

Under the CAA, the most straightforward way for the EPA to address climate change would be to add carbon dioxide to its list of seven "criteria pollutants," the most significant sources of harm to human health. This would allow the agency to set a national standard for atmospheric carbon dioxide concentration—say, 350 parts per million, the limit that inspired the 350.org climate advocacy group—and then to implement permitting requirements to enforce that standard. This is the process that has successfully lowered levels of carbon monoxide and ozone in the air,[14] and it would be a direct way of pegging climate policy to the warming limits suggested by the Intergovernmental Panel on Climate Change (1.5 degrees Celsius)[15] and agreed upon at the Paris climate talks (two degrees, with an aspiration for 1.5).[16]

Think about it in reverse: if we had such a national standard for an acceptable concentration of atmospheric carbon dioxide, we would force anyone releasing the gas—car drivers, manufacturers, even homeowners—to keep their emissions under a certain level. This would have a direct beneficial effect on the climate, as less heat would be trapped by greenhouse gases. As a side effect, demand for fossil fuels would go down—you can't use them without releasing

14 Environmental Protection Agency, "Our Nation's Air: Status and Trends Through 2018." (2018). https://gispub.epa.gov/air/trendsreport/2019/#summary.

15 Intergovernmental Panel on Climate Change. "Summary for Policymakers." *Global warming of 1.5°C. An IPCC Special Report on the impacts of global warming of 1.5°C above pre-industrial levels and related global greenhouse gas emission pathways, in the context of strengthening the global response to the threat of climate change, sustainable development, and efforts to eradicate poverty.* V. Masson-Delmotte, P. Zhai, H. O. Pörtner, D. Roberts, J. Skea, P. R. Shukla, A. Pirani, W. Moufouma-Okia, C. Péan, R. Pidcock, S. Connors, J. B. R. Matthews, Y. Chen, X. Zhou, M. I. Gomis, E. Lonnoy, T. Maycock, M. Tignor, T. Waterfield, eds. (Geneva: World Meteorological Organization, 2018), https://www.ipcc.ch/sr15/.

16 Paris Agreement to the United Nations Framework Convention on Climate Change, Art. 2, sec, 1(a), Dec. 12, 2015, T.I.A.S. No. 16-1104.

carbon dioxide—while demand for cleaner energy sources would go up.

But the EPA hasn't done this.[17] Instead, the agency has attempted to deal with global warming through a series of more indirect, politically palatable strategies. There are good legal and practical reasons for this piecemeal approach. Making carbon dioxide a "criteria pollutant" would require each state to keep its own atmospheric concentration below the agency-determined limit of what's healthy. But given the diffuse nature of global carbon emissions, the states would have little ability to do so on their own: so long as Canada drills oil and India burns coal, the amount of CO_2 in Illinois air will remain unsafe. Given the near-impossibility of satisfying a realistic carbon limit—each state would find itself unable to lower the atmospheric concentration—such an effort would likely run into immediate implementation problems, and courts would probably strike down the agency effort as unreasonable.

Then there's the problem of politics: even the EPA's modest efforts to address climate change through strategies like mileage requirements for select classes of motor vehicles have met with stiff resistance from industry and conservatives. A far more ambitious, one-size-fits-all approach like a national standard would be doomed in today's Washington.[18]

17 Howard M. Crystal, Kassie Siegel, Maya Golden-Krasner, and Clare Lakewood. "Returning to Clean Air Act Fundamentals: A Renewed Call to Regulate Greenhouse Gases under the National Ambient Air Quality Standards (NAAQS) Program," *Georgetown Environmental Law Review* 31 (2019), 233-284; see Center for Biological Diversity and 350.org, "Petition to Establish National Pollution Limits for Greenhouse Gases Pursuant to the Clean Air Act" (Dec. 2, 2009), https://perma.cc/SU4Q-5GGE.

18 For pro-environmentalist arguments against setting a national standard for the atmospheric concentration of carbon dioxide, see Brigham Daniels, Hannah Polikov, Timothy Profeta, and James Salzman, "Regulating Climate:

A brief pause: it's actually not that useful to refer to *the* EPA. The agency's attitude toward climate change has vacillated dramatically in tandem with changing presidential administrations. Trump's second EPA administrator banished climate science from his agency's website and worked to reverse emissions reductions outlined by his own office just a few years ago.[19] Just as important as the legal efforts that the EPA has undertaken to address global warming are the political priorities dictating, and often undoing, these efforts. This is why it's important to know which administration we're dealing with when we read case titles involving the agency and its administrators—*Train v. NRDC, Whitman v. American Trucking*—because it may not be obvious whose interests the agency is protecting.

Take *Massachusetts v. EPA* (2007), still the preeminent U.S. climate change case. The Bush administration—led by two former fossil fuel executives, and, until the Trump regime, the closest thing we've had to direct rule by Big Oil—did not want to discourage carbon dioxide emissions. Its EPA had refused to issue any regulations related to greenhouse gases even as evidence of their effect on temperatures piled up, a policy that was the direct result of lobbying by

What Role for the Clean Air Act?," *Environmental Law Reporter* 39 (2009), 10837-10841.

19   Oliver Milman, "'It's a ghost page': EPA site's climate change section may be gone for good," *The Guardian* (Nov. 1, 2018), https://www.theguardian.com/us-news/2018/nov/01/epa-website-climate-change-trump-administration; Nadja Popovich, Livia Albeck-Ripka, and Kendra Pierre-Louis, "95 Environmental Rules Being Rolled Back Under Trump," *The New York Times* (Dec. 21, 2019), https://www.nytimes.com/interactive/2019/climate/trump-environment-rollbacks.html.

oil companies and a general culture of fossil-friendly corruption in the administration.[20]

The agency was sued by several states, cities, and environmental organizations who claimed that climate change and the agency's inaction in addressing it were causing environmental damage like coastal erosion. They demanded that the EPA respond to a petition for limits on carbon dioxide from motor vehicles (at the time, the U.S. transportation sector accounted for 6 percent of total global emissions). At the Supreme Court, the EPA argued that the CAA had never been intended to give the agency the sort of industry-shaping power that regulating the gas would entail, and said that its only legal option was to refuse to consider the issue altogether.

The Supreme Court didn't buy it. Writing for a 5–4 majority, Justice John Paul Stevens found that anthropogenic global warming was real, that it was causing serious damage, and that the agency had to decide one way or another whether excessive carbon dioxide was harmful. On the basic question of whether carbon dioxide qualifies as an "air pollutant" under the Clean Air Act, the Court was clear: it is, and the agency has the authority to regulate it. The Court also rejected the government's arguments that it wasn't responsible for the problem, that climate science was still murky, and that any regulations would be insufficient to redress the states' and cities' injuries.[21]

Massachusetts v. EPA was most significant for clearing up certain questions about process, the biggest constraint on the filing of climate change lawsuits. The Supreme Court found that the

20   Mary Wood, *Nature's Trust* (Cambridge University Press, 2013), 24-33.

21   *Massachusetts v. EPA*, 549 U.S. 497 (2007).

plaintiffs were being harmed by the effects of global warming and that they had a right to sue over this injury. This was a rebuke to the government's position that, given the diffuse and uncertain nature of climate change effects, court proceedings were an inappropriate forum for resolving the issue. By providing an opening on the process front, the Supreme Court also dealt a political defeat to the oil industry and its allies, and created an important precedent for climate advocates, who could point to the nation's highest court in support of their claims that climate change was serious and that it was the government's responsibility to do something about it. In the end, though, the practical effect of the decision was limited: the EPA was simply directed to consider the issue, not to take any specific action.[22]

The Dawn of Climate Regulation?

Massachusetts v. EPA narrowly allowed climate regulation to proceed, and so presented a real threat to companies like ExxonMobil. For a few years, it seemed as though the federal government was finally getting into the game of global warming policy. Shortly after the decision, the EPA released an endangerment finding on carbon dioxide. The Obama administration used this legal hook to issue the first direct federal effort to cap greenhouse gas emissions: the 2010 Tailpipe Rule, which set gas-mileage standards for new vehicles.[23] Even the automotive industry supported the new scheme.

22 Richard Lazarus's *The Rule of Five* (Harvard University Press, 2020) is the authoritative account of this case, examining the tension between political demands and environmental legal standards and the difficult strategic decisions faced by environmental lawyers trying to address new problems using outdated laws.

23 40 CFR Parts 85, 86, and 600; 49 CFR Parts 531, 533, and 536 (May 7, 2010).

Building off this success, the government sought next to cap carbon dioxide emissions from stationary sources.

It's important to grasp how technical climate law can be, so let's get into the weeds again. The Obama EPA's Tailpipe Rule reinterpreted a CAA provision allowing regulation of sources that released "any air pollutant" in excess of 100 or 250 tons per year, depending on industrial category. The rule triggered other sections of the law that would allow greenhouse gas limits on stationary sources like coal plants. But, as noted above, carbon dioxide is far more prevalent than other pollutants; regulating at these levels would have made millions of facilities, including schools and churches, subject to permit requirements. The agency decided to adjust the threshold for regulation to 100,000 tons per year in order to reflect this reality.

This did not go off without a hitch. Industry groups joined with conservative state attorneys general to challenge the new stationary source rule, and climate change soon found itself back on the docket of the Supreme Court.

This time—perhaps because the justices were considering an actual exercise of regulatory power rather than the more speculative question of whether to acknowledge the problem at all—the court largely sided against the environmentalists. In *Utility Air Regulatory Group v. EPA (UARG)*, the justices held that the agency's interpretation of the CAA, represented an "enormous and transformative expansion in EPA's regulatory authority without clear congressional authorization."[24] If the EPA were allowed to create a whole new category of regulated entities—those that emit at least

24   573 U.S. 302, 324 (2014).

100,000 tons of carbon dioxide—then the agency would have the power to reshape the economy, as such sources are fundamental to our existing fossil fuel-driven system. Congress had never signaled that reducing greenhouse gases was a policy meriting such disruption.

In an admirable moment of jurisprudential finesse, the court majority nonetheless saved the regulatory program by allowing the EPA to accomplish its goal in a more roundabout way. Rather than applying a universal standard to all stationary sources, the agency would limit the new carbon dioxide permit requirements to sources already emitting another "criteria pollutant" such as sulfur dioxide. Because Congress *had* approved broad regulatory efforts to control these criteria pollutants, it was appropriate to issue new restrictions for sources that emitted them. Practically, because so many of the plants and factories that emit 100,000 tons of CO_2 also emit another criteria pollutant, this tweak had nearly the same effect as the rule that the agency had originally proposed. But the Court's rebuke was a shot across the bow for the Obama EPA: by discouraging creative fixes to an antiquated law, the court had suggested that the CAA provided limited resources for addressing global warming.[25]

The Obama administration built on this mixed victory to issue the most significant federal climate effort yet: the 2015 Clean Power Plan. The Plan aimed to phase out coal-burning electrical plants, relying on Section 111(d) of the CAA, which governs how states regulate non-hazardous and non-"criteria" pollutants. Because of the

25   Jody Freeman, "Why I Worry About UARG," *Harvard Environmental Law Review* 39, no. 9 (2015), 9-22.

CAA's complexity and lack of provisions directly addressing CO_2, the agency again had to find creative ways of targeting a gas that the law was never meant to handle. It encouraged untraditional interventions "outside the fence line" of the polluting sources themselves, such as improvements in electrical grid efficiency, incentives for natural gas, and subsidies for renewable energy. All told, the Plan aimed by 2030 to reduce power sector carbon emissions to 32 percent of 2005 levels.[26]

As expected, conservatives maligned the Plan as regulatory overreach, and twenty-seven states, joined by energy companies, sued to stop it. (One leader of this effort, Scott Pruitt, then the attorney general of Oklahoma, would soon head the agency he was attacking.) Their arguments were familiar: the EPA was overstepping its authority and interfering in economic activity it had no right to disturb. Even Laurence Tribe, a leading liberal lawyer who was hired by Peabody Energy to fight the Plan, said that the agency was "burning the Constitution."[27] The case wound its way up the court system as the 2016 presidential election approached, and several states, anticipating that some version of the Plan would survive, began implementing its changes.

Then, in February 2016, the Supreme Court made a radical move. It intervened in the ongoing case and, without any legal findings, halted the Plan before a lower court had a chance to review it.[28] The Court had never done this before; in every other instance,

26   80 Fed. Reg. at 64,661-64,120 (to be codified at 40 CFR Part 60) (Oct. 23, 2015).

27   Erica Martinson, "Laurence Tribe, Obama's legal mentor, attacks EPA power plant rule," *Politico* (March 20, 2015), https://www.politico.com/story/2015/03/epa-power-plant-rule-laurence-tribe-116258.

28   *West Virginia v. EPA*, No. 15A773 (U.S. Feb. 9, 2016) (interim order granting

a regulation goes into effect unless and until some court finds it legally problematic.[29] Though the Court provided no justification for its extraordinary "stay" of the Plan, it wasn't difficult to conclude that the justices had reached the limits of their tolerance for creative regulation under the CAA. In *Massachusetts v. EPA*, the Court had narrowly forced the EPA to make a decision on CO_2's dangers. In *UARG*, it had limited carbon reduction regulations to sources already regulated under another part of the law. The Clean Power Plan aimed to impose a more generalized CO_2 suppression policy, a goal in line with Congress's goal of reducing air pollution but one whose specific and wide-ranging application had never received legislative approval. The lack of a clear legislative signal probably motivated the Supreme Court's intervention. As happens again and again in federal courts, restraining regulatory ambition took precedence over badly needed reform.

The death knell for the Clean Power Plan came with another unprecedented development: Donald Trump's election. The Trump administration was a bulwark of fossil fuel boosterism and climate change denial, positions that dovetail with white nationalism and the consolidation of oligarchic power. Trump campaigned on a fantasy of "clean coal," suggested that global warming is a "Chinese hoax," and, once the Koch brothers' political machine got over its initial distaste for his protectionist rhetoric, earned the unstinting

stay of the Clean Power Plan).

29 See Adam Liptak and Coral Davenport, "Supreme Court Deals Blow to Obama's Efforts to Regulate Coal Emissions," *The New York Times* (Feb. 9, 2016), https://www.nytimes.com/2016/02/10/us/politics/supreme-court-blocks-obama-epa-coal-emissions-regulations.html ("[T]he Supreme Court had never before granted a request to halt a regulation before review by a federal appeals court.").

support of fossil fuel companies and their Washington mouthpiec-
es.[30] Pruitt, a man who's made a career of protecting big business
from accountability, was installed as head of the EPA. Rex Tillerson
left ExxonMobil to assume his first public position as secretary
of state, neatly signaling the fossil fuel industry's role as global
hegemon. Across the federal government, climate change initiatives were stalled or canceled, and within months of entering office
Trump announced his intention to withdraw the United States
from the Paris Agreement (more on Paris in a bit). The Supreme
Court never had to review the Clean Power Plan because the EPA
cancelled it.

Some highlights from the Trumpocene: in December 2018,
new performance standards for coal plants were rolled back.[31] In
June 2019, the EPA announced its final plan to replace the Clean
Power Plan with the Affordable Clean Energy Rule, which—under
the cover of abiding by the agency's previous finding that carbon
dioxide emissions posed a health threat—essentially abandoned
the goal of reducing emissions from power generation. Binding
pollution limits were eliminated and the focus on "outside the
fence line" measures was scrapped.[32] Obama-era motor vehicle
regulations were stalled, replaced with a new Safer, Affordable,
Fuel-Efficient Vehicles Rule that froze gas-mileage targets at the

30 Brian Kahn and Bobby Magill, "A Trump Budget Could Decimate Climate
    Funding," *Climate Central* (Nov. 23, 2016), https://www.climatecentral.org/
    news/trump-budget-climate-funding-20907.

31 "Trump's EPA Plans To Ease Carbon Emissions Rule For New Coal Plants,"
    NPR (Nov. 6, 2018), https://www.npr.org/2018/12/06/674255402/trumps-
    epa-plans-to-ease-carbon-emissions-rule-for-new-coal-plants.

32 Lisa Friedman, "States Sue Trump Administration Over Rollback of Oba-
    ma-Era Climate Rule," *The New York Times* (Aug. 13, 2019), https://www.
    nytimes.com/2019/08/13/climate/states-lawsuit-clean-power-ace.html.

2020 level, around thirty-seven miles per gallon on average.[33] Meanwhile, the EPA endeavored to make it easier to frack without controlling for emissions of methane and other pollutants.[34]

Unsurprisingly, the Trump administration used the COVID-19 pandemic to prop up the U.S. fossil fuel industry which, in early 2020, faced severe economic threats in the form of plunging oil prices (a result of a Saudi effort to wrest back control of the global market), the collapse of the fracking bubble, and competition from renewables. With executive branch support, oil, gas, and coal companies benefited from bailout payouts, favorable changes to tax law, and the waiver of several environmental standards.[35]

These rollbacks were met with legal resistance, of course. Environmental advocates enjoyed a bit of a grace period in the first half of the administration, as Pruitt's anti-regulatory zeal and penchant for petty self-enrichment caused him to commit a series of legal and political blunders. For a while, nearly all of the administration's hasty efforts were overturned in court.[36]

---

33 49 CFR 85, 86, 523, 531, 533, 536, and 537 (March 30, 2020); Juliet Eilperin and Brady Dennis, "Trump administration to revoke California's power to set stricter auto emissions standards," *The Washington Post* (Sep. 17, 2019), https://www.washingtonpost.com/climate-environment/trump-administration-to-revoke-californias-power-to-set-stricter-auto-emissions-standards/2019/09/17/79af2ee0-d97b-11e9-a688-303693fb4b0b_story.html.

34 Marianne Lavelle, "Trump EPA Tries Again to Roll Back Methane Rules for Oil and Gas Industry," *Inside Climate News* (Aug. 30, 2019), https://insideclimatenews.org/news/29082019/methane-regulation-oil-gas-storage-pipelines-epa-rollback-trump-wheeler.

35 "Pro-Polluter Pandemic Priorities," *Climate Power 2020* (May 28, 2020), https://www.climatepower2020.org/resources/pro-polluter-pandemic-priorities/; Gregory Brew, "Saudi Arabia's Weaponization of Oil Abundance," *Middle East Research and Information Project* (March 20, 2020), https://merip.org/2020/03/saudi-arabias-weaponization-of-oil-abundance/.

36 Andy Kroll, "Meet the Lawyers Beating Back Trump's Reckless Environmental Policies—and Winning," *Rolling Stone* (Sep. 20, 2019), https://www.rollingstone.com/politics/politics-features/meet-the-lawyers-beat-

One strength of our environmental law system is its heavy research and procedural requirements: rules need to be backed up with reams of scientific evidence, which makes it hard for administrations to push through policy changes that directly contradict the evidence already on record. Taking advantage of this, states, cities, and environmental organizations sued to stop the Trump EPA's every move. Most notably, the administration found itself in a high-profile fight with the state government of California, which has long enjoyed a special exemption allowing it to set its own rules for vehicle gas mileage. Under the EPA's new rule, the entire nation had to follow one plan, and any state effort to set stricter standards was presumptively illegal.[37]

No doubt the Biden administration will unwind many of these anti-regulatory measures. The new president has signaled a commitment to reducing carbon pollution, bringing back Obama-era environmental advisers and creating new climate advisory positions. He has promised a plan to reduce emissions to net-zero by 2050.[38] And already at the end of 2020, the second COVID-19 relief bill included expanded funding for renewable energy and a measure to severely reduce the release of warming-intensive hydrofluorocarbons.[39]

ing-back-trumps-reckless-environmental-policies-and-winning-887321/.

37   Coral Davenport, "California Sues the Trump Administration in Its Escalating War Over Auto Emissions," *The New York Times* (Sep. 20, 2019), https://www.nytimes.com/2019/09/20/climate/california-auto-emissions-lawsuit.html.

38   Scott Detrow, Tamara Keith, and Jennifer Ludden, "Biden To Name Gina McCarthy, Former EPA Chief, As Domestic Climate Coordinator," *NPR* (Dec. 15, 2020), https://www.npr.org/sections/biden-transition-updates/2020/12/15/945937035/biden-to-name-gina-mccarthy-former-epa-chief-as-domestic-climate-coordinator.

39   Coral Davenport, "Climate Change Legislation Included in Coronavirus

What hasn't changed is the tenor of the legal debate. Fossil fuel supporters and judicial conservatives bemoan regulatory interference in the market, while environmental advocates promote complicated schemes built on shaky legislative authority. Despite the CAA, despite *Massachusetts v. EPA*, and despite the Clean Power Plan, federal regulation of greenhouse gas emissions remains at roughly the same place it was a half century ago.

To better understand this impasse, it's worth returning to *Massachusetts v. EPA* for a moment. In that case, Chief Justice Roberts wrote a dissenting opinion. Dissents are, by definition, non-binding: they express the loser's side of a case. But in our system of common law, judges often reprise these losing ideas in future decisions. Roberts's dissent, which contains many of the main arguments still leveled against climate legal advocacy, is particularly troubling because it came in a closely decided case—5 to 4—and because the Court is more in line with Roberts's anti-regulatory position today than it was in 2007: after Trump's successful nomination of three remarkably conservative justices, the nation's highest tribunal will likely remain solidly right-wing for many years. We can thus consider Roberts' words as a summary of the main pillars of a still dominant fossil law.

Roberts maintained that the states and cities had no standing to bring their case against the EPA—a classic process argument. The rules for standing require harms and remedies to be "particularized" (specific to the litigants in a case). But global warming affects everyone, so, Roberts reasoned, there was no way to distinguish the

Relief Deal," *The New York Times* (Dec. 21, 2020), https://www.nytimes.com/2020/12/21/climate/climate-change-stimulus.html.

petitioners from the public at large. What's more, the effects of climate change are too distant in the future to be considered "imminent," another requirement for standing. Roberts found it doubtful that any action by the EPA would significantly reduce warming anyway: other countries, notably China, were already surpassing the United States in their greenhouse gas contributions. What this all amounted to for the chief justice was "the evident mismatch between the source of [the plaintiffs'] alleged injury—catastrophic global warming—and the narrow subject matter of the Clean Air Act provision at issue in this suit."[40] In other words, the climate crisis was so massive that it didn't make sense for the EPA to do anything about it.

This reasoning is common in pro-fossil fuel and anti-regulatory circles. If global warming is too large and diffuse to effectively target using existing laws, then we have no choice but to sit on our hands and wait until Congress passes a new statute. Considered in light of the need for urgent climate action, the best way to describe Roberts's argument is that he favored form over fact and abstract legal principles over the public good. At least in matters that threaten established economic power, these are hallmarks of conservative jurisprudence and fossil law.

But if we sever Roberts's ideas from their context and consequences, even leftist lawyers might agree with their gist. The CAA wasn't written to address climate change, and it's not well-equipped to do so. The statute's provisions are mostly geared toward small releases of particularly noxious chemicals, not enormous emissions of a gas that, like carbon dioxide, forms the

40   *Massachusetts v. EPA*, 535–548 (Roberts, J., dissenting).

basis for life on Earth (this was the issue in *UARG*).[41] Current rules on standing, which forced the states and cities in *Massachusetts v. EPA* to distinguish themselves from the public at large by arguing that their climate-related harms merit special attention, are also a poor fit for the massively distributed problem of global warming. And the federal government's response to climate change should be more comprehensive, and should have greater political force behind it, than a set of regulations based upon interpretations of a law more than forty years old. Most people would agree that there is indeed an "evident mismatch" between the crisis and the laws we have to address it: we need a better legal process for entertaining climate claims, and we need much stronger precedent and legislative authority to justify regulatory action (ideas for how to do this are discussed in Chapter 4).

On the other hand, if we adopt a pragmatic approach to the law, then it makes no sense to ignore the climate crisis just because we lack the perfect legal tools to stop it. The history of progressive legal activism in the United States has shown time and again that social and ecological values can trump inherited common law principles and the legal system's internal norms of procedure. In 1905, the Supreme Court ruled in *Lochner v. New York* that states couldn't limit working hours because such regulations violated the freedom

---

41   For the countervailing view that the Clean Air Act was in fact designed to provide the EPA with flexibility to regulate public health threats like climate change and that the Clean Power Plan perfectly accords with this statutory intent, see the amicus brief submitted by Thomas C. Jorling in a legal challenge to the Trump administration's repeal of the Plan: Corrected Brief of Thomas C. Jorling as Amicus Curiae in Support of State and Municipal, Public Health Environmental, Power Company, and Clean Energy Trade Association Petitioners, *American Lung Association v. EPA*, No. 19-1140 (D.C. Cir. Apr. 20, 2020).

to contract, a cherished common law ideal.[42] Had labor activists agreed to abide by this purportedly inviolable principle, *Lochner* would still be the law of the land, and we would have no minimum wage laws or rules on overtime pay. But, despite the property-protecting imperatives of ostensibly sacrosanct principles, idealistic lawyers and organizers have continued to fight corporate power and government inaction. Their approach is to take the law's precedent, process, and politics not as eternal verities to be obeyed, but as constraints to be overcome and reimagined. This is precisely the attitude we need in order to dismantle fossil law.

The Periphery of Public Law

The CAA is the still the starting point for a study of the U.S. law of climate change, but it's not the only bit of statutory environmental law that lawyers and regulators have used to confront global warming. Advocates have had some success in using provisions of the Endangered Species Act to push back against projects whose greenhouse gas emissions will harm rare animals' habitats. They continue to cite the National Environmental Policy Act, which requires government agencies to assess the environmental impact of their projects: since 1990, courts have sometimes found that the impact statements required under the law must include an assessment of climate change consequences, such as when a new railroad will increase the amount of coal available on the market. The Obama administration even made agency review of global warming impacts mandatory. In 2020, though, the Trump administration made significant changes to ways in which federal agencies

---

42   198 U.S. 45 (1905).

implement the statute, imposing limits on the length and preparation time of environmental impact statements and eliminating the requirement to consider the cumulative environmental effects of federal actions—an especially important consideration for global warming.[43] In the midst of the coronavirus crisis, the administration further instructed agencies to expedite infrastructure projects and to waive environmental review requirements when possible,[44] although the order was rather vague and unlikely to result in serious changes to existing standards.[45]

It is also important to consider state laws, especially given the policy volatility at the federal level. State legislators have recently started to act with some degree of urgency and, in six states, have passed laws that mandate a near-total elimination of fossil fuels in power generation. California's SB 100, passed in 2018, commits the state to totally renewable electricity production by 2045.[46] The 2019 New York Climate Leadership and Community Protection Act mandates carbon-free electricity by 2040 and net-zero emissions by 2050. Hawaii, New Mexico, Nevada, and Washington have passed similar legislation.[47] Because they recognize the scope of the crisis and

---

43   Council on Environmental Quality, Update to the Regulations Implementing the Procedural Provisions of the National Environmental Policy Act, 85 Fed. Reg. 43304 (July 16, 2020) (codified at 40 C.F,R § 1500-1508 and 1515-1518).

44   Exec. Order 13,927, 85 Fed. Reg. 35165 (June 4, 2020).

45   Dan Farber, "Trump's Latest Deregulatory Ploy: Emergency Waivers," *Legal Planet* (June 8, 2020), https://legal-planet.org/2020/06/08/trumps-latest-deregulatory-ploy-emergency-waivers/

46   Jennifer Lu, "California is set to go carbon-free by 2045," *Popular Science* (Sep. 10, 2019), https://www.popsci.com/california-100-percent-renewable/.

47   David Roberts, "New York just passed the most ambitious climate target in the country," *Vox* (July 22, 2019), https://www.vox.com/energy-and-environment/2019/6/20/18691058/new-york-green-new-deal-climate-change-cuomo.

propose concrete commitment to eliminating fossil fuels, these laws represent significant progress and serve as a model for federal legislation. At the very least—even if the initial emissions reduction targets are missed—advocates can use them to hold leaders accountable.

In court, activists have also used state laws to demand that state governments take climate into consideration on everything from power purchasing agreements to forest conservation plans, and they've pushed back on state approvals for pipelines and natural gas facilities, citing the dangers of global warming.[48]

One of the more successful statute-based strategies has been the Sierra Club's Beyond Coal campaign. Relying upon an array of technical and procedural requirements in state laws and the CAA, Beyond Coal lawyers have forced the shutdown or blocked the opening of hundreds of coal plants across the country. They've done this by showing that a coal plant would threaten an endangered clover, convincing utilities that the cost of required pollution controls would be prohibitive for taxpayers, or pointing out when operations permits are expired. A classic environmental law strategy—heavy on expert knowledge and devoted to the devil in the law's details—the campaign has found an ingenious way of targeting emissions without the need for comprehensive climate regulation. Its success is built on the fact that, in the absence of sustained scrutiny, government officials regularly approve fossil fuel projects despite legal violations.[49]

48   The best collection of information on climate change cases is the Columbia
      University Sabin Center for Climate Change Law's Climate Change Litiga-
      tion Database, which provides updates on all the efforts mentioned here:
      http://climatecasechart.com/us-climate-change-litigation/.

49   Michael Grunwald, "Inside the war on coal," *Politico* (May 26, 2015), https://
      www.politico.com/agenda/story/2015/05/inside-war-on-coal-000002/;

But these efforts, important as they are—and, in the case of Beyond Coal, as effective as they've been at preventing particularly noxious pollution—suffer from the same weakness as the long and tortuous campaign to instrumentalize the CAA: they use yesterday's weapons to fight today's war. Statutory environmental law by and large looks at discrete impacts and encourages cost-benefit analysis and economic stability. It has proven inadequate for coping with the large, long-term, and diffuse nature of greenhouse gas pollution, let alone the fundamental challenges that the climate crisis poses to our current economic and political order. Much of this failure must be laid at the feet of politicians who have recoiled from using the legal tools that do exist to attack global warming. But if many conservative Supreme Court justices and federal judges view even the Clean Power Plan as an illegitimate application of environmental law, then, in addition to pushing the law's current limits, we also must radically update its ambition and scope.

"This Egregious State of Affairs Is No Accident"

But wait—didn't we just see Rex Tillerson, ex-CEO of ExxonMobil and ex-secretary of state, sitting in a Manhattan courthouse and defending his record on global warming? That case was a securities fraud action, distant from the sort of lawsuit that directly addresses emissions regulation under the CAA. But it was an important reminder that there are other options for climate lawyers, and other reasons why fossil fuel executives might be worried about their legal exposure.

Sierra Club, "America, Let's Move Beyond Coal" (2019), https://content. sierraclub.org/coal/.

Recall that most modern environmental law derives from statutes passed since the 1970s. Alongside this main current of environmental law, litigation rooted in the common law—judge-made law with English roots—persists. In recent years, it's become one of the main areas of climate legal creativity, and, so long as conservative interpretations of the CAA constrict the EPA's power to combat emissions, it's the most likely source of progressive global warming jurisprudence.

The main item to consider on the common law side of things is the law of torts, or private wrongs and injuries. This is an area of the legal system with which most Americans are passingly familiar: tort cases involve private harms like cutting down your neighbor's tree or selling a defective space heater, as well as the complicated toxics litigation seen in movies like *A Civil Action* and *Erin Brockovich*. People suffering from the effects of climate change have understandably turned to tort as a way to seek compensation for their injuries and to stop the activities that cause them.

Such cases usually involve one or more of the following claims: *nuisance* (property damage caused by another's irresponsible actions), *negligence* (failing to control for the foreseeable effects of an activity or product), or *trespass* (unauthorized encroachment on land, usually referring in this instance to rising sea levels). Unlike the CAA provisions applied to carbon dioxide emissions, these are age-old legal principles that judges feel comfortable picking apart and applying because they don't involve sticky questions about agency authority and congressional intent, at least not on their face.

Take a classic of environmental law courses: in *Boomer v. Atlantic Cement*, an upstate New York cement company was sued for the nuisance it caused to its neighbors—clouds of dust, persistent vibrations, excruciating noise. The court ordered the company to pay local residents damages to compensate for these harms, but, balancing the economic benefits of the plant, stopped short of shutting down the factory's operation. No questions of constitutional authority or agency discretion were involved: just a group of private parties, an injury, and a court reasoning its way to the best solution.[50]

The analogy to fossil fuels is easy. Say you live by the coast. Your house, formerly safe from the high-tide line, now floods every year. Certain companies knowingly sell products that contribute to sea level rise, and you ask a court to find them liable. With the degree and clarity of our knowledge about the effects of climate change, and with research demonstrating the outsize responsibility of a small number of firms, it'd be reasonable to think that such tort claims are an ideal legal tool for climate advocates. Oil, gas, and coal companies could be made to pay for the foreseeable effects of their products' use, and some cases might even result in injunctions, or court orders to cease the harmful behavior.

A major test of this strategy came in *American Electric Power Co. v. Connecticut (AEP)*, a Supreme Court case decided in 2011. Eight states, along with New York City and a group of land trusts, sued utilities for climate-related harms to human and natural health. The EPA, in its 2009 endangerment finding, had recently acknowledged that excessive carbon dioxide was a problem, though it had yet to issue its major climate regulations. The plaintiffs asked the court to apply tort principles to the electric utilities' emissions of

50   26 N.Y.2d 219 (1970).

greenhouse gases and to make the defendants pay for their noxious consequences.

You might think that the court would look favorably on these claims in light of *Massachusetts v. EPA*. But the justices cited a doctrine known as "displacement," according to which the judiciary should get out of the way of the legislature and its delegates once they've signaled their intent to deal with an issue. In the area of climate change, the court reasoned, the CAA covered the territory, and it was left to the EPA to figure out the best way to deal with the plaintiffs' problems; judges are simply too inexpert to deal with the scientific complexities involved, and it's not proper for them to intervene in such an economically consequential issue. Going forward, the court ruled, climate change claims could no longer be brought under "federal common law": any avenues for redress opened up by tort law were now foreclosed.[51]

Note the irony here. In 2007, the Supreme Court found that the EPA was bound to make some sort of decision about the dangers of carbon dioxide emissions. This seemed to herald an era of

51   546 U.S. 410. *AEP* followed *California v. General Motors*, a 2007 case in which the state sought damages from vehicle manufacturers for their contributions to global warming. A federal district court dismissed the state's nuisance claims, ruling—like the Supreme Court in *AEP*—that any finding of liability would require it to improperly interfere in policy decisions. No. C06-05755 MJJ (N.D. Cal. Sept. 17, 2007). In 2012, a related case reached the Ninth Circuit Court of Appeals, where Alaskan native villagers sought damages from energy companies for melting sea ice and coastal erosion that were destroying their homes. The Ninth Circuit cited *AEP* to toss the case out. But there was a silver lining: the court did not accept the energy companies' arguments that any sort of judicial ruling on climate change would improperly interfere in a "political question," or that any future defendants making similar claims would lack standing because of the complications of global warming causation. This left the door open to litigation not blocked by the displacement doctrine: namely, state cases in which the EPA's actions do not foreclose further action based on state common law. *Native Village of Kivalina v. ExxonMobil Corp.*, 696 F.3d 849 (9th Cir. 2012).

judicial attention to global warming. But, once the justices had told the agency to make a decision, the EPA—whether it confronted the problem, as with its Clean Power Plan, or whether it ignored it, as with its Trump-era reversals—now officially owned the issue. People couldn't come seeking help in federal courts anymore. Principle of process and politics—administrative law trumping tort law, and the legislative branch trumping the judicial branch—stood in the way of effective climate action.

R. Henry Weaver and Doug Kysar attribute the Supreme Court's reluctance to entertain common law climate claims to a broader judicial failure to engage with the issue. "[C]limate change plaintiffs have obliged courts to choose between denial and nihilism," Weaver and Kysar write. "Most judges have preferred the latter." These judges use "a variety of self-limiting procedural and jurisdictional doctrines" to toss climate plaintiffs out of court, sticking to old-fashioned notions of individual action and strict causation rather than "thinking ecologically"—that is, confronting honestly the complex problems of attribution, responsibility, and harm that the climate crisis involves.[52] The point is not that judges should lead the charge in defining the perpetrators and victims of global warming; it's that they should follow the facts.

The question of how active the federal courts should be in deciding major social issues is one that's been around since the country's founding. It has no obvious ideological valence: conservatives cry judicial activism when the Supreme Court leads the way in racial and gender justice, while liberals call foul when the Court

52   "Courting Disaster: Climate Change and the Adjudication of Catastrophe," *Notre Dame Law Review* 93, no. 1 (2017), 295-356, 313, 340, 354.

expands corporate rights or sanctions presidential lawbreaking. To repeat a point, the problem—what the law should do about climate change—can't be resolved by reference to abstract principles. Courts don't exist in a vacuum.

Luckily, *AEP* didn't shut down climate tort cases altogether. The Supreme Court has its say over *federal* common law; *state* common law is a different matter, one in which federal courts have limited authority. The "displacement" problem arising from federal legislation and regulation disappears: state courts can, at least in theory, continue to consider matters that federal agencies are also responsible for addressing, like whether plastic bags are a public health hazard, and they can make their own decisions about whether climate harms are being adequately addressed by the other branches of government.

A new generation of climate cases is built on this possibility. Their claims are not so different from those in *AEP*: fossil fuel companies have knowingly peddled a product that's damaging public health and property, and they should pay for it. Starting in 2017, a slew of city and county lawsuits were filed using this premise: *County of Santa Cruz v. Chevron, City of Oakland v. B.P., Rhode Island v. Chevron, New York City v. B.P.*, and others. These cases point out that oil giants have devoted massive sums to preventing any action on climate, and so—especially in light of the $649 billion in subsidies that their products receive from the federal government[53]—it seems fair for them to chip in for measures like seawalls and cooling centers. As stated in the Oakland lawsuit: "This

---

53   Tim Dickinson, "Study: U.S. Fossil Fuel Subsidies Exceed Pentagon Spending," *Rolling Stone* (May 8, 2019), https://www.rollingstone.com/politics/politics-news/fossil-fuel-subsidies-pentagon-spending-imf-report-833035/.

egregious state of affairs is no accident . . . Even today, with the global warming danger at a critical phase, Defendants continue to engage in massive fossil fuel production and execute long-term business plans to continue and even expand their fossil fuel production for decades into the future."[54]

As in any other tort law case, the cities and counties need to prove that the fossil fuel companies had a legal *duty*: they're not allowed to knowingly destroy coastlines, for instance. They also have to show a *violation*: the companies did in fact destroy the coastlines. This violation must have resulted in an *injury*: the coastline's destruction harmed people and their property. As we know, the science is pretty tight on these questions. So the companies will dance around the issue by contesting *causation*—you can't draw a direct line between pumping oil and flooding in lower Manhattan; argue against *attribution*—we contributed only a tiny part of all the carbon dioxide in the atmosphere; and wave away *responsibility*—we only sold these products, it's the consumers who actually burned them.

These cases are still ongoing, so it's premature to predict where the courts will finally land. Some judges have followed the Supreme Court's lead in *AEP* and ruled that Congress should deal with the issue, while others have kicked the cases back to the federal judiciary because they think that global warming is a national rather than local problem. (When federal law trumps state law like this, it's called *precedence*. Follow the precedence path, and you find

54 *Oakland v. BP P.L.C.*, Complaint for Public Nuisance, No. RG17875889 at 2 (Cal. Super. Ct. Sep. 19, 2017).

yourself back before the wall of *displacement*: statutory law trumps judge-made law. If there's no good statutory law, you're out of luck.)

On the other hand, some of the new lawsuits are proceeding apace, and there are promising signs that these will soon be litigated in more environmentally friendly state courts. For example, in March 2020, the federal Fourth Circuit Court of Appeals ruled that the City of Baltimore's lawsuit against BP and other oil companies belonged in state court, where it is sure to face better odds. The case now appears set for a state court trial on theories of nuisance, strict liability, negligent product design, and violation of consumer protection laws.[55] The Ninth Circuit made a similar decision in the California lawsuits two months later.[56] In all these cases, appeals will likely drag on for years, and it's worth noting that the Trump Department of Justice worked behind the scenes with oil industry defendants to defeat the cases.[57]

The CAA, other environmental laws, tort law: these represent the climate law core. Efforts to halt global warming in this core have had mixed results at best. There's been no major court ruling ordering a draw-down in greenhouse gas emissions and federal regulatory efforts have been entirely inconsistent; on the other hand, action at the state level is ramping up and showing signs of rapid progress.

---

55   *Mayor and City Council of Baltimore v. BP p.l.c.*, No. 19-1644 (4th Cir. Mar. 6, 2020).

56   *Oakland v. BP P.L.C*, No. 18-16663 (9th Cir. May 26, 2020).

57   David Hasemyer, "Emails Reveal U.S. Justice Dept. Working Closely with Oil Industry to Oppose Climate Lawsuits," *Inside Climate News* (Jan. 13, 2020), https://insideclimatenews.org/news/10012020/emails-show-us-justice-department-working-closely-oil-industry-oppose-climate-lawsuits.

But not all legal victories occur in obvious places. Sometimes tangential matters prove pivotal in a courtroom, as with Al Capone's famous conviction on tax fraud. Might there be cause for hope at climate law's margins?

Let's return to Rex Tillerson's star turn in the Manhattan courthouse. That case, a securities fraud action, was not strictly about ExxonMobil's contribution to climate change. Instead, it was about whether the company had lied to its stockholders when it predicted the effect that potential climate regulation might have on the value of its fossil fuel holdings. While such a question obviously involves some of the fundamental facts about global warming and its origins, the ultimate outcome would have nothing to do with the propriety of extractive activities or the duty of the government to address them. Instead, it would have to do with the company's denial and misinformation. The attorneys general of Massachusetts, Minnesota, and the District of Columbia have brought similar cases, all of which are in their early stages.[58] Despite ExxonMobil's victory in New York, this type of lawsuit might force accountability and eventual changes in corporate behavior, even as the main question of climate change harms remains unaddressed.

In a related vein, environmentalists have sued ExxonMobil and its peers for failing to protect infrastructure against sea-level rise; for causing property damage via forest fires; for harming the Oregon crab industry; and for a suite of other injustices.[59] Like the

58 *Massachusetts v. ExxonMobil Corp.,* No. 1984CV03333 (Mass. Super. Ct. Oct. 24, 2019); *Minnesota v. American Petroleum Institute,* No. 62-CV-20-3837 (Minn. Dist. Ct. June 24, 2020); *D.C. v. ExxonMobil Corp.,* No. 2020 CA 002892 B (D.C. Super. Ct. June 25 2020).

59 *Conservation Law Foundation v. ExxonMobil Corp.,* No. 1:16-cv-11950 (D. Mass. Sept. 29, 2016); *Van Oeyen v. Southern California Edison Co.,* No.

one in New York, these cases are important insofar as they target the usual corporate routine of dumping costs onto other people. Maybe, if the industry wasn't receiving more public money than the Pentagon,[60] such efforts would pose a serious threat. But, as things stand now, it's very unlikely that a lawsuit will put any oil companies out of business.

There's an important qualification to be made here, a low rumble emerging from the other side of the courthouse. Some creative activists and lawyers have decided that the best play is to start a different game altogether, and they've sought new sources for climate law: the Fifth Amendment of the Constitution, the public trust doctrine, and the rights of nature. Because these arguments are so new and so different, they'll be treated separately in Chapter 4.

A New World Order?

But wait. What about the rest of the world? Maybe *international law* will finally put an end to the use of fossil fuels?

The global community has had something to say about global warming, to be sure. In fact, international pronouncements on the importance of environmental protection have been a rare source of inspiration in the legal realm: the U.N. World Charter for Nature proclaims that "Nature shall be respected and its essential processes shall not be disturbed,"[61] and efforts like the Montreal Protocol to repair the ozone layer have made a real difference.

19STCV04409 (Cal. Super. Ct. Feb. 8, 2019); *Pacific Coast Federation of Fishermen's Associations, Inc. v. Chevron Corp.*, No. 3:18-cv-07477 (N.D. Cal. Nov. 14, 2018); see the Sabin Center Climate Change Litigation Database for other cases.

60 Dickinson, "Study: U.S. Fossil Fuel Subsidies Exceed Pentagon Spending."

61 G.A. Res. 37/7, Annex I.1, U.N. Doc. A/RES/37/7 (Oct. 28, 1982).

In 1988, the United Nations Framework Convention on Climate Change (UNFCCC) was established, creating an umbrella instrument under which initiatives like the Paris Agreement have been launched. Here's the official line of the UNFCC, to which 197 countries, including the United States (where it was signed into law as a treaty), are parties: "The ultimate objective of this Convention and any related legal instruments that the Conference of the Parties may adopt is to achieve . . . stabilization of greenhouse gas concentrations in the atmosphere at a level that would prevent dangerous anthropogenic interference with the climate system."[62] Had the spirit of the convention been followed, we might be in better shape. The 1997 Kyoto Protocol, which currently has 192 signatories, extended the UNFCCC and mandated 5 percent reductions in major greenhouse gases from 1990 levels by 2012 and 18 percent by 2020. Crucially, Kyoto required bigger emissions cuts from rich nations.[63] But a big red flag was raised when the U.S. Senate voted unanimously to refuse any treaty that would "result in serious harm to the economy of the United States."[64] Without the participation of one of the world's largest emitters, Kyoto's reach was limited.

There's another problem with the UNFCCC: its mandates aren't enforceable. Commitments to reduce greenhouse gas emissions exist on paper, but there's no mechanism—no world police, no economic sanctions regime, no reciprocal obligation scheme—that compels countries to do what they say. This is a process and

---

62   S. Treaty Doc No. 102-38, 1771 U.N.T.S. 107, Art. 2 (May 9, 1992).

63   United Nations Framework Convention on Climate Change [UNFCCC], "What Is the Kyoto Protocol?" (2019), https://unfccc.int/kyoto_protocol.

64   Senate Resolution 98 (1997).

politics problem. (Some of the provisions of the Kyoto Protocol include penalties for non-compliance, but these are limited to exclusion from an emissions trading scheme; regardless, Kyoto has largely been superseded by Paris.)

Let's focus on the most recent major UNFCCC agreement. The 2015 Paris talks—which welcomed oil giants to the proceedings but excluded climate activists, many of whom were surveilled and jailed by French authorities[65]—represent the high-water mark of human cooperation on warming. The Paris Agreement required signatories to develop national plans for reducing emissions and to assist poorer nations in mitigation and adaptation. It aimed to cap warming at two degrees Celsius, and acknowledged that 1.5 degrees would be safer. The most substantive part of the Agreement, the emissions targets, are not legally binding, while the reporting and procedural requirements, such as maintaining "Nationally Determined Contributions" to emissions reductions, are. (Signatories are also bound to "pursue domestic mitigation measures.")[66]

Jump forward six years. The vast majority of countries have failed to put forward plans—which, remember, aren't even enforceable—that would meet the Paris Agreement goals.[67] Even the Clean Power Plan—our country's most ambitious climate

---

65　Sewell Chan, "France Uses Sweeping Powers to Curb Climate Protests, but Clashes Erupt," *The New York Times* (Nov. 29, 2015), https://www.nytimes.com/2015/11/30/world/europe/france-uses-sweeping-powers-to-curb-climate-protests-but-clashes-erupt.html.

66　Paris Agreement Art. 2, sec. 1(a), Arts. 3, 4.

67　Sir Robert Watson, Dr. James J. McCarthy, Dr. Pablo Canziani, Prof. Dr. Nebojsa Nakicenovic, Liana Hisas, "The Truth Behind the Climate Pledges," *Universal Ecological Fund* (2019), https://drive.google.com/file/d/1nFx8UKTy-jEteYO87-x06mVEkTs6RSPBi/view.

regulation to date—would have fallen far short of U.S. obligations, resulting in 17 percent cuts in 2005 emission levels by 2025 rather than the 26 to 28 percent promised.[68] President Trump withdrew the United States from the Agreement— something he was allowed to do because the Agreement was never voted on by the Senate and thus never became an official treaty under U.S. law[69]—a move that President Biden will surely reverse.[70]

At COP25 in Madrid, the latest round of UNFCC talks, even those countries that did offer plans admitted that they fell short of what had been agreed in Paris. The UN Environment Programme noted that existing commitments under the Agreement would cause warming of 3.2 degree Celsius, and that the 1.5 degree goal was "on the brink of becoming impossible."[71] The U.S. refused to submit to even non-binding targets, and activists were expelled from the talks again as corporate leaders pushed the discussion toward profit-making and palatable carbon taxes.[72]

68   Earth Institute, Columbia University, "What Is the U.S. Commitment in Paris?" *State of the Planet* (Dec. 11, 2015), https://blogs.ei.columbia.edu/2015/12/11/what-is-the-u-s-commitment-in-paris/.

69   Lisa Friedman, "Trump Serves Notice to Quit Paris Climate Agreement," *The New York Times* (Nov. 4, 2019), https://www.nytimes.com/2019/11/04/climate/trump-paris-agreement-climate.html; Steven P. Mulligan, "Withdrawal from International Agreements: Legal Framework, the Paris Agreement, and the Iran Nuclear Agreement," *Congressional Research Service,* R44761 (2018).

70   Frank Jordans and Jeff Schaeffer, "As leaders set fresh climate goals, Biden pledges US support," *Associated Press* (Dec. 12, 2020), https://apnews.com/article/europe-climate-climate-change-paris-france-6e21f86b5c4af-faee8ee04e870a1ea6c.

71   United Nations Environment Programme, *Emissions Gap Report 2019,* (Nairobi: United Nations Environment Programme, 2019), https://www.unenvironment.org/interactive/emissions-gap-report/2019/.

72   Kate Aronoff, "Rich Nations, After Driving Climate Disaster, Block All Progress at U.N. Talks," *The Intercept* (Dec. 18, 2019), https://theintercept.com/2019/12/18/un-climate-cop25/.

What explains this gap between ambition and actualization? One reason is that international law is marked by a surfeit of rhetoric and an absence of force. This is not to denigrate rhetoric: it's enormously useful to have the countries of the world on record as supporting environmental protection and other progressive values, especially for political activists who can cite such commitments as they battle oppressive regimes. But the mere existence of international institutions does nothing to change the hierarchy of power among nations, nor the nature of a world structured on imperial and colonial relations. These relations often negate fine intentions, as when the United States flatly refuses to turn its war criminals over to the International Criminal Court. To the degree that the world's richest nations and their biggest industry are to blame for the climate crisis, international institutions are comparatively impotent to hold them to task.

Related to this inherent impotence is the fact that the global climate talks are designed to promote and protect a specific vision of economic well being. Multinational corporations are given a prominent role in negotiations. GDP growth is a nonnegotiable desideratum. The political economic status quo—capitalism—is the only framework within which "alternatives" are considered, so the options for change are restricted from the outset. Ideas like a carbon tax get lots of play while notions like decentralized communal ownership of energy production are ignored. So the climate crisis is discussed even as its fundamental causes and conditions are left off the agenda. This is like holding the first meeting of the French Estates General in 1789 to discuss only those reforms that would leave the absolute monarchy in place.

An example: Article 6 of the Paris Agreement allows for countries to enter into carbon pricing agreements and emissions trading schemes. Such approaches use market forces to regulate the cost of contributing to climate change. Whereas fossil fuel producers generally pay no price for the harm caused by their products, market-based efforts like those under Article 6 try to send a price signal that discourages harmful activity, either by imposing a tax on emissions or by financially rewarding those who keep their emissions below the legal limit. Not a bad idea, if the free market is our only framework for action. But these schemes have a checkered history replete with inefficiency and corruption, not to mention human rights abuses stemming from climate-friendly projects like dam-building.[73] As the Indigenous Environmental Network and the Climate Justice Alliance have noted, market-based efforts also "promote the ideology that if something is not given a price then it does not have a value, and that if pollution can be treated as a measurable commodity, it can be managed and controlled." Such measures are designed to stop short of transformations in the energy system: "in order to make climate regulation cheap enough for capital's requirements, the price of pollution permits can never be allowed to rise high enough to achieve structural change."[74]

73   Notably, negotiators at the 2019 COP25 in Madrid removed language from Article 6 that would have strengthened human rights protections. Jocelyn Timperley, "Carbon offsets have patchy human rights record. Now UN talks erode safeguards," *Climate Home News* (Sep. 12, 2019), https://www.climatechangenews.com/2019/12/09/carbon-offsets-patchy-human-rights-record-now-un-talks-erode-safeguards/.

74   Tamra Gilbertson, *Carbon Pricing: A Critical Perspective for Community Resistance*, vol. 1 (Bemidji, Minnesota: Indigenous Environmental Network, 2017), 37-8.

We can find one sign of hope amid this global lethargy: many "subnational" governments like states and cities have pledged to go beyond the Paris Agreement's commitments in order to keep warming below 1.5 degrees. Groups like the Local Leaders Climate Change Summit and the We Are Still In coalition, which bring together thousands of leaders from municipalities, tribal nations, universities, and businesses, have agreed to use their own powers to reduce warming and to limit the effect of the United States' withdrawal from Paris.[75] If such efforts pan out, they would represent an inspiring effort to organize climate policy outside the paradigm of nation-state negotiation that currently defines international law.

You might be noticing a similarity here between the international climate talks and the fate of climate litigation in the United States. Both have run up a limit of imagination: the only permissible moves are those that don't change the rules of the game. And those rules tend to protect capital and its search for profit—profits that it discovers even in emissions reductions. When climate advocates encounter the legal system, then, they are forced to fight with one hand behind their backs, making only those arguments and proposals that will not threaten the global balance of economic and political power. That balance tilts heavily in favor of fossil fuel companies and their cronies.

But is this the case in every country? While the story of climate law in the United States has been bleak, and while this bleakness infects the UNFCCC talks, other nations have made some progress. According to the Climate Change Laws of the World

75   Daniel C. Esty and Dena P. Adler, "Changing International Law for a Changing Climate," *AJIL Unbound* 112 (2018), 279-284, 280.

database at Grantham Research Institute on Climate Change and the Environment, Brazil has passed regulations under its National Policy on Climate Change to reduce emissions by 2020 by at least 36.1 percent from 2010 levels; China's thirteenth Five-Year Plan aims to cut emissions per unit of GDP by 15 percent from 2015 to 2020; and Papua New Guinea passed its United Nations Paris Agreement (Implementation) Act in 2016.[76] It's still too early to tell whether actual reductions in most places will be accomplished, but the European Union, at least, is actually on track to meet its 2020 target of reducing 1990 emissions levels by 20 percent, and seems set to cut 40 percent by 2030, as it promised at Paris.[77]

So much for top-down climate regulation abroad. Are there international legal efforts similar to the U.S. litigation against energy companies and the EPA?

Short answer: yes. From Peru to Pakistan to the Netherlands, there's been an explosion in climate litigation aimed at both governments and corporations, forming the first elements of an important new body of climate law. Because this wave of legal action is just picking up, and because it relies largely on novel legal ideas such as environmental human rights, it will be revisited in Chapter 4, when the focus moves from a discussion of what the law of climate change *is* to what climate legal activists are hoping it *might be.*

The need for this change is obvious. At whichever point you enter the legal system—as an oil executive wondering about your

76   Grantham Research Institute on Climate Change and the Environment, *Climate Change Laws of the World* (London School of Economics, 2020), https://climate-laws.org/cclow.

77   European Commission, "Progress made in cutting emissions" (2020), https://ec.europa.eu/clima/policies/strategies/progress_en.

exposure, as a regulator hoping to design a creative new emissions fix, as an activist excluded from COP25—you'll find a notable lack of urgency and a strange adherence to the status quo. An attorney advising an oil executive would tell her that there's not much to worry about right now: fossil law remains strong. Courts have failed to take significant action on warming, and, as Hawaii Senator Brian Schatz recently remarked, the fossil fuel industry has "structural control of Congress."[78]

On the other hand, if an attorney were to be retained by planet Earth and asked what protection the law provides, professional ethics would oblige her to provide one answer:

"Find a new tenant."

---

78   Justin Mikulka, "Senate Hearing Calls out the Influence of Dark Money in Blocking Climate Action," *Desmog Blog* (Oct 29, 2019), https://www.desmog-blog.com/2019/10/29/dark-money-climate-senate-hearing-whitehouse.

The Valve Turners Part 1:
Breaking the Law to Make the Law

Is there anything we can do about climate change?

The previous chapter offered a pretty bleak diagnosis, at least so far as the law goes. Damage to the climate system is legal and promoted by the state. Incipient efforts to hold warming-mongers to account, and to make policies that reflect the warnings of climate science, are piecemeal and weak. If ever conditions existed in which resistance to the legal system was justified, these are they. And the past decade has in fact seen an exponential rise in protest and direct action against the fossil fuel industry and its protectors. From small island nation protesters in Paris to "kayaktivists" in Seattle, the climate justice movement has become one of our millennium's most urgent sources of anti-establishment mobilization.

The climate activists in this story came from the heart of this tendency. What makes the saga of the so-called "Valve Turners" particularly interesting for a study of climate law is the fact that they directed their protest not only at a source of greenhouse gas emissions—in this case, Canadian tar sands oil—but at the legal system itself. Using a coordinated legal and media strategy, they brought their fight into the courtroom. They demanded a judicial reckoning of their cause. And they sought a declaration—in the voice of the jury, a stand-in for society at large—that true justice requires direct interference with the fossil fuel system.

How did they do this? How did courts respond? And what possible connection could a handful of small criminal trials in local courthouses have with the larger phenomenon of climate law?

Climate Conflict in Oceti Sakowin Country

Autumn 2016 was a transformative period in U.S. politics. Black Lives Matter protests had grown throughout the summer in response to the police shootings of Alton Sterling in Baton Rouge and Philando Castile in St. Paul. September saw three days of uprising and violence in Charlotte.[79] Over twenty thousand inmates participated in the largest prison strike in the nation's history.[80] The country officially joined the Paris Agreement.[81]

In presidential politics, two very different representatives of the global elite battled for dominance: on the one hand, a con man and TV star who called global warming a "Chinese hoax"; on the other, a neoliberal ex-attorney who'd spent years promoting

---

79   Max Blau and Eliott C. McLaughlin, "Backlash to police shootings resonates beyond Charlotte, Tulsa," *CNN* (Sep. 22, 2016), https://www.cnn.com/2016/09/22/us/police-shootings-charlotte-tulsa-boston-st-louis-baltimore/index.html.

80   Alice Speri, "The Largest Prison Strike in U.S. History Enters Its Second Week," *The Intercept* (Sep. 16, 2016), https://theintercept.com/2016/09/16/the-largest-prison-strike-in-u-s-history-enters-its-second-week/.

81   Mark Landler and Jane Perlez, "Rare Harmony as China and U.S. Commit to Climate Deal," *The New York Times* (Sep. 3, 2016), https://www.nytimes.com/2016/09/04/world/asia/obama-xi-jinping-china-climate-accord.html.

fracking around the world. Their first two debates featured no questions about climate change or the environment.[82]

Most significant for students of climate justice was the mobilization at Standing Rock. Beginning as a fight against an obscure pipeline, the protest developed into an anti-colonial uprising and the largest gathering of Native Americans in over a century. Drawing together struggles for Indigenous rights, environmental well-being, and democratic control of the energy system, Standing Rock struck at the heart of the legal and political consensus regarding fossil fuels and exposed the industry's naked reliance on state violence.

The Standing Rock Indian Reservation lies in Oceti Sakowin (Sioux) country, on the border of the present-day states of North and South Dakota. Belonging to the Standing Rock Sioux— whose members have included Sitting Bull and the lawyer-activist Vine Deloria, Jr.—the land has been at the center of several disputes between its native population and the United States government. In 2014, Energy Transfer Partners finalized plans to build the Dakota Access Pipeline [DAPL], which would carry oil from the Bakken fields in North Dakota to a terminal in Illinois and pass within half a mile of the reservation. In 2016, Standing Rock Sioux members established the Sacred Stone Camp to protest the project.[83]

---

82 Oliver Milman, "Why has climate change been ignored in the US election debates?," *The Guardian* (Oct. 19, 2016), https://www.theguardian.com/us-news/2016/oct/19/where-is-climate-change-in-the-trump-v-clinton-presidential-debates#maincontent.

83 For the best survey of the events at Standing Rock and their historical context, *see* Nick Estes, *Our History is the Future* (New York: Verso, 2019).

There were many grounds for resistance. Energy Transfer Partners had adjusted the initial pipeline route to avoid risks to the majority white city of Bismarck, North Dakota, and now planned to ship its oil across the reservation's water sources in Lake Oahe and the Missouri River. The dangers posed to public health, and the potential damage to crucial hunting and fishing areas, were enormous. Pipeline construction would involve the destruction of dozens of sites of historical, religious, and cultural significance to the Standing Rock Sioux, and the company's asserted right to use surrounding lands for pipeline construction and operation violated the Treaty of Fort Laramie, in which the U.S. recognized Oceti Sakowin dominion over the area.[84]

As thousands of Indigenous activists and their allies gathered at Sacred Stone, the courtroom battle unfolded in ways that neatly captured the legal system's timidity on climate change. The federal government's environmental impact statements—which initially had treated DAPL as a series of individual construction projects rather than one massive infrastructure development—ultimately concluded that the risk to Standing Rock's water sources was acceptable. Challenges based on tribal sovereignty, historical preservation, and the right to religious expression were rejected. After some waffling, a federal court allowed construction to proceed.[85] The Obama administration paused the project in response to the protests, but President Trump reversed this as soon as he

---

84   Carla F. Fredericks and Jesse D. Heibel, "Standing Rock, the Sioux Treaties, and the Limits of the Supremacy Clause," *University of Colorado Law Review* 89 (2018), 447-532.

85   Memorandum Opinions of 14 June, 9 Sep., and 4 Dec., *Standing Rock Sioux Tribe v. U.S. Army Corps of Engineers*, 205 F. Supp. 3d 4 (D.D.C. 2016).

came to power. For a time, DAPL was carrying nearly half a million barrels of crude oil every day.[86] Then, in July 2020, the same federal court ordered the pipeline shut down after it found that the Army Corps of Engineers had improperly failed to prepare an environmental impact statement, as required under the National Environmental Policy Act.[87] (See Chapter 3 for a fuller discussion of the Standing Rock conflict and the government's violent clampdown on activists).

But the real action at Standing Rock did not take place in a courtroom or agency headquarters. Instead, the conflict was fought in brutal confrontations between armor-clad state police and unarmed Water Protectors, which resulted in over eight hundred arrests and, in just one incident involving the use of water cannons, over three hundred injuries.[88] The protesters—whose ranks swelled to ten thousand, including members of three hundred Native American nations and three thousand U.S. military veterans who arrived to defend "the human rights warriors of the Sioux tribes"[89]—became the most visible front line against the fossil fuel system.

---

86   "FAQ: Standing Rock Litigation," *Earthjustice* (Nov. 8, 2019), https://earthjustice.org/features/faq-standing-rock-litigation.

87   *Cheyenne River Sioux Tribe v. U.S. Army Corps of Engineers*, No. CV 16-1534 (D.D.C. July 6, 2020).

88   "Standing Rock Case Updates & Information." *Water Protective Legal Collective* (Feb. 25, 2018), https://waterprotectorlegal.org/; Julia Carrie Wong, "Dakota Access pipeline: 300 protesters injured after police use water cannons," *The Guardian* (Nov. 21, 2016), https://www.theguardian.com/us-news/2016/nov/21/dakota-access-pipeline-water-cannon-police-standing-rock-protest.

89   Tracy Matsue Loeffelholz, "The Numbers That Tell the Story of This Standing Rock Victory," *yes!* (Dec. 4, 2016), https://www.yesmagazine.org/democracy/2016/12/04/numbers-tell-the-story-of-the-standing-rock-sioux2019s-victory/; Sandy Tolan, "The Next Battle of Standing Rock Is Protesters vs. Tribes," *Daily Beast* (Apr. 11, 2017), https://www.thedailybeast.com/the-next-

In early October, these resisters issued a call for the International Days of Prayer and Action, asking allies around the world to target fossil fuel projects.[90] A group of climate activists from the Pacific Northwest heard the call and responded with an unprecedented intervention.

The Valve Turner Solidarity Action

For the most part, the Valve Turners did not resemble the most active protesters at Standing Rock, who tended to be young and Indigenous. The Valve Turners are all white. They skew older. If you saw them on the street, you might think them more likely to host the neighborhood book club than to launch an audacious strike on dangerous energy infrastructure. As the activists have publicly noted, this profile is part of their motivation and their strategy: more insulated from the harms of climate change than most of the world's population and less likely to bear the brunt of the legal system's racist, sexist, and classist biases, they felt a special sense of responsibility to take action.[91]

The group had come to know each other through climate activists circles in Seattle and Portland, including groups like 350.org and the Shell No! and Break Free From Fossil Fuels

battle-of-standing-rock-is-protesters-vs-tribes; Adam Linehan, "Why They Went: The Inside Story Of The Standing Rock Veterans," *Task & Purpose* (Dec. 19, 2016), https://taskandpurpose.com/went-inside-story-stand-ing-rock-veterans.

90   "Event: Standing Rock International Day Of Prayer & Action (Hosted by ECHO Action NH: A #FossilFree603 for Environmental Justice)," *Facebook. com* (Oct. 8, 2016), https://www.facebook.com/events/166377043809956/.

91   Alleen Brown, 'Environmental Extremism' or Necessary Response to Climate Emergency? Pipeline Shutdown Trials Pit Activists Against the Oil Industry," *The Intercept* (Mar. 21, 2018), https://theintercept.com/2018/03/21/pipeline-protest-necessity-defense-tar-sands/.

campaigns. Some had already been arrested for protesting fossil fuels and climate policy, and all were well-versed in traditional forms of environmental advocacy. Emily Johnston, a fifty-year-old poet and editor, had written and spoken extensively about global warming as a member of the Seattle climate justice scene. Annette Klapstein, sixty-four, a retired attorney for the Puyallup Nation, had been involved in anti-war and environmental activism for decades. Michael Foster, a fifty-two-year-old therapist, had organized climate lobbying and litigation efforts with young people for years. Leonard Higgins, sixty-three, who began to question his middle-class values after he retired from a thirty-one-year career as an Information Techology manager with the Oregon state government, had devoted himself full-time to organizing in the movement. Ken Ward, fifty-nine, a veteran of mainstream environmentalism, had worked at Greenpeace, the National Environmental Law Center, and U.S. PIRG before turning to direct action.

The sense of frustration and futility engendered by these years of advocacy had set the Valve Turners on their path toward civil disobedience. As Leonard Higgins would later testify at his trial: "Nothing was getting done. And in fact, it was getting worse. What we were doing is just a drop in a bucket. We were not getting any traction . . . I felt responsible to stand up for what was right. Sometimes what is right is not necessarily what is legal. It was a really hard conclusion to come to."[92]

Michael Foster, who for decades had taken every step he could to eliminate fossil fuels from his daily life—he avoids fossil-based

92   Transcript of Trial, vol. 3 at 13, *Montana v. Higgins*, No. DC-16-18 (12th Jud. Dist. Ct., Choteau Cty., Mont. Nov. 22, 2017).

travel whenever possible and keeps his monthly budget below $500[93]—wrote on the group's website that "I am here to generate action that wakes people up to the reality of what we are doing to life as we know it. All of our climate victories are meaningless if we don't stop extracting oil, coal and gas now."[94]

So the Valve Turners sought a more direct and immediate means of reducing emissions. If the government wouldn't stop the flow of poisonous fuels, then the activists would have to do it themselves—and without any of the powers of persuasion or coercion available to the state. They considered the measures at their disposal. They studied the vulnerabilities of the fossil fuel system. And they arrived at the same conclusion reached by generations of protesters: their best tools were themselves.

This radical reliance on principled individual action took two forms. On the one hand, the Valve Turners realized that many pipelines were open to quick and simple disruption. This vulnerability is the flip-side of fossil fuel infrastructure's ubiquity and invisibility: as soon as we realize that it's all around us, we discover how easy it can be to turn off.

On the other hand, the Valve Turners believed that the effect of their intervention would go far beyond the immediate decrease in the flow of fossil fuels. The activists—many of them rooted in faith traditions—saw bold action as a prerequisite to mass mobilization. In order to convince people that, with a little organization

93   Michelle Nijhuis, "'I'm Just More Afraid of Climate Change Than I Am of Prison,'" *The New York Times Magazine* (Feb. 13, 2018), https://www.nytimes.com/2018/02/13/magazine/afraid-climate-change-prison-valve-turners-global-warming.html.

94   "Activist Bios," *Shut It Down Today: Climate Direct Action* (2020), http://www.shutitdown.today/activist_bios.

and a little sacrifice, the tide could be turned, the world needed examples of political risk taking. This theory of change, based on a study of historical social movements, was ground-up: start with direct action, and a sense of moral urgency will in time produce the desired reforms at the top.

Building on their research and inspired by interventions against Enbridge Line 9 in Canada,[95] the group split up and traveled to sites across the west. They were concerned about Canadian tar sands oil, an especially noxious and polluting fossil fuel that flows from the fields of Alberta, where its extraction causes enormous ecological damage, toward U.S. refineries, where it is converted into a combustible fuel source. The Valve Turners targeted the four points at which this fuel enters the country via pipeline: Emily Johnston and Annette Klapstein traveled to Enbridge Lines 4 and 67 in Leonard, Minnesota; Michael Foster went to the TransCanada Keystone XL Pipeline in Walhalla, North Dakota; Leonard Higgins approached the Spectra Express near Coal Banks Landing, Montana; and Ken Ward aimed at the Kinder Morgan TransMountain Pipeline in Anacortes, Washington.

In the early morning hours of October 11, 2016, their website went live with dramatic video streams: in each state, the activists, wearing orange safety vests and work helmets, cut padlocks, took hold of safety valves, and cut off the flow of the climate-wrecking fuel.

Take the action of Emily Johnston and Annette Klapstein. At 7:30 in the morning, under an immense grey sky and against a

---

95   David Gray-Donald, "Canadian Protesters Keep Shutting Down the Line Nine Oil Pipeline," *Vice* (Dec. 22, 2015), https://www.vice.com/en_us/article/wd7y85/protesters-keep-shutting-down-the-line-9-oil-pipeline.

landscape of brown-green grass and scattered, leafless, trees, they cut a padlock to open a chain-link gate. Ben Joldersma, filming with his phone, called the company's pipeline operations center in Alberta, Canada and read a message:

> I'm here with Emily Johnston and Annette Klapstein. We're calling from Leonard, Minnesota. We're currently at the block valve sites for Lines 4 and 67, just ten miles southeast from the Clearbrook Pumping Station. For the sake of climate justice, to ensure a future for human civilization, we must immediately halt the extraction and burning of Canadian tar sands. For safety, I am calling to inform you that when I hang up this phone we are closing the valves. Please shut down these two pipelines now for safety and for our future.[96]

Notice having been given, Johnston and Klapstein maneuvered around two valves that stood level with their heads and turned large orange wheels. A high-pitched whir like a bandsaw signaled the flow of oil being cut off below their feet. Johnston and Klapstein placed flowers on the wheels. The site went silent. Enbridge Lines 4 and 67 were down.

And then the activists waited. Steve Liptay, a journalist on the scene, filmed. Many miles away, officers at the Clearwater County Sheriff's Office began receiving calls from Enbridge and the news media. By 10:30, five officers were on scene. Johnston and Klapstein told them that they were protesting for an end to fossil fuels. The officers said that they respected their right to protest but that they had to stay within the law. The Valve Turners responded that

---

96 "Climate Direct Action short films," *Shut It Down Today: Climate Direct Action* (2020), http://www.shutitdown.today/videos.

they'd tried that and it didn't work. Then Johnston and Klapstein were arrested and taken back to the station. (Joldersma and Liptay were notified of criminal charges later.)

This action, like the ones in North Dakota, Montana, and Washington, was precise and well planned. As would become evident in the course of the legal cases, the group's methods posed no risk of causing a spill, and the pipeline companies were alerted before the activists turned the valves. In fact, in Washington and Minnesota, the pipeline companies responded to the call by remotely turning off the pipelines themselves: the shut-down that Johnston and Klapstein felt may have resulted not from their valve-turning but from a remote signal sent from company headquarters.

Each Valve Turner also carried a copy of a letter to President Obama that they had sent to the White House earlier in the day. The letter, quoted in the Introduction, explained that the activists had "tried every avenue by which engaged citizens might advance such concerns—in this case, ecological—in public policy, and nothing has worked. There is no plausible means or mechanism by which the extraction and burning of coal and tar sands oil from existing mines and fields can be halted on the timeline now required by any ordinary, legal means." The letter asked the president to invoke his emergency powers to make the pipeline shutoff permanent, to immediately phase down coal and tar sands extraction, and to introduce a national mobilization plan to transition to renewable energy.[97]

---

97 "Dear President Obama," *Shut It Down Today: Climate Direct Action* (2020), http://www.shutitdown.today/dearobama.

These coordinated actions cut off 15 percent of the country's crude oil supply for a day. Reuters called it the "biggest coordinated move on U.S. energy infrastructure ever undertaken by environmental protesters."[98] It resulted in the arrest of eleven Valve Turners, supporters, and journalists, who now found themselves at the mercy of the states' criminal legal apparatuses.

Of course, the Valve Turners expected this. The very notion of civil disobedience involves breaking the law (though the arrest of the journalists was a different and more troubling matter). But the Valve Turners didn't think that what they were doing was wrong. If anything, they thought their actions abided by the most fundamental principles of justice: protection of the common good, advocacy for the oppressed, and resistance to unjust authority. So they decided to carry their campaign to trial and to force the legal system to reckon with its own complicity.

There was a useful legal strategy waiting for the Valve Turners as they sought to justify their conduct: the necessity defense. Over the course of the next few years, their courtroom battles would help to bring this strategy to the attention of the movement at large, and, in time, make it an important legal weapon in the fight against fossil fuels.

The Political Necessity Defense

Necessity has been a part of the criminal law for as long as criminal law has been around. Its basic idea—that the law should sometimes allow people to break the law when doing so serves the greater

98   Nia Williams and Laila Kearney, "Daring U.S. pipeline sabotage spawned by lobster boat coal protest," *Reuters* (Oct. 13, 2016), https://www.reuters.com/article/us-usa-canada-pipeline-activists-idUSKCN12D2R7.

good—exists as the principle of justification in almost every legal tradition. Some typical examples: a house is on fire, and there's a child trapped on the top floor. You're legally justified in breaking and entering into the house to save the child's life. Or say you've had a few drinks and your friend has a heart attack—you can argue that it was necessary to drive under the influence to reach the hospital. In such cases, there's a good chance that you'll be acquitted.

Recall the discussion in Chapter 1 about the U.S. legal system's roots in the English common law. The necessity defense comes from that tradition, and some of the earliest judicial opinions on necessity deal with matters such as sea captains tossing cargo to avoid shipwreck. After independence from Britain, each state developed its own version of the common law, and there are now at least fifty-one slightly different versions of the necessity defense across the country (this includes all fifty states as well as the federal circuits courts, which have their own versions, as well as slightly distinct traditions in legal sub-fields like administrative law).[99]

Say you're a climate activist facing charges for protesting the use of fossil fuels. You think what you did was right, and you want to make that argument in court. In whatever state you find yourself, the first question you'll ask is: does the necessity defense exist here? The answer is almost always yes, though some states such as Alabama and New Mexico have combined the necessity defense into the broader defense of "justification," or have assimilated it with the slightly different coercion or duress defenses.[100] These

99 See "Political Necessity Defense Jurisdiction Guide," *Climate Defense Project* (Aug. 12, 2021), available at https://climatedefenseproject.org/resources/.

100 *Id.*

distinctions are important, as they determine what type of evidence you'll be permitted to offer in court.

Next, you'll need to ask about the elements of your state's necessity defense. These are the building-blocks of any defense theory: they define what you need to prove in order to win acquittal. Here's a definition of the most common elements of the necessity defense by the U.S. First Court of Appeals: "The necessity defense requires the defendant to show that he (1) was faced with a choice of evils and chose the lesser evil, (2) acted to prevent imminent harm, (3) reasonably anticipated a direct causal relationship between his acts and the harm to be averted, and (4) had no legal alternative but to violate the law."[101]

This should sound intuitive. Think back to the burning house example. First, you had a choice between two bad options or "evils": breaking and entering, or letting a child die. You chose the lesser evil. Second, you acted to prevent an imminent harm: the death of the child. Third, you reasonably anticipated a direct causal relationship between entering the house and saving the child's life. Finally, there were no good options that didn't involve breaking the law.

On their face, these elements have little to do with civil disobedience. But it's worth noting that, even in its most basic articulation, the necessity defense implies a political critique: it's a direct challenge to the law's claim of universality. There are situations that the law as written cannot adequately handle, and the straightforward application of criminal statutes sometimes produces injustice. It's not hard to see how, expanded beyond the realm of burning houses

---

101   *United States v. Maxwell,* 254 F.3d 21, 27 (1st Cir. 2001).

and storm-tossed ships, necessity might disturb the established legal order.[102]

This radical potential began to be developed in the twentieth century. Activists, seeking community approval for their acts of civil disobedience, began arguing that their protest actions satisfied the four corners of necessity law, and asked juries to acquit them. This approach harkened back to colonial days, in which juries frequently acquitted opponents of the crown. (There's also a darker side to this history of so-called "jury nullification," involving white juries that routinely acquitted murderers of black people, primarily in the South.)[103] The use of the so-called "political necessity defense" gained speed in the 1970s among anti-war and anti-nuclear circles, and, for a time, the strategy enjoyed significant success. Anti-apartheid protestors won a necessity case after occupying the Washington State Capitol; California anti-nuclear activists were found not guilty when they argued that their protests at a nuclear plant were justified; and President Jimmy Carter's daughter Amy was acquitted by reason of necessity after disrupting CIA recruitment at the University of Massachusetts alongside Abby Hoffman.[104] A non-scientific survey by my organization, Climate Defense Project, has found over thirty instances of juries acquitting political activists on a theory of necessity.[105] The number is likely much higher: political necessity defense acquittals, because they

102 *See* Shaun P. Martin, "The Radical Necessity Defense," *University of Cincinnati Law Review* 73 (2005), 1527-1607, 1541-42.

103 Lance N. Long and Ted Hamilton, "The Climate Necessity Defense: Proof and Judicial Error in Climate Protest Cases," *Stanford Environmental Law Journal* 38 (2018), 57-115, 71-73.

104 "Political Necessity Defense Jurisdiction Guide," *Climate Defense Project.*

105 *Id.*

tend to occur in small criminal courts and because they are usually resolved by a jury that is not required to justify its reasoning, rarely leave behind much in the way of written law.

The political necessity defense is not the exclusive purview of progressive activists. Perhaps the first use of the theory in the United States involved a posse of anti-labor vigilantes who rounded up thousands of striking International Workers of the World miners in southern Arizona in 1917 and forcibly deported them to Mexico on cattle cars. At court, they were acquitted on the idea that such extra-judicial action was necessary to preserve the republic from radicals.[106] Much later, anti-abortion activists repeatedly tried to assert the political necessity defense when facing charges of trespass at abortion clinics. Such efforts tended to fail because courts would not accept that a "choice of evils" existed between breaking the law and allowing an abortion to go forward: the latter involves a constitutionally protected activity.[107]

By and large, though, political necessity defendants in the United States have sought to win public and legal approval for actions that promote social justice. Consider *People v. Gray,* a 1991 case from New York City. Commuters and public health advocates were outraged that the city had allowed vehicles to use a bicycle and pedestrian lane on the Queensboro Bridge. They argued that the bridge's heavy traffic posed serious risks to air quality and road safety. Fed up with the failure of officials to hold a public hearing on the issue, and after a sustained campaign of leafletting, petitioning,

106   "Editorial: The Law of Necessity as Applied in the Bisbee Deportation Case," *Arizona Law Review* 3 (1961), 264–279.

107   "Political Necessity Defense Jurisdiction Guide," *Climate Defense Project.*

and lobbying, they finally decided to stage a protest in which they remained in the contested lane until they were arrested. After being charged with disorderly conduct, they went to trial and argued necessity. Luckily, New York's special system for adjudicating such low-level charges, in which the judge takes on the role of the jury and lays out all legal and factual findings in writing, has left us with a remarkable opinion. Judge Laura Safer-Espinoza recognized the long and beneficial history of civil disobedience in the United States, and noted that success in such endeavors cannot be precisely predicted. She concluded, in language auspicious for the present analysis: "The defense does not legalize lawlessness; rather it permits courts to distinguish between necessary and unnecessary illegal acts in order to provide an essential safety valve to law enforcement in a democratic society.[108]

This is a clear-eyed analysis of how the common law of necessity dovetails with the public-minded civil disobedience of political activists. Unfortunately, most other judges haven't seen it like Judge Safer-Espinoza. Since the 1980s, a conservative judicial backlash—contemporaneous with the conservative assault on environmental law—has restricted the use of the political necessity defense in many jurisdictions and has made it much harder for activists to avail themselves of the strategy. The reasoning behind this backlash is familiar from Chapter 1: politics don't belong in the courtroom, it's wrong to interfere with business activities, and judges shouldn't have to decide matters of social controversy. What's more, in a very curious interpretation of U.S. history, many judges have decided that "real" civil disobedience requires protesters to

108 *People v. Gray*, 571 N.Y.S.2d 851, 866 (N.Y. Crim. Ct. 1991).

accept whatever punishment the law imposes, and that there's something inappropriate about trying to justify your actions and seeking an acquittal. Such an argument—which admits that extra-legal action is sometimes good but still insists that the law cannot abide exceptions—would seem to obviate the need for the ancient doctrine of necessity in the first place.

A particularly trenchant version of this legalistic mindset exists in the federal courts. In *United States v. Schoon*, the Ninth Circuit issued the strongest condemnation of political necessity to date, opining that "[w]hat these cases are really about is gaining notoriety for a cause—the defense allows protestors to get their political grievances discussed in a courtroom."[109] The result of such resistance is that judges often block the necessity defense as "a matter of law," exercising their power to prevent legally problematic material, such as hearsay evidence, from reaching the jury. When the jury then decides the facts of the case, it doesn't get to hear any evidence supporting the four elements of necessity. This means that, in the majority of cases, the political necessity defense dies before it gets a fair hearing in court. (The constitutional implications of this restriction, which became a central point of debate in each of the Valve Turner trials, will be discussed later.)

Still, despite this judicial resistance, activists have never let go of the necessity defense. Social movement lawyers, particularly those associated with the National Lawyers Guild, continue to press it in courthouses across the country, taking advantage of the legal system's ostensible commitment to justice to advocate for the morality of civil disobedience. When these defenses actually go

---

109 *United States v. Schoon*, 971 F.2d 193, 199 (9th Cir. 1991).

before a jury, defendants tend to be acquitted.[110] A small exercise in radical democracy takes place: the community decides that its laws are inadequate to the crisis at hand, and it approves the conduct of those who resist.

The Climate Necessity Defense

Once activists began being arrested for their efforts to address global warming, it was only a matter of time before the political necessity defense took a climate turn. The first high-profile use of the climate necessity defense came in England in 2008, when six Greenpeace protesters were charged with trespass and criminal damage after painting the prime minister's name on a chimney at the Kingsnorth coal plant.

Relying on a special English version of necessity called "lawful excuse"—by which defendants argue that they damaged one bit of property in order to save another—they brought in experts such as climate scientist James Hansen and politician and editor Zac Goldsmith to prove that carbon dioxide emissions were harming coastal regions, including sensitive Inuit territory, and that political efforts to address the problem had failed. A jury acquitted them of all charges.[111]

Later that year, the Bureau of Land Management (BLM), the agency responsible for administering mining on federal lands, held an oil lease auction in Salt Lake City, Utah. Despite its failure

110   *See* William P. Quigley, "The Necessity Defense in Civil Disobedience Cases: Bring in the Jury," *New England Law Review* 38 (2003), 3-72.

111   *See* entry for "Kingsnorth 6" in "Climate Necessity Defense Case Guide," *Climate Defense Project* (Aug. 12, 2021), available at https://climatedefense-project.org/resources/ .

to properly assess the likely consequences—a recurrent theme in environmental law—the BLM had decided to open up 150,000 acres of pristine red-rock country to drilling. A local college student named Tim DeChristopher, concerned about global warming and the government's failure to act on it, decided to register for the auction without any clear plan for what he might do there. As the agency began accepting bids for the leases, DeChristopher decided to raise his paddle. He bid $500 and won a parcel. Then he bid $25,000 on another, and won again. Then again. And again. By the time the auction was called off, DeChristopher had pledged $1.8 million dollars on fourteen leases. DeChristopher—who, backed by a circle of fundraisers, offered to pay the bids, an offer that the BLM rejected—was later arrested and charged with planning to defeat the Federal Oil and Gas Lease Reform Act and with making a false statement on his bidder registration form.

Because DeChristopher had protested at a federal agency auction, he found himself in federal court, where political activists tend to do poorly. In a pretrial filing called a "proffer," DeChristopher and his attorneys (one of whom was a former BLM director) offered evidence on each element of the necessity defense, describing how oil drilling contributes to climate change, the connection between civil disobedience and social change, and the impossibility that any alternative legal action, such as filing a lawsuit or organizing a rally, would have averted the lease sale. Importantly, DeChristopher stressed that he wasn't simply protesting a policy that he disagreed with. The federal government's promotion of oil drilling on public lands, based as it was on flagrant violations of environmental and procedural laws and grounded in a well-documented culture of corruption involving government and industry officials, was an "evil" regardless of DeChristopher's political views.

Subsequent developments would prove DeChristopher right. Media attention around the protest sparked an investigation that verified the claim that environmental assessments had been inadequate, and, after the federal government admitted its mistake, all drill leases in the area were canceled.[112] DeChristopher's action was thus directly effective, proving how civil disobedience is often necessary to protect the environment and climate.

But the judges weren't swayed. In line with the federal trend in political cases, DeChristopher was barred from presenting necessity evidence before the trial started, and he was convicted. On appeal, the court found that an agency auction could not be a "harm" under the law, and that there were plenty of legal alternatives to protest.[113] DeChristopher spent twenty-one months in prison.[114]

Thanks to this case and to the increasing prevalence of direct action against fossil fuels, climate necessity defenses began popping up around the country. The defense was attempted in Montana, where protesters were arrested at the state capitol as they inveighed against coal leases in the Powder River Basin; in Washington, where activists blocked train tracks used to export

---

112 MSNBC.com Staff and News Service Reports, "Bush-era energy drilling leases in Utah canceled," *MSNBC* (Feb. 4, 2009), http://www.nbcnews.com/id/29017638/ns/us_news-environment/t/bush-era-energy-drillingleases-utah-canceled#.Xrb-oZopBlA.

113 *United States v. DeChristopher*, 695 F.3d 1082, 1087-88 (10th Cir. 2012).

114 Brian Maffly, "Activist Tim DeChristopher to be freed after 21 months in custody," *The Salt Lake Tribune* (Apr. 17, 2013), http://archive.sltrib.com/story.php?ref=/sltrib/news/56159854-78/dechristopher-tim-bidder-prison.html.csp.

coal abroad; in Oklahoma, where a man locked himself to equipment used on the Keystone XL pipeline extension; and in Michigan, where resisters shut down a construction site for a tar sands pipeline. All of these attempted necessity defenses were blocked by a judge prior to trial.

In Massachusetts, Jay O'Hara, a crucial support team member for the future Valve Turners, and Ken Ward, who would become a Valve Turner himself, piloted a lobster boat named the *Henry David T.* to obstruct a shipping channel through which mountaintop coal was delivered to a power plant. On September 8, 2014, they were prepared to present their climate necessity case in court when the district attorney announced that he was dropping the charges. The prosecutor then gave a speech on the courtroom steps commending the activists and urging the crowd to take action to address global warming.[115]

In only two cases were defendants actually given the chance to present a climate necessity defense to a jury. The first occurred in Florida in 2008, where activists with Everglades Earth First! protested a Palm Beach power plant and based their defense in part on the plant's harmful effect on the climate. They were convicted by a jury and sentenced to short terms in jail. In 2016, the so-called "Delta 5" were allowed to present a necessity defense in a case stemming from the blockade of railroad tracks used to transport Bakken crude oil in Everett, Washington. After the close of evidence, the trial judge barred the jury from considering the necessity defense, and the activists were convicted.[116]

---

115 "Climate Necessity Defense Case Guide," *Climate Defense Project.*

116 *Id.*

By late 2016, these cases had given the Valve Turners a good playbook for amplifying their action through a legal defense strategy. But it was still a risky maneuver: no U.S. jury had ever acquitted someone on the theory of climate necessity, and in almost every case a judge had blocked activists from presenting their case in the first place. Many of the reasons for these instances of judicial reluctance were identical to those seen in the court battles over EPA regulations and in lawsuits against industry: global warming is "too political," reform efforts belong in the legislature rather than the courtroom, and the problem is too big for any one case to handle.

Preparing the Case

Precedent wasn't the Valve Turners' only legal problem. Lacking any attorneys on the ground—the activists were arrested in rural areas distant from their traditional bases of support—a legal team had to be assembled on the fly. So the Valve Turner support crew, some members of which had been arrested, worked around the clock to broadcast the action to the world, to solicit donations to a legal fund, and to reach out to friendly lawyers.

Lauren Regan, who leads the Civil Liberties Defense Center in Eugene, Oregon, soon came on as lead attorney for the effort. A celebrated social justice lawyer who has practiced since the 1990s, Regan has defended hundreds of radical environmental and animal rights activists, including many caught up in the Bush administration's "Green Scare" (more on this in Chapter 2). Climate Defense Project, which had been founded weeks prior by myself and two other recent law graduates, Alex Marquardt and Kelsey Skaggs, signed up. Over the following weeks, the Valve Turners also retained attorneys barred in the jurisdictions where their trials would take place: Tim Phillips in Minnesota; Mike Hoffman and William Kirschner in North Dakota; Herman Watson IV in Montana; and Ralph Hurvitz in Washington.

The oil had been stopped and the Valve Turners had inspired activists around the world, including the protesters camped out at Standing Rock. Now it was time to face the judicial system and to see who would be judged accountable in the eyes of the law: the purveyors of fossil fuels, or those who sought to stop them.

As anyone who has been arrested knows, the criminal legal system is designed to secure convictions as quickly as possible. The high-minded principles of the Bill of Rights and Supreme Court jurisprudence—the right to counsel, the right against self-incrimination, the burden on the government to prove charges beyond a reasonable doubt—often disappear in a haze of confusing procedures, hefty administrative fines, and the disconnect between ordinary people and overworked court staff, lawyers, and judges.

In this system, prosecutors have nearly all the power: 97 percent of all criminal cases are resolved by plea deals rather than trials, and those who choose to exercise their trial right suffer from much higher punishments when convicted.[117] This means that very few defendants ever get to the point of even arguing what a jury should hear in their case, let alone getting them to hear it. This

---

117 Rick Jones, Gerald B. Lefcourt, Barry J. Pollack, Norman L. Reimer, and Kyle O'Dowd, *The Trial Penalty: The Sixth Amendment Right to Trial on the Verge of Extinction and How to Save It* (Washington, DC: National Association of Criminal Defense Lawyers and Foundation for Criminal Justice, 2018), https://www.nacdl.org/getattachment/95b7f0f5-90df-4f9f-9115-520b3f58036a/the-trial-penalty-the-sixth-amendment-right-to-trial-on-the-verge-of-extinction-and-how-to-save-it.pdf.

oppressive state of affairs is felt especially by poor people and by racial and sexual minorities.

Such facts make it difficult to see how or why anyone would seek to use a criminal trial to make a political point. But acknowledging the deep injustices in our criminal legal system shouldn't lead us to the conclusion that activism within its strictures is impossible. For example, many political defendants choose to subvert the system by representing themselves, proving how—despite the anti-democratic bias of the legal profession—regular people can still confront power on their own terms. Although there's a gap between theory and practice, the existence of the rights to confront one's accusers and to test the prosecution's evidence in court remain crucial bulwarks against government persecution. And the state's tendency to break its own rules in the pursuit of dissidents means that political trials sometimes expose crucial information about surveillance and other constitutional violations.[118]

Pushing back against the inertia of the carceral state requires a lot of work. As the Valve Turners embarked on a speaking tour to explain their action and strategy to audiences across the western United States, they collaborated with their attorneys on gathering evidence of the harms of climate change and the need for civil disobedience, recruiting expert witnesses to testify to these facts, and outlining the legal arguments they would use to rebut the inevitable resistance to their defense.

Let's return to the Minnesota Valve Turners. The criminal process at the Ninth Judicial District Court in Clearwater County moves

---

118   For example, see the description of the West Roxbury and Iron Eyes climate necessity trials below.

slowly, as it does in every other courthouse. While Emily Johnston and Annette Klapstein were still in detention, the state announced its charges against them. They faced four charges each: two were felonies carrying a maximum of ten years in prison (criminal damage to the property of critical public service facilities, utilities, or pipeline, and aiding and abetting such damage), and two were gross misdemeanors punishable by up to a year of jail time (trespass on a critical public service facility, utility, or pipeline, and aiding and abetting such trespass). Ben Joldersma, who called the pipeline to warn of the action and then live-streamed it, was charged with felony conspiracy and aiding and abetting criminal damage (both felonies), while Steve Liptay, the independent journalist filming and photographing the scene, was charged with trespass and aiding and abetting trespass (both misdemeanors).

These charges were announced through a document called a "complaint," which the prosecutor files with the court and which lists the basic facts justifying the accusation of criminal conduct. In their first court date, the arraignment, the activists were put on notice that the state would be seeking to punish them for what they'd done, and that they were legally bound to show up for the subsequent hearings that would determine their fate.

Between the arraignment and their next day in court—scheduling delays, all too typical in criminal cases, moved the expected start of trial from April to August—the Minnesota activists retained Tim Phillips, an attorney from Minneapolis with experience representing area protesters. The Valve Turners in the other states were also finding local counsel, and over the course of the fall the legal team came together as an integrated unit. The attorneys from the

Civil Liberties Defense Center and Climate Defense Project put together a primer on climate science and the justification for civil disobedience, which included a comparison of the necessity law in the different states where trials would take place and outlined some of the legal arguments they might offer in each jurisdiction. All of the attorneys and defendants signed a joint defense agreement, in which—in contrast to the usual practice in which one attorney represents one client and looks out solely for that client's interests—the team agreed to work together as a whole. This agreement grounded the legal strategy in the solidarity that had given rise to the action in the first place and allowed the attorneys leeway in sharing documents and information.

Under Minnesota law, defendants must notify the prosecution if they plan to bring certain defenses at trial, including self-defense and necessity.[119] The legal team did so on December 20; this triggered a response from the state, which, on January 23, 2017, filed a memorandum in opposition, or what's commonly known as a motion "*in limine*" ("at the threshold"). The purpose of such a motion is to prevent the other side from presenting evidence that might be irrelevant or prejudicial, and to do so before a jury enters the room. Although motions *in limine* began as defense tool to prevent the government from bringing in embarrassing or incriminatory facts about a defendant—such as evidence of past convictions which, though irrelevant, might prejudice a jury—it has in recent years became a favorite prosecutorial tool for clipping the wings of

119   Minn. R. Crim. Proc. 9.02 Subd. 1(5).

an unfavorable defense strategy.[120] In political necessity cases, it's the reef on which most defenses founder.

The prosecutor's *motion in limine* argument in *Minnesota v. Klapstein* began like this: "The use of necessity as a defense in protestor cases has been uniformly rejected by courts."[121] This statement is demonstrably false—think back to *People v. Gray* for only one example—but it's been repeated again and again by prosecutors and judges, as though they could simply wish away an entire tradition of social movement law. The state's motion went on to describe necessity as a "controversial" defense, and then turned to the elements.

According to the prosecution, the imminence element can never be satisfied if defendants have "time to ponder alternatives," as in the case of a protest. As for legal alternatives, the motion cited a federal case for the proposition that "legislative action can always mitigate the 'harm,'" so civil disobedience is never really justified. Finally, the prosecutor argued that protest can never have a sufficient causal relationship to averting a harm: because some sort of policy change is required before something like climate change is addressed, there's simply no way in which civil disobedience accomplishes anything. The motion put its final emphasis on the presumed legitimacy of the state and industry's inaction on climate change: "The necessity defense was never intended to excuse criminal activity by those who disagree with the decisions and

---

120   Douglas L. Colbert, "The Motion in Limine in Politically Sensitive Cases: Silencing the Defendant at Trial," *Stanford Law Review* 39 (1987), 1271-1327, 1280-83.

121   State's Memorandum in Opposition to Affirmative Defense of Necessity at 2, *Minnesota v. Klapstein*, No. 15-CR-16-413 (9th Jud. Dist. Ct., Clearwater Cty. Minn. Jan. 23, 2017).

policies of the lawmaking branches of government, who, in turn, allow regulated conduct by private enterprise."[122]

As we follow the saga of the Valve Turners, these arguments will become depressingly familiar. Like the musty assertions marshaled by opponents of judicial action to address global warming, they rely on a series of seemingly contradictory premises: climate change is serious, but it's not so serious that we need to take immediate action; if we do need to take immediate action, we should trust the legislature to take it; if the legislature doesn't take it, then nothing else will work anyway. This leads to the inevitable conclusion that the only rational—or legal—response is to do nothing.

Sixteen days later, the Valve Turners' legal team filed their "Response to State's Memorandum in Opposition to Affirmative Defense of Necessity." This was not only a refutation of the prosecution's reasoning; it was also an effort to couch the Valve Turners' legal argument in the broader moral context in which their action had taken place. In order to see what this sort of legal activism looks like in practice, it's worth reading the entire first section of the brief:

STATE OF MINNESOTA
COUNTY OF CLEARTWATER
IN DISTRICT COURT
NINTH JUDICIAL DISTRICT

STATE OF MINNESOTA,

     Plaintiff,   Case FILE NO. 15-CR-16-413
     15-CR-16-414
     15-CR-16-425
     15-CR-17-25

---

122 *Id.* at 3-6 (citing *Schoon,* 971 F. 2d at 198).

DEFENSE RESPONSE TO STATE'S
MEMORANDUM IN OPPOSITION
TO AFFIRMATIVE DEFENSE OF NECESSITY

ANNETTE MARIE KLAPSTEIN,
EMILY NESBITT JOHNSTON,
STEVEN ROBERT LIPTAY,
BENJAMIN JOLDERSMA
              Defendants

INTRODUCTION

The defendants' charges in this case stem from an act of civil disobedience at an Enbridge tar sands pipeline facility on October 11, 2016. Their actions were motivated by the need to mitigate catastrophic climate change and its effects on public health and the natural environment. Climate change, caused by greenhouse gas emissions leading to global warming, has already caused severe injuries to people and the environment such as rising sea levels, volatile weather patterns, and increased drought. Scientific consensus points to a rapid increase of such harms in the near future in Minnesota and around the world, unless immediate and drastic action is taken to alter our patterns of energy consumption. The emission of CO_2 from the burning of fossil fuels is a major driver of global warming, and the vast majority of the world's gas and oil reserves must be left in the ground to avoid catastrophic temperature increases. The successful burning of Alberta's tar sands resources alone would lock humanity into a cycle of dangerous warming from which it would not be able to escape.

Yet all levels of government have failed to respond to the climate crisis. Despite scientific clarity regarding the severity of the problem, international agreements to cap warming, and persistent lobbying by activists such as the defendants, federal, state, and local governments have remained in thrall to fossil fuel interests. The economic power of oil, gas, and coal companies, exacerbated by corruption and the evisceration of public participation in policymaking, have blocked governmental action on climate change, leaving no reasonable legal alternative for individuals seeking to avert its ongoing harms.

Faced with the decision regarding whether to sit passively and watch global warming ravage the planet or to take action to address this crisis, the defendants decided to engage in the long American tradition of civil disobedience. Since before the founding of the Republic, individual moral action taken in violation of the law and in furtherance of the public good has proven a crucial driver of social progress. From the Boston Tea Party, to women's suffrage protests, to the lunch counter sit-ins, individuals committing civil disobedience have advanced the nation's interests and provided a democratic check on the abuse of power.

Through the common law defense of necessity, the state of Minnesota provides protection for individuals, such as the defendants, who have broken the law for the greater good. Necessity has for centuries guided courts in ensuring that the spirit of the law trumps inflexible application of criminal statutes. As an essential aspect of government by and for the people, jury deliberation provides a method for the community to weigh the justification arguments of necessity defendants, as well as for the defendants to avail themselves of the right to be judged by their peers. In this case, the defendants can offer sufficient proof on each element of the necessity defense to present their evidence to a jury.[123]

The memorandum went on to describe the events of October 11, 2016, before launching into an extended discussion of why the facts of the case lined up with the elements of the necessity defense.

Placing the discussion in a broader frame, the "Legal Standard" section noted that the necessity defense "is prudential and reflects courts' understanding that strict enforcement of the law must sometimes give way to practical and moral considerations, as happens elsewhere in the criminal justice process, such as in prosecutorial charging decisions and sentencing hearings." Next, the brief stated that "it is incontrovertible that the common law allows the necessity defense for acts of civil disobedience"—an assertion backed up with a footnote documenting nineteen instances of successful political necessity defenses. The defense then pushed back on the government's argument that legal alternatives are always available in our political system, arguing that the existence of alternatives is a fact-dependent question that requires an inquiry into what sorts of legal options the defendants have actually attempted—in this case, many—and which have actually proven effective—in this case, none. As for imminence, the memorandum argued that this element requires a simple showing that a harm is "substantially certain to occur." Finally, the brief shifted emphasis away from whether civil disobedience is guaranteed to prevent a

123 Defendant's Response to State's Memorandum in Opposition to Affirmative Defense of Necessity at 1-2, *Minnesota v. Klapstein* (Feb. 3, 2017).

given harm to the likelihood that it will do so and to the reasonableness of the protesters in anticipating this causal connection.[124]

The heart of the defense brief came in the "Analysis" section,
where an overwhelming amount of evidence—including IPCC
reports, EPA studies, and even *Massachusetts v. EPA*—demonstrated
the existence and imminence of climate change harms. Indeed,
the fact that the "severe effects of climate change are already felt
in Minnesota and around the world" made this a moot point: climate change isn't just imminent, it's already occurring. The brief
also discussed at length the efforts of Annette Klapstein, Emily
Johnston, Ben Joldersma, and Steve Liptay to address global warming through legal channels, including testifying at local hearings,
meeting with elected officials, and organizing rallies. At the same
time, the activists' personal experiences, which included the successful use of civil disobedience to end Shell's efforts to drill in the
Arctic, demonstrated the efficacy of direct action. The defense also
quickly parried the prosecution's claim that the ravages of climate
change are perfectly legal: even if a pipeline operator has secured a
permit, the effects of its actions, including "sea level rise, extreme
weather events, drought, species extinction, air quality degradation, agricultural collapse, property damage, and many others"
violate core principles of our constitution and environmental statutes (more on these principles in Chapter 4).[125]

The final section of the defense brief offered what may have
been the most palatable argument for a judge. Given the evidence
listed above, the brief argued, the defendants had a constitutional

124   *Id.* at 3-10.
125   *Id.* at 10-28.

right to proceed to trial. Under the Sixth Amendment and the Supreme Court cases that have interpreted it, defendants have a right to a complete defense and the right to try their case as they see fit. Judges may exclude irrelevant evidence, but, once a substantial offer of proof on every element of a defense has been made, it's up to the jury to decide whether to believe it. The brief cited Minnesota's own highest court for the proposition that it is "fundamental that criminal defendants have a due process right to explain their conduct to a jury."[126]

The Valve Turner cases in North Dakota, Montana, and Washington proceeded in similar fashion. Scheduling orders were issued, the prosecution filed motions to block all evidence of necessity, and the defense team prepared legal arguments and scientific evidence. Expert witnesses in climate science and social change were recruited. Legal funds were raised. And the Valve Turners continued making their case to the public, waiting to find out whether they would be spending the coming years in jail as the world burned.

Meanwhile, the ground was shifting outside the courtroom. Donald Trump was elected president, signaling a giant step backwards in efforts to address the climate crisis and a consolidation of the forces of anti-environmentalism, white nationalism, and corporate control. The Standing Rock uprising reached a peak of violence on November 21, as police used rubber bullets, pepper spray, and water cannons to attack unarmed protesters.[127]

---

126   *Id.* at 31-4 (quoting *State v. Brechon,* 352 N.W.2d 751 (Minn. 1984)).

127   Alleen Brown, "Medics Describe How Police Sprayed Standing Rock Demonstrators With Tear Gas and Water Cannons," *The Intercept* (Nov. 21, 2016), https://theintercept.com/2016/11/21/medics-describe-how-police-sprayed-

As though reflecting the inscrutable mix of fear, hope, and confusion raging in the country, two momentous court cases made the news just as the Valve Turners prepared for their own trials. On October 27, a Portland, Oregon jury acquitted the Bundy brothers, who, along with a group of anti-government followers, had staged an armed occupation of a federal wildlife sanctuary in outrage over efforts to regulate their cattle grazing.[128] This acquittal, which signaled the government's inability to stop violent attacks on environmental regulation, stood in stark contrast to the legal fate of nonviolent protesters battling fossil fuels. Then, two days after the presidential election, in a suit brought by a group of young people against the federal government for inaction on climate change, the federal district court in Oregon recognized a right to "a climate system capable of sustaining human life"—the first time a court had recognized anything remotely like a fundamental duty to prevent global warming[129] (more on this case in Chapter 4).

As they got ready to face their judges, then, the Valve Turners found themselves in a time of radical uncertainty. Their best way forward, they decided, was simply to stick to their principles and to stand up in court for their actions. As Emily Johnston wrote in an op-ed published on the day of the action: "When we are old, what will we wish we had done? What will *you* wish you had done? How do we wake each other out of this?" She concluded with a simple, if

standing-rock-demonstrators-with-tear-gas-and-water-cannons/.

128 Courtney Sherwood and Kirk Johnson, "Bundy Brothers Acquitted in Takeover of Oregon Wildlife Refuge," *The New York Times* (Oct. 27, 2016), https://www.nytimes.com/2016/10/28/us/bundy-brothers-acquitted-in-takeover-of-oregon-wildlife-refuge.html.

129 *Juliana v. United States*, 217 F. Supp. 3d 1224, 1250 (D. Or. 2016). This case is discussed at length in Chapter 4.

infernally difficult, solution: "Direct action by itself, of course, won't be enough to set us on the right path. But when you're in a hole, the first thing you do is stop digging. So we have to stop digging."[130]

---

130   Emily Johnston, "The Time for Direct Action on Climate Change Is Now," *Truthout* (Oct. 11, 2016), https://truthout.org/articles/the-time-for-direct-ac-tion-is-now/.

CHAPTER 2

Law at the Origins of the Climate Crisis

Chapter 1 provided a map to climate law: its instruments, its possibilities, its gaps. This map showed that there are several possible ways to address climate change using existing law—the Clean Air Act, tort cases, state legislation—but that political opposition has exploited inadequacies of precedent and process to block climate remedies. Though we can see how the business activities that cause global warming remain legal, we have yet to really understand why this is the case. To do so, we need to look back to the origins of fossil law, and to provide a sort of historical atlas that will make sense of the lay of the land today.

The point of this history is to tie together the design of fossil law with its actual application. The fossil economy's legal infrastructure has emerged over centuries of economic growth and technological innovation. Policies designed to lower energy costs, increase industrial production, and expand the power of imperial nations were linked to laws that protect private property and

immunize corporate shareholders against the risks of investment
and the costs of environmental damage. Many of these laws originated in movements for social justice and individual liberty. But the
means of emancipation can in time become the methods of control:
legal principles once wielded against state tyranny are now often
exploited to defend established economic power and to encourage
ever-greater fossil-based consumption. Later in the chapter, we'll
see how environmental law, which seeks to contain the unantici-
pated consequences of such consumption, has had a difficult time
escaping from this bind.

A few legal ideas have been crucial to the growth in the use of
fossil fuels, and today they are important obstacles to a just transition. Think of them as a key to the atlas of fossil law:

- *Private property rights.* The idea that people and corporations
  should exercise exclusive dominion over individual pieces of
  territory, and that they alone are responsible for what happens there, doesn't work well in a world in which private
  economic activity has global consequences and in which
  climatic changes are experienced in diffuse, unpredictable
  ways. While the law doesn't only recognize this extreme
  form of ownership, property rights—especially those of
  fossil fuel companies—prove time and again to be a major
  impediment to effective climate regulation. This critique can
  be extended to private ownership of extraction technology,
  transmission equipment, and energy generation, as the law's
  bias toward the profit-making of private holdings hampers
  the use of this property for the collective good.

- *Corporate privilege.* Fossil fuel companies, like other corporations, enjoy an array of legal rights and protections, from the ability to exist in the first place—by no means a natural fact, but a deliberately designed legal strategy to facilitate the growth of private industry—to the "free speech" right to contribute to political campaigns. Of course, companies can't be arrested, and they can exploit loopholes in tax laws more easily than most individuals. This favorable set-up tends to enshrine the interests of the private sector over the public good.

- *Rules of standing.* The basic assumption in every legal case is that there are two parties involved in a conflict. One did wrong and the other seeks redress. This assumption has always made it hard to hold polluters accountable, as courts often question whether plaintiffs have suffered distinct injuries that entitle them to standing (remember the odd arguments that the states and cities had to put forth for standing in *Massachusetts v. EPA*). Relatedly, defendants in environmental suits often claim that they can't be made to answer for problems in which proof of causation and attribution is difficult. These issues are exacerbated in the case of climate change, where the problem is everywhere and nowhere at once and where the traditional model of direct, immediate harm is scientifically inaccurate. So long as the law imposes a threshold test inherited from an antiquated model of conflict, the prospects for holding fossil fuel companies are limited.

These are ostensibly neutral norms of legal procedure. How did they come to exert so much influence over the state of the world's climate?

A New Legal Infrastructure

As Andreas Malm documents in *Fossil Capital*, there was nothing inevitable about the world economy's shift to fossil fuels. Coal, the first widely-used fossil fuel, had been burned for centuries in Europe and China, but industrial applications did not emerge until the eighteenth century. This was a result of specific business strategies. British textile mill owners, who relied on cheap water power, began to grow frustrated with the seasonal fluctuations of rivers and the ability of workers at fixed mill sites to organize, walk off work, and control the rhythms of their labor. Seeking a situation more amenable to productive regularity, capitalists turned to coal. This energy source—which, after the invention of the steam engine, could power a mill at any time and in any place—offered consistent, predictable power. When transported into urban centers where pools of cheap labor were available, coal also gave owners the ability to favorably negotiate hours and wages. In short order, dirtier and more expensive coal proved a better lubricant of industrial efficiency than clean, cheap water.[131]

Property rights were a fundamental enabling condition for this transformative shift to industrial coal use. Individuals were able to own machinery and the land on which to operate it. Capitalists were able to combine money into joint stock companies to buy expensive steam engines and workers' time. If someone tried to

131   Andreas Malm, *Fossil Capital* (New York: Verso, 2016), 121-125.

break a work contract, steal a steam engine, or hold an investor individually liable for a company's losses, the state would intervene on the side of the property owner.

Such phenomena may seem as natural today as the burning of coal, but, from a historical perspective, they are exception rather than the rule. Other coal-rich regions like China lacked the sort of legal market structures that would enable wealthy individuals to experiment with corporate design and workplace models. Even in Britain, these reforms were the relatively recent product of centuries of middle-class ascendancy, and were actionable only because of other legal factors conducive to the rise of industrialization: the Enclosure Acts had kicked millions of agricultural workers from common lands and into city labor markets, and there were few penalties for the "externalities" of coal combustion such as air and water pollution.[132] When added to the appearance of the steam engine and, soon, the emergence of the steam engine-driven railroad—which was developed in large part to ease the transport of coal and finished mill products[133]—these legal facts created conditions ripe for profit-making. Michael Tigar, a famed radical attorney and legal historian, writes that, by 1750, "the fundamental changes in social structure, and new laws to define these changes, had been accomplished to the extent that the English bourgeoisie could take advantage of the innovations in technique and revolutionize the process of manufacture."[134]

132 E. P. Thompson, *The Making of the English Working Class* (New York: Vintage, 1966), 201, 213-231, 445.

133 Wolfgang Schivelbush, *The Railway Journey: The Industrialization of Time and Space in the Nineteenth Century* (University of California Press, 2014), 22-24.

134 Michael Tigar, *Law and the Rise of Capitalism*, (New York: Monthly Review Press, 2d ed. 2000), 242.

Britain thus became the first home of fossil law by offering a legal structure favorable to the exploitation of coal. But fossil law was not only applied in the industrial heartland: Britain's new economy depended on the reach of its empire. In the colonies, wealth was extracted from subject populations and sent home to be invested in new enterprises. Slaves grew cotton to be turned into textiles, and this remained the case even after the United States gained independence and Britain outlawed slavery. As the global market economy expanded, and as industrialization spread from Britain, raw materials—including, in time, oil—flowed to Europe and the United States and facilitated ever-greater consumption.

Law was an important part of this order, too, even if we're more likely to see the fundamental relation between colonizer and colonized as one of brute force. In the Americas, invading nations justified divvying up Indigenous lands with the "doctrine of discovery," which gave legal title to the supposedly more enlightened Europeans. This doctrine still serves as one of the foundations of U.S. Indian law, which recognizes the federal government's legal right to determine the fate of its Indigenous "wards."[135] In Latin America, Spanish colonizers and their descendants mostly ignored the 1512 Laws of Burgos that held Indigenous people to have human and property rights, preserving pseudo-feudal property regimes until the land reform wave of the twentieth century. Even after the wave of independence struggles in the nineteenth and twentieth centuries, the world continues to be largely defined by colonial legal relations, as nominally sovereign nations are held to

135 Joseph William Singer, "Sovereignty and Property." *Northwestern University Law Review* 86, no. 1 (1991-1992), 1-56.

agreements, backed by international law, that require the export of natural resources in exchange for development funds. Chief among these resources are oil, coal, and natural gas, whose trade is highly regulated at the international level and whose continued and increasing extraction is a top priority for those in command of the global economy.

The colonial nature of fossil law is intimately linked to the racial inequities that lie at the heart of the fossil fuel system. As we'll explore further in the next chapter, the growth of capitalist economies is dependent upon the raiding of Indigenous lands for resources and energy, a project that becomes increasingly important as industry seeks new reserves. Similarly, the legacy of slavery can be seen in how the effects of fossil fuel processing and combustion, such as toxic emissions from coal plants and oil refineries, are often felt much more severely by low-income communities of color.[136] These inequities are the result of a legal bias towards private enterprise and rising consumption and against other legal principles like the rights of self-determination and environmental well-being that might have provided a restraint on fossil law.

Growing from the coal-run British mills, the link between large-scale industry and the legal structure of the market—namely, laws that allowed capitalists to buy wage labor, fuel, and machines—reinforced itself as productivity increased. Wage

136   Adrian Wilson, *Coal Blooded: Putting Profits Before People* (Baltimore: National Association for the Advancement of Colored People, 2012), https://www.naacp.org/wp-content/uploads/2016/04/CoalBlooded.pdf; Lesley Fleischman and Marcus Franklin, *Fumes Across the Fenceline: The Health Impacts of Air Pollution from Oil & Gas Facilities on African American Communities* (Baltimore: National Association for the Advancement of Colored People, 2017), http://www.naacp.org/wp-content/uploads/2017/11/Fumes-Across-the-Fence-Line_NAACP_CATF.pdf.

relations were extended to other areas of the globe and industry's use of fossil fuels exploded, a process that continues today. For example, China's greenhouse gas emissions have risen in direct correlation to the country's embrace of capitalism; while involving a unique and more state-driven approach to economic growth and entrepreneurship than seen in the case of British industrialization, this process has depended upon the embrace of legal rules conducive to the profitable use of property and the engagement of labor contracts.[137]

Historian Timothy Mitchell argues that, beginning with the growth of the British coal economy, fossil fuels also played a determinative role in the formation of the modern liberal democratic nation-state and its distinct mode of managing class conflict. Coal facilitated the growth of industrial labor and commodity consumption in imperial metropoles, while at the same time encouraging a colonial system in which dependent foreign economies relied on solar energy to produce raw products like cotton and grain.[138] But coal, in Mitchell's account, was vulnerable to a major inconvenience: labor activism. Whereas early mill owners had favored the bituminous fuel because they could move it to central locations and avoid the natural and social inconstancies of dispersed workers at

137 Yonglong Lu, Yueqing Zhang, Xianghui Cao, Chenchen Wang, Yichao Wang, Meng Zhang, Robert C. Ferrier, Alan Jenkins, Jingjing Yuan, Mark J. Bailey, Deliang Chen, Hanqin Tian, Hong Li, Ernst Ulrich von Weizsäcker, Zhongxiang Zhang, "Forty years of reform and opening up: China's progress toward a sustainable path," *Science Advances* 5, no. 8 (Aug. 7 2019), https://advances.sciencemag.org/content/5/8/eaau9413; Ding Chen, Simon Deakin, Mathias Siems and Boya Wang, "Law, trust and institutional change in China: evidence from qualitative fieldwork," *Journal of Corporate Law Studies* 2 (2017), 257-290, https://www.tandfonline.com/doi/full/10.1080/14735970.2016.1270252.

138 Timothy Mitchell, *Carbon Democracy* (New York: Verso, 2013), 15-18.

rivers, their capitalist successors found themselves exposed to the threat of strikes at the massive mines and narrow transit routes that delivered their products to market. In fact, the physical concentration of miners and railroad workers played a major role in the emergence of working-class consciousness, as a small population of proletarians developed modes of organization and solidarity to exploit their power over capitalism's energy flows.[139] Still, miners met with repression and were often defeated: in 1914, efforts to set up a union at a coal mine in Ludlow, Colorado broke out into open battle between miners and the National Guard, triggering a wide-ranging regional conflict that left at least seventy-five people dead.[140]

Luckily for the capitalist class, a fix to the confrontational class politics of coal presented itself: oil. Beginning with wells in Pennsylvania in the 1850s, and accelerating with the development of reserves in present-day Azerbaijan, Saudi Arabia, and Iraq, imperial powers and Western corporations developed an energy system in which oil extraction occurred mostly at remote locations staffed by culturally and geographically isolated workers. Transoceanic and pipeline transport avoided the logistical pitfalls of railroad fuel shipment. The rise of combustion engines created a consumer class dependent upon energy companies who, thanks to new systems of control, were able to manipulate output to suit their needs. A new world order evolved in which colonial powers outsourced the conquest and defense of energy resources to imperial armies and local

---

139 *Id.* at 19-27.

140 Thomas G. Andrews, *Killing for Coal: America's Deadliest Labor War* (Harvard University Press, 2008), 13-14.

elites.[141] The twentieth century saw repeated instances of overt colonial violence aimed at maintaining the flow of oil, from the U.S. overthrow of democratic governments in Iraq and Iran to Shell Oil's campaign of war and dispossession in Ogoniland, Nigeria. Today, the United States military is the biggest consumer of fossil fuels in the world,[142] and that military's intervention in oil-producing nations like Iraq represents an estimated $81 billion in additional annual industry subsidies.[143] The link between state power and extraction becomes even clearer when we take note of the fact that 55 percent of the world's oil and gas is produced by governments themselves (national oil companies also control an estimated 90 percent of existing reserves).[144]

Where fossil fuel extraction occurred within the borders of colonial powers, the use of state violence took another form. For example, geographer Matthew T. Huber documents how the Texas and Oklahoma state governments imposed martial law in 1931 to prevent overproduction and maintain a high price for oil.[145] Throughout the twentieth and early twenty-first centuries,

141 Mitchell, *Carbon Democracy*, 31-42.

142 Neta C. Crawford, *Pentagon Fuel Use, Climate Change, and the Costs of War* (Providence, Rhode Island: Watson Institute, Brown University, 2019), https://watson.brown.edu/costsofwar/files/cow/imce/papers/Pentagon%20Fuel%20Use%2C%20Climate%20Change%20and%20the%20Costs%20of%20War%20Revised%20November%202019%20Crawford.pdf.

143 Securing America's Energy Future, *The Military Cost of Defending the Global Oil Supply* (Sep. 21, 2018), http://secureenergy.org/wp-content/uploads/2018/09/Military-Cost-of-Defending-the-Global-Oil-Supply.-Sep.-18.-2018.pdf.

144 National Resource Governance Institute, *The National Oil Company Database* (April 2019), https://resourcegovernance.org/sites/default/files/documents/national_oil_company_database.pdf.

145 Matthew T. Huber, *Lifeblood: Oil, Freedom, and the Forces of Capital* (University of Minnesota Press, 2013), 48-50.

national governments in the Americas have repeatedly invaded Indigenous territories to extract oil, a phenomenon analyzed in the next chapter.

The sharp uptick in emissions that accompanied the turn to a consumer-based economy in the United States also relied upon crucial legal changes. The "rule of capture," articulated by the Pennsylvania Supreme Court during that state's oil boom in the 1880s, gives ownership of a body of oil to whomever first taps it, regardless of whose land lies on top.[146] The 1935 Wagner Act, which recognized various workers' rights, helped the oil and oil-consuming industries by tamping down labor insurrections and uniting workers and management in a policy of ever-greater fossil-driven production and consumption. Later, initiatives like the Federal Housing Act and federal investment in bridges and highways encouraged the growth of suburbs and the widespread use of automobiles.[147]

The transportation of oil and gas is also facilitated by an array of legal rights and privileges. Defined as common carriers (oil)—a term for businesses like trains or telecommunications networks that transport public goods—or public utilities (gas), pipelines are often built after companies seize private property, which they can do under the power of eminent domain, the same power that allows the government to tear down houses in order to build highways. The Federal Energy Regulatory Commission is responsible for approving interstate gas pipelines, and as a general rule promotes the expansion of fossil fuel infrastructure over all other values; its

146 *Westmoreland & Cambria Natural Gas Co. v. DeWitt*, 18 A. 724 (Pa. 1889).
147 Huber, *Lifeblood*, 35-36, 38-42.

budget is entirely funded by industry and it has approved over 99 percent of the pipelines it has reviewed in the last two decades.[148]

Following the fuel on its path, there are laws that promote the use of automobiles, as in urban planning schemes that give car owners free street parking and devote tax dollars to road maintenance. The composition of the energy grid—how power is produced and where it flows—is highly regulated, with many energy companies operating as semi-public entities. The law says how much energy should be produced by natural gas versus coal, and what proportion of renewables utilities must use. The law also goes into minute detail on energy standards for vehicles and appliances. Then there are the more overt policy decisions codified into law: the fossil fuel industry enjoys tax write-offs for drilling costs, and federal agencies regularly issue permits and approvals for oil imports and oil and gas development on federal lands.

The idea behind these laws is that the government should help make energy cheap and readily available. But this policy has become an impediment to climate regulation and a giant giveaway to the fossil fuel industry. In Texas, for example, opponents of the Keystone XL Pipeline found that pipeline companies could take people's land simply by attesting that they were common carriers: no government review or approval was needed.[149]

One can think of this corner of the legal system—which sets rules for the production, transport, and use of energy—as an

---

148 Steve Horn, "FERC, Which Rejected 2 Gas Pipelines Out of 400 Since 1999, to Review Approval Policy," *Desmog Blog* (Dec. 26, 2017), https://www.desmog.com/2017/12/26/ferc-2-gas-pipelines-denied-400-approved-1999-rule/.

149 Alexandra B. Klass & Danielle Meinhardt, "Transporting Oil and Gas: U.S. Infrastructure Challenges," *Iowa Law Review* 100 (2015), 947-1053, 984.

institutional counterpart to the machines that drill, pump, and burn fuel. Like those machines, fossil law came into being in the late eighteenth and nineteenth centuries, and was largely exported from the industrial North Atlantic to the rest of the world by the middle of the twentieth. This apparatus generally runs smoothly, delivering corporate profits and the cheap energy that we use every day. And like its technical counterpart, we rarely pay it much mind.

Of course, state power can be exercised in the opposite direction. For example, the Obama administration included $90 billion for clean energy support in the stimulus package following the 2008 financial crisis. While the effort would have been better if it had included a comprehensive plan for a green grid or if bank bailouts had been conditioned on financing renewable energy,[150] this use of legal measures to erode fossil fuels' market power demonstrates that governments are not incapable of escaping the bind of fossil law.

Note that the legal changes that facilitated the consumption of oil, gas, and coal partly caused and partly accompanied changes in economic scale and structure. The ability of a mill-owner to enlist the state in enforcing labor contracts allowed for, but didn't fully explain, that owner's expanded use of coal to power his looms. Laws that protect U.S. corporations drilling for oil in the Middle East and Latin America enable their success, but so too do military interventions and energy demand at home. Most obviously, technological innovation has driven the rise of the fossil fuel economy, while transformations in culture and worldview—which accommodated

150 Kate Aronoff, Alyssa Battistoni, Daniel Aldana Cohen, and Thea Riofrancos, *A Planet to Win* (New York: Verso, 2019), 11-14.

and even promoted the introduction of industry and fossil fuel use into everyday life—were also crucial. So the role of law should not be overstated, even as its presence is evident in every step of industrial development. Law has been a necessary but not sufficient condition in the ever-increasing emissions of greenhouse gases.

In short, the adoption of fossil fuels to power the world economy has depended upon a fossil law that arranges a particular type of market and enforces a particular balance of power.

So who's to blame?

Law Under Capitalism

From a left critical perspective, the answer is clear: law is the handmaiden of capital, and so by definition it facilitates the deleterious effects of unbridled economic growth on the planet. Marxists and anarchists have long viewed both domestic and international legal systems as extensions of capitalist control over the workplace. Leading Soviet legal theorist Evgeny Pashukanis argued in *The General Theory of Law and Marxism* that the law is derivative of property relations, and that, historically, public law developed from the regulation of conflicts between owners: "the economic relation in its actual workings is the source of the legal relation, which comes into being only at the moment of dispute."[151] In other words, once commodity exchange becomes the governing logic of society—determining how we live, work, and interact with our environment—law develops as the regulatory mechanism that keeps this exchange system in place. This is the case even in areas of

151   Evgeny B. Pashukanis, *The General Theory of Law and Marxism*, trans. Barbara Einhorn (New Brunswick, NJ: Transaction Publishers, 2002), 93

the law that seem to have nothing to do with property conflict, such as prohibitions on incest or free speech; all of these, in this Marxist account, are based on a concepts of abstract rights and abstract legal subjects whose basis is the economic relationship: "legal fetishism complements commodity fetishism."[152] For Pashukanis, the arrival of communism would mean "the withering away of law altogether."[153]

Moving further to the left, anarchist critique typically views the law as an irredeemable instrument of coercion. The state, often in allegiance with capital, oppresses the people through its courts and police, and justifies its domination with pretty language about justice and rights. Peter Kropotkin, a prominent Russian anarchist of the nineteenth century, wrote that "[t]he law [is] nothing but an instrument for the maintenance of exploitation, and the domination of the toiling masses by rich idlers."[154] The climate crisis, a conjoined natural and social disaster visited by the wealthy on the poor, is in this picture just the latest in a series of injustices facilitated by the legal system.

A more recent left critical perspective more overtly concerned with nonhumans and planetary health renders a similar judgment. In this account, capitalism inexorably destroys natural systems and pollutes the Earth: this is the result of an inherent anti-ecological tendency and not a mere side effect of class oppression. The law's failure to do much about this—indeed, its seeming blindness to the well-being of the Earth system and its promotion of environmental

152 *Id.* at 14.

153 *Id.* at 61.

154 Pierre Kropotkine [Peter Kropotkin], *Law and Authority: An Anarchist Essay* (London: International Publishing Co., 1887), 17.

abuses—places it squarely on the side of the destroyers, and nothing short of an ecosocialist revolution will reverse this.[155]

Whether or not you agree with these theoretical prescriptions, it's easy to see how fossil law's market design creates ecological problems. Price signals have trouble capturing environmental values like breathing clean air or avoiding extinction, so production and consumption are systematically privileged over less quantifiable interests. Furthermore, it's hard to avoid harming the environment when you work in a capitalist economy. The need for most workers to sell their labor time in a competitive market makes it very difficult to simply choose greener jobs: coal miners and gas station attendants are forced to think primarily in terms of dollars and cents, not community and environmental well-being. And market-driven solutions for ecological crises leave much to be desired. For example, "lifestyle environmentalism"—the idea that we will create a more ecologically just society through individual behavioral changes rather than through political and legal reform—necessarily relies upon the market power of more affluent consumers, which provides them the flexibility to choose more environmentally-friendly commodities, or, to a limited extent, live outside commodity chains altogether. This is not an option for most people. So long as the law creates and enforces a commodity- and class-based economy, then, the best climate policies are usually just tweaks at the margins.[156]

---

155 See e.g., Joel Kovel, *The Enemy of Nature: The End of Capitalism or the End of the World?* (New York: Zed Books, 2007), 88-91, 270.

156 For an analysis of the class dynamics of environmental and climate politics, see Matt T. Huber, "Ecological Politics for the Working Class," *Catalyst*, 3 no. 1 (Spring 2019), https://catalyst-journal.com/vol3/no1/ecological-politics-for-the-working-class.

Still, this story might strike you as a bit too neat. Was the law ever really "designed" to promote global warming? Of course not. The inventors of the joint stock enterprise knew nothing of the greenhouse effect. To the extent that we can attribute intent to a centuries-long tradition involving millions of legislators, litigants, and jurists, we would say that the fundaments of fossil law were put in place to promote economic growth and individual autonomy. These are fine principles in themselves, but they can easily become instruments of oppression or disaster. Maybe we can forgive the law's support of the emergence of the fossil-fuel system. But let's not overlook its complicity in its perpetuation.

Environmental Law?

If we want to overturn fossil law, then, we need a legal response that will address that complicity and promote a vision for a better-ordered society. The first candidate that comes to mind is environmental law, which has made some significant strides in regulating industrial activity and in translating the lessons of the ecological sciences into policy. But, for reasons that will be discussed in a moment, environmental law has so far proven inadequate. Focusing on the United States, this section addresses a few myths that cause us to invest so much hope in environmental law as it currently exists, and explains why this hope is largely misplaced.

As mentioned in Chapter 1, U.S. environmental law only came into being as a coherent entity at the end of the 1960s, with the passage of the first major environmental statutes and the emergence of the first self-described environmental lawyers. Actually, "coherent" is a mischaracterization. The field is notoriously complicated, diffuse, and immune to conceptual reduction. This difficulty isn't the result of a conspiracy to keep laypeople away; rather, it's a testament to the patchwork approach to environmental policy generally. Remember, the United States has yet to endorse environmental values at the constitutional level.

The birth of modern U.S. environmental law presents a conundrum. If our legal and political institutions really are committed to economic growth and the protection of private property, how was it that the Congress unanimously approved—and a business-friendly Republican administration signed into law—legislation designed to curb industrial activity in favor of environmental health?

For one thing, the ostensible contradiction between economic and environmental well-being was not as sharply felt in the late 1960s and early 1970s as it is today. Business leaders and conservationists often agreed that capitalism was best served by mild government intervention to preserve public resources like clean air and water; this was seen not as a threat to the established order but as a guarantee of its survival. Another explanation is that early supporters of environmental legal initiatives, including President Nixon, didn't understand the monster they were creating. The enforcement of laws like the National Environmental Policy Act, the Clean Water Act, and the Endangered Species Act produced unexpected regulatory and production demands on private business, and, within a few years, many early advocates for the statutes were condemning them. Corporate and conservative messaging began promoting the idea of a zero-sum game between protecting profits and protecting the planet. It's also important to note that, for a brief moment, environmentalists were able to present their cause as a bipartisan one, and politicians bowed to their demands out of fear of losing votes. But as environmental regulation became a wedge issue over the course of the 1970s, the field's political neutrality disappeared.[157]

One thing did unify environmental law in its beginnings, however: it was committed to the protection of the natural world and the promotion of humans' environmental well-being. This seems obvious. Environmental law, like civil rights law, seems to be as much a project as it is a discipline or a profession: its values are built in.

But it turns out that many, if not most, environmental lawyers actually work against the field's original commitments, largely in the employ of industry.[158] (The same goes for other areas of the law: the best professional and financial opportunities lie in defending *against* civil rights or sexual harassment claims, or in forcing tenants out of their homes.) Give credit where it's due: businesses and their political backers got organized in the 1980s, developing a strategy that confronted environmentalism head-on while co-opting its messaging and strategies. Furthermore, as Robert Gottlieb and Mark Dowie describe in their histories of U.S. environmentalism, professionalization and market-centered approaches have changed the culture of the movement's legal wing from a "sue the bastards" approach to a more accommodationist stance.[159] A

---

157 *See* Richard Lazarus, *The Making of Environmental Law* (University of Chicago Press, 2004); Mark Dowie, *Losing Ground: American environmentalism at the close of the twentieth century* (MIT Press, 1996).

158 *See* Law Students for Climate Accountability, *The 2020 Law Firm Climate Change Scorecard* (Oct. 2020), https://static1.squarespace.com/static/5f53fa556b708446acb4dcb5/t/5f755753f217027860728759/1601525603800/Law+Firm+Climate+Change+-Scorecard.pdf.

159 Robert Gottlieb, *Forcing the Spring: The Transformation of the American En-*

major effect of this shift has been to deepen the divide between mainstream environmentalism, with its better-funded and mostly white leadership, and environmental justice movements, which tend to be more ethnically diverse and shorter on resources.

So, first myth dispelled: environmental law isn't so much law *for* the environment as it is law *about* the environment.

Second myth: environmental law has been a huge success.

There is a definite triumphalist tone in many depictions of the field. Consider the assessment by Richard Lazarus, an accomplished litigator and professor of environmental law at Harvard: "In many respects, the quality of the natural environment in the United States is better on an absolute scale than it was over three decades ago, notwithstanding the tremendous increased in economic activity during the same period . . . [T]he far worse environmental catastrophes experienced by many other industrialized nations offer compelling testimony to what environmental law has spared the United States."[160]

It's easy to see why environmental lawyers turn to this argument. Their skin is in the game. They've achieved some remarkable victories against long odds, and, when reasoning from counterfactuals, they make the fair point that things could have been much worse: for example, U.S. air today contains much less lead and sulfur dioxide, and twice as many U.S. waterways are swimmable or fishable, than was the case in the 1960s.[161] Who knows how bad

vironmental Movement (Washington, DC: Island Press, 2005), 216-7; Dowie, *Losing Ground* 116.

160   *The Making of Environmental Law*, xiv.

161   Emily Greenhalgh, "Five successes to celebrate this Earth Day," *National Oceanic and Atmospheric Association: Climate.gov* (Apr. 22, 2016), https://www.climate.gov/news-features/features/five-successes-celebrate-earth-day.

things would have been without our existing system of environmental regulation?

But this is a gaze from within. It mostly accepts our currently existing political and economic systems as given, and assesses the success of environmentalist efforts based on the limited possibilities currently available. Even when celebrating truly laudable advances like those mentioned above, or more specifically legal victories like the recognition of citizen standing to assert general harms to natural resources[162] and the Endangered Species Act's explicit valuation of wildlife health over economic utility,[163] the assumption of environmental law triumphalism is that progress should be measured against a background of unchecked economic growth.

If we take a step back, the picture is much darker. The lifespan of U.S. environmental law has coincided with the largest die-off of species in sixty-six million years.[164] The Environmental Law Institute celebrated its fiftieth anniversary in the same year that Amazon deforestation spiked to its greatest rate in a decade.[165] And

162 "Citizen suit" provisions are included in many environmental statutes. *United States v. Students Challenging Regulatory Agency Procedure*, 412 U.S. 669 (1973) allowed environmental organizations to sue over injury to their members' recreational interests. The question of standing has grown substantially more complicated as judicial conservatives seek to limit standing, as in *Lujan v. Defenders of Wildlife*, 504 U.S. 555 (1992), where a majority led by Justice Scalia ruled that an environmental organization had failed to show how its members would be effected by a decision not to apply the Endangered Species Act review provisions to international projects.

163 16 U.S.C. § 1533(b)(1)(A). Not surprisingly, the Trump administration proposed injecting economic considerations into decisions to list endangered species. 50 CFR Part 17 (July 25, 2018).

164 Michael Greshko and National Geographic Staff, "What are mass extinctions, and what causes them?" *National Geographic* (Sep. 26, 2019), https://www.nationalgeographic.com/science/prehistoric-world/mass-extinction/.

165 Jonathan Watts, "Amazon deforestation 'at highest level in a decade,'" *The*

environmental law has done almost nothing to stop the climate crisis from spiraling out of control. If we take into account the fact that wealthy nations have made modest progress in reducing greenhouse gas emissions in part because they have outsourced fossil fuel-intensive production to countries like India and China—the so-called "carbon loophole" or "emissions transfer" problem[166]—then the capacity of our existing regulatory systems to handle the problem is thrown into even greater doubt. It's simply impossible to reconcile a truly positive assessment of environmental law with the dire state of Earth systems today.[167]

Third myth: environmental law offers a viable alternative to fossil law's dominion.

Here's where we get back to the structural questions with which this chapter began and to a specific focus on climate change. The social phenomenon of global warming, as a by-product of explosive economic expansion since the Industrial Revolution, is traceable to a basic code at the root of the capitalist world system, one that vaunts property rights, individualism, and private enterprise. Environmental law shares this code. It has mostly acted not

Guardian (Nov. 18, 2019), https://www.theguardian.com/environment/2019/nov/18/amazon-deforestation-at-highest-level-in-a-decade.

166 *See* Daniel Moran, Ali Hasanbeigi, and Cecilia Springer, "The Carbon Loophole in Climate Policy: Quantifying the Embodied Carbon in Traded Products" (KG&M Associates Pty Ltd., Global Efficiency Intelligence, LLC, and ClimateWorks Foundation 2018), https://buyclean.org/media/2016/12/The-Carbon-Loophole-in-Climate-Policy-Final.pdf; Brad Plumer, "A closer look at how rich countries 'outsource' their CO2 emissions to poorer ones," *Vox* (Aug. 18, 2017), https://www.vox.com/energy-and-environment/2017/4/18/15331040/emissions-outsourcing-carbon-leakage.

167 For a balanced account of U.S. environmentalism's successes and failures since the first Earth Day in 1970, *see* Brad Plumer and John Schwartz, "50 Years of Earth Day: What's Better Today, and What's Worse." *The New York Times* (April 21, 2020), https://www.nytimes.com/interactive/2020/climate/earth-day-history.html/.

to prevent ecological damage, but to mitigate it—at best, a patch on the underlying system. Consider how different the assessment of environmental law is when approached from this perspective— asking not what the field has accomplished as a *restraint* on the expansion of capitalist relations, but as a *participant* in it.

Michael M'Gonigle and Louise Takeda, professors at the University of Victoria who advocate for a new paradigm of legal-ecological relations, write that

> stable economic management lies at the core of modernist state politics with its attendant need for ever more energy, ever more consumption, and ever more extractions from nature, all at the least possible cost. Thus does a seemingly irresolvable conundrum between economic production and environmental protection pervade the modern state ... Environmental law was born not to resolve this conundrum but to bolster one side of it by providing a bulwark against ecological erosion.[168]

This pattern is clearly manifested in the dominance of cost-benefit analysis. As an approach to designing regulations and predicting their effects, cost-benefit analysis seeks to quantify all aspects of human-environmental interaction. In recent decades, it has become a leading paradigm for regulators and the judges who review their work. In considering whether to ban an industrial toxin, for example, the EPA will calculate the likely economic cost of this ban and compare it to the environmental and public health benefits, rendered in dollars: how much a clean river or a human life is worth. This method has been useful in addressing macro-level

168 Michael M'Gonigle and Louise Takeda, "The Liberal Limits of Environmental Law: A Green Legal Critique," *Pace Environmental Law Review* 30, no. 3 (2013), 1005-1115 1012.

planning and measurement problems, as in the ecosystem services approach to monitoring global ecological trends, and it has helped to describe humanity's reliance on healthy Earth systems. It's also important to demonstrating that climate regulation is financially sound: the savings in job growth, infrastructure maintenance, and health care spending, to name just a few considerations, far outweigh the costs of overhauling our energy system.[169]

But cost-benefit analysis tends generally to disfavor such regulation by prioritizing short-term monetary gain. When elevated to a universal management solution, it tips the scales in favor of economic growth and anthropocentric value: the environment becomes merely a source of "natural capital," and all questions of well-being and justice are reduced to an accounting exercise.[170]

Environmental law's allegiance to the economic status quo can also be seen in the capture of regulatory agencies by business interests. Mary Wood — a professor of environmental law at the University of Oregon and one of the pioneers of the "atmospheric trust doctrine," which will be analyzed in Chapter 4 — identifies the "illusion of environmental law" as the fact that, while the field

---

169 *See* Nadra Rahman and Jessica Wentz, "The Price of Climate Deregulation: Adding Up the Costs and Benefits of Federal Greenhouse Gas Emission Standards" (Columbia Law School Sabin Center for Climate Change Law 2017), http://columbiaclimatelaw.com/files/2016/06/Rahman-and-Wentz-2017-08-The-Price-of-Climate-Deregulation.pdf.

170 For studies of the growing role of cost-benefit analysis in environmental regulation and its problematic effects, see Laurence Tribe, "Ways Not to Think About Plastic Trees: New Foundations for Environmental Law," *Yale Law Journal* 83 (1974), 1315-1348; Douglas Kysar, *Regulating from Nowhere: Environmental Law and the Search for Objectivity* (Yale University Press, 2010); and Giulia Wegner and Unai Pascual, "Cost-benefit analysis in the context of ecosystem services for human well-being: A multidisciplinary critique," *Global Environmental Change* 21, no. 2 (2011), 492-504.

aims to protect the environment, it has been enlisted by industry to help destroy it:

> We can pass any new environmental law we want, but no matter what it says, if it stays bounded by the frame in which we've operated for the last four decades, government will continue to impoverish natural resources until our society can no longer sustain itself . . . Environmental statutes do not declare a purpose of allowing rampant natural resource destruction, but we know from experience that they will accomplish precisely that result if the agencies stay captive to the industries they are supposed to regulate.[171]

The discussion above has already given us enough evidence to support this assessment. Recall the major impediment to climate change lawsuits: judges are wary of appearing to interfere with the economy, either via agency regulation or court orders. Recall the EPA's disastrous inconsistency on greenhouse gas emissions, a direct result of fossil fuel industry influence over government. Recall the fate of global climate talks, where negotiations are oriented toward minimizing interference with profits.

Finally, consider the matter of environmental justice. Since the 1980s, activists have made great strides in addressing and ameliorating the disproportionate impact of environmental harm on racial minorities and poor people. In 1991, the First National People of Color Environmental Leadership summit issued its groundbreaking Principles of Environmental Justice, which asserted the need to ground environmental policy in progressive racial, social,

171   *Nature's Trust*, xvii

and economic values.[172] In 1994, President Clinton issued an executive order requiring each federal agency to "make achieving environmental justice part of its mission," largely through information-gathering.[173] This increased the visibility of environmental justice issues without producing definite changes in policy. The Obama administration strengthened such measures, though they still remained mostly administrative.[174] In the courts, the reception of environmental justice has been colder, largely as a result of procedural obstacles to civil rights claims based on environmental injuries. In 1983, the Supreme Court ruled that plaintiffs alleging racial discrimination in federal actions—such as the permitting of hazardous sites—must prove discriminatory intent, which is much harder to prove than discriminatory effect.[175] In 2001, the Court imposed another barrier, ruling that there is no right to bring a lawsuit to challenge the disparate racial impact of such federal actions.[176] In short, environmental justice has received plenty of official lip-service, while the law falls well short of giving injured individuals and communities legitimate avenues for redress.

This is what environmental law, and fossil law, look like. The point of this reckoning is not to sow despair, but to encourage honesty. If we want laws commensurate to the scale of the climate crisis, we simply cannot accept what we've inherited. We need legal

---

172   The Principles of Environmental Justice (Oct. 1991), available at https://www.nrdc.org/sites/default/files/ej-principles.pdf.

173   Exec. Order 12,898, 59 Fed. Reg. 32 (Feb. 11, 1994).

174   Environmental Protection Agency, "Memorandum of Understanding on Environmental Justice and Executive Order 12898" (2011), https://www.epa.gov/sites/production/files/2015-02/documents/ej-mou-2011-08.pdf.

175   *Guardians Ass'n v. Civil Service Commission*, 463 U.S. 582 (1983).

176   *Alexander v. Sandoval*, 532 U.S. 275 (2001).

thinking that doesn't limit itself to its own self-understanding, but instead places itself within a larger world of social and natural relations.

Can the Law Be Redeemed?

So what is the law of climate change? One answer suggested in these first two chapters: there isn't much. This is true quantitatively, if you consider the numbers of statutes, regulations, and court opinions dealing with global warming, at least in the United States. The fact that the Clean Air Act doesn't even address the problem is a sign of this general reticence. Climate law is a remarkably underdeveloped field. The professionals have their work cut out for them.

But there's another answer that is perhaps more instructive. The law of climate change is fossil law: the system of rules and concepts that have historically facilitated the rise of the fossil-based economy, and which today support the continued use of fossil fuels to the detriment of other energy sources. This law—which rarely mentions greenhouse gas emissions directly—mostly operates in favor of the oil, gas, and coal industries, and protects a series of rights, privileges, and customs that make a just transition to renewables very difficult. Designed to make cheap energy readily available, this system, like other areas of politics and the economy, is captured by wealthy interests resistant to change.

You'd be justified if, at this point, you get the feeling that climate legal activism is a fool's errand. Filing lawsuits and going to global climate talks can feel like beseeching a bully to let your head up from the ground. It's fair to say that attorneys who spend their time looking for creative angles in the law have little to show in terms of lowering the atmospheric concentration of carbon dioxide.

But, *but*—the situation is not quite this simple. As in any social sphere, the law is shot through with competing interests and antagonistic values. And it isn't static: it changes constantly, sometimes even in its core commitments, and often against the desires of those it ostensibly serves.

To use a classic example from another area of the law: consider how civil rights developed in the century after the Civil War. The Thirteenth, Fourteenth, and Fifteenth Amendments abolished slavery and aimed to grant full political rights to black males. In the ensuing decades, federal courts allied with reactionary racists to thwart this effort, culminating in the Supreme Court's 1896 *Plessy v. Ferguson* decision which ruled that segregation in public accommodations was lawful.[177] Two generations later, the same court reversed itself in *Brown v. Board of Education,* ruling that "separate but equal" in unconstitutional and that schools and places of business cannot segregate by race.[178] This sequence makes it difficult to flatly declare just what the legal system's attitude toward race relations is. Given the law's endorsement of white supremacy—from the text of the Constitution to judges' refusal to stop racial gerrymandering today—it would certainly be accurate to say that U.S. law is shot through with racism. But this categorical statement cannot explain how the judiciary has at the same time embraced racial progress, often in advance of the other branches of government.

177   163 U.S. 537 (1896).
178   347 U.S. 483 (1954).

Similarly, while we see many courts rejecting efforts to advance climate justice, others embrace them. Our discussion of climate law therefore needs a bit of nuance, even if the overall picture of power and privilege is clear. Luckily, there are other resources from the left critical tradition that can help us.

The thinking of Italian theorist Antonio Gramsci is especially useful for considering institutions like the law as semi-autonomous fields in which social classes fight for "hegemony." Using a Gramscian analysis, you would say that the fossil fuel industry exerts hegemony over the law, but that counter-hegemonic projects launched by environmentalists, Indigenous people, climate change-affected communities, and even some nation-states seek to reverse this.[179] These counter-hegemonic projects have a real chance of stealing the legal system away from its current masters, and this victory could be linked to counter-hegemonic projects in politics and the economy. This picture is an alternative to the one that views the law as part of a monolithic system of oppression that must be overthrown all at once. It also recognizes the fact that, even should an ecosocialist or climate justice revolution occur, there will continue to be battles of hegemony within the more enlightened social systems that have been created. The question of what the law *is* cannot be answered once and for all: it's always a matter of contention. Climate law is a mix of fossil law and its antithesis: the law of a just transition.

179 Antonio Gramsci, *Prison Notebooks*, trans. Joseph A. Buttigieg and Antonio Callari (Columbia University Press, 1991). *See also* Alan Hunt, "Rights and Social Movements: Counter-Hegemonic Strategies," *Journal of Law and Society* 17, no. 3 (Autumn 1990), 309-328.

The breathing-room this accounts allows makes it possible to acknowledge real successes on the climate law front, some of which have been described above. Many cities and states, often in conjunction with non-U.S. governments, have passed laws or made pledges to overhaul their energy networks. These plans would directly challenge fossil fuel dominance and, in some cases, address the deep inequalities associated with the disparate impacts of climate change. At long last, there are also signs of hope on the litigation front, as seen in the wave of tort lawsuits against fossil fuel producers and in the development of novel legal tools like the atmospheric trust doctrine and the rights of nature (these will be more fully explored in Chapter 4).

At the level of the law's deep bias toward fossil fuel development, courts have recently started to question private companies' power to seize land for pipelines: New Jersey has successfully pushed back on PennEast's effort to take control of state property,[180] and the town of Oberlin, Ohio has convinced the D.C. Circuit Court of Appeals to question the Federal Energy Regulatory Commission's grant of eminent domain to a pipeline, a process which up until now has been a matter of routine approval.[181] Under the Trump administration, some federal courts began to look more closely at the permitting of fossil fuel infrastructure, requiring deeper environmental reviews and cancelling drilling leases.[182] Notably, the Dakota Access Pipeline was ordered to cease operations after

---

180 *In Re: PennEast Pipeline, Co, LLC,* No. 19-1991 (3rd Cir. Sep. 10, 2019).

181 *City of Oberlin, Ohio v. Federal Energy Regulatory Commission,* No. 18-1248 (D.D.C. Sep. 6, 2019).

182 Matthew Brown, "Trump's fossil fuel agenda gets pushback from federal judges," *Associated Press* (May 28, 2020).

a federal court found that the Army Corps of Engineers' environmental analysis of the project under the National Environmental Policy Act was insufficient.[183] In April 2020, the federal district court of Montana ruled that a long-standing practice whereby the Army Corps of Engineers granted blanket permission for discharging dredged material from pipeline construction into federal waters was unlawful, disturbing the traditional rubber-stamp process for such projects.[184] The Atlantic Coast Pipeline was then aborted by its owners, who claimed that "a series of legal challenges to the project's federal and state permits has caused significant project cost increases and timing delays. These lawsuits and decisions have sought to dramatically rewrite decades of permitting and legal precedent."[185] Although the Supreme Court later reversed the Montana ruling for the majority of the country's pipelines—with the notable exception of the Keystone XL pipeline, whose construction was temporarily suspended[186]—the prospect of "legal uncertainty" in the construction of fossil fuel infrastructure has scared investors, who are increasingly turning to other forms of energy development.[187] And there are even signs that more explicit climate

183 *Cheyenne River Sioux Tribe*, No. CV 16-1534 (D.D.C. July 6, 2020).

184 *N. Plains Res. Council v. U.S. Army Corps of Engineers*, No. CV-19-44-GF-BMM (D. Mont., Apr. 15, 2020).

185 "Dominion Energy and Duke Energy cancel the Atlantic Coast Pipeline," *Duke Energy* (July 5, 2020), https://news.duke-energy.com/releases/dominion-energy-and-duke-energy-cancel-the-atlantic-coast-pipeline?utm_source=TWITTER&utm_medium=DukeEnergy&utm_term=--multimedia&utm_content=3470104365-20200705-20200705190705&utm_campaign=Evergreen.

186 *N. Plains Res. Council*, No. 19A1053 (U.S. July 6, 2020)

187 "Dominion Energy and Duke Energy cancel the Atlantic Coast Pipeline," *Duke Energy*; Jonathan Mingle, "How Overreach by Trump Administration Derailed Big Pipeline Projects, *Yale Environment 360* (July 15, 2020), https://e360.yale.edu/features/how-overreach-by-trump-administration-de-

justice questions are finally meriting serious judicial notice: in early 2020, a federal appeals court vacated a state permit granted to the Atlantic Coast Pipeline due to concerns that a compressor station would disproportionately affect a black community.[188]

This short list shows that the story of climate law is not as simple as the state's sanctioning of climate injustice, even if that remains the story's major theme. Obstacles are obstacles, and we should seek to remove them. While staying true to some fundamental principles such as the right of every human to a healthy environment—more on that in Chapter 4—advocates needs to embrace an instrumental approach to climate law, seizing on victories where they can and opening new arenas of conflict on their enemies' turf.

One area of the law where this is happening is in criminal courts. This may be a surprising place for a study of climate law, because problems of environmental law have generally been considered separate from the state's prosecution of individual wrongdoing. But with resistance to the fossil fuel system increasing, activists and protesters have increasingly found themselves hauled off to jail and made to answer for their actions in defense of the climate.

This is a greatly understudied and crucially important part of the legal system's encounter with global warming. Government persecution of climate activists—often in tandem with corporate

railed-big-pipeline-projects.

188 *Friends of Buckingham v. State Air Pollution Board*, No. 19-1152 (4th Cir. Jan. 7, 2020) (this decision followed a series of others that blocked the pipeline on environmental review grounds). *See also* Gregory S. Schneider, "As court challenges pile up, gas pipeline falls behind," *The Washington Post* (Dec. 21, 2018), https://www.washingtonpost.com/local/virginia-politics/as-court-challenges-pile-up-gas-pipeline-falls-behind/2018/12/29/8637dbd2-0549-11e9-b5df-5d3874f1ac36_story.html.

efforts—occurs at the front line of the fight for an environmentally just future. When this persecution makes it into court, and when the fight is dramatized in the form of a trial, the battle for legal hegemony reaches a point of ultimate clarity. The legal saga of the Valve Turners is a paradigmatic instance: in their cases, issues of state capture by industry, the inadequacy of the law in the face of the climate crisis, and the possibility of change in the legal system come to a head.

To get a handle on why these court battles are so important and instructive, it's time to shift the discussion away from a focus on climate regulation *per se*. Just as determinative as what the law says or doesn't say about the climate crisis is what the legal system— including, crucially, the police—does in the middle of the fight for our future. State repression is one of the main faces that the law wears in its engagement with global warming, and it's the topic of Chapter 3.

The Valve Turners
Part 2: Climate on Trial

The phenomenon mentioned at the end of the previous chapter—state violence used to protect and promote the fossil fuel system—was the major theme of the Valve Turner cases. This was most obviously true in the simple fact that the activists were arrested and required to attend court under penalty of imprisonment. The use of coercion against people trying to stop climate catastrophe rather than against the people causing it is a striking inversion of ecological and humane values.

But it is a well-known fact of social progress that tomorrow's heroes are often today's criminals. Consider this another lesson about the law's functioning: to metabolize change, the legal system first ignores a plea for justice, then attacks it, and finally adopts it as its own. The law was blind to climate change for decades; now it persecutes those who take it too seriously. The Valve Turners' story tells us a bit about how long this second phase might last, and what a real judicial reckoning with warming would look like.

But first, the reaction. On December 9, 2016—less than two months after the Valve Turners' action, and as the legal teams in each state were preparing their pre-trial filings—the federal Pipeline and Hazardous Materials Safety Administration (PHMSA) issued an advisory bulletin to pipeline owners and operators. The bulletin alleged that, on October 11, "several unauthorized persons accessed and interfered with pipeline operations in four states, creating the potential for serious infrastructure damage and significant economic and environmental harm, as well as endangering public safety. While the incidents did not result in any damage or injuries, the potential impacts emphasize the need for increased awareness and vigilance." The bulletin went on to encourage pipeline operators to keep an eye out for suspicious activity, to increase security patrols, and to invest in better locks and fencing. The agency reminded its audience that "a strong relationship with local law enforcement is extremely beneficial for safe pipeline operations."[189]

This rather banal bureaucratic notice was a sign that the government was playing close attention to the Valve Turners. Indeed, the bulletin noted that federal law imposes a maximum penalty of twenty years in prison on "any person that willingly and knowingly injures or destroys, or attempts to injure or destroy a pipeline facility"[190]—a signal that federal law enforcement was considering its options for dealing with anti-pipeline protests. In 2018, *The Intercept* reported on a Department of Homeland Security (DHS) "Field Analysis Report" issued on May 2, 2017 that described the Valve Turners as "suspected environmental rights extremists" who "showed a high level of pre-operational planning." The report

189　81 FR 89183.

190　49 CFR 190.291.

portrayed the activists as sophisticated violent actors, and also commented on the clashes at Standing Rock, a mobilization that the DHS viewed as "environmental rights extremists exploit[ing] Native American causes in furtherance of their own violent agenda."[191]

On October 23, 2017, eighty-four congresspeople, the vast majority of them Republicans, sent a letter to then-Attorney General Jeff Sessions asking him why the Department of Justice had not prosecuted the Valve Turners, and inquiring whether their actions were punishable under federal terrorism statutes or the Patriot Act. The letter raised the red herring of pipeline safety— the Valve Turners had in fact created no risk of a spill or explosion, as their evidence at trial (when they were allowed to present it) would demonstrate—and closed with the typical association of fossil fuels and state interest: "maintaining safe and reliable energy infrastructure is a matter of national security."[192] In the wake of the letter, the American Petroleum Institute, the industry's lead trade group, said that it had been working with the Department of Justice, the FBI, and the PHMSA to press for federal charges,[193] and

---

191   Alleen Brown, "'Environmental Extremism' or Necessary Response to Climate Emergency? Pipeline Shutdown Trials Pit Activists Against the Oil Industry," *The Intercept* (Mar. 21, 2018), https://theintercept.com/2018/03/21/pipeline-protest-necessity-defense-tar-sands/; "May 2017 Field Analysis Report," *Department of Homeland Security* (May 2, 2017), available at https://theintercept.com/document/2017/12/11/may-2017-field-analysis-report/.

192   Letter from Members of Congress to Attorney General Jeff Sessions Re: Pipeline Infrastructure, Congress of the United States (Oct. 23, 2017), available at https://buck.house.gov/sites/buck.house.gov/files/wysiwyg_uploaded/Protecting%20Energy%20Infrastructure.pdf.

193   Jeremiah Shelor, "Group of Lawmakers Suggests Calling Pipeline Sabotage Domestic Terrorism," *NGI's Daily Gas Price Index* (Oct. 25, 2017), https://www.naturalgasintel.com/articles/112211-group-of-lawmakers-suggests-calling-pipeline-sabotage-domestic-terrorism.

the Department of Justice later issued a message of non-committal support for the effort.[194] This risible characterization of nonviolent climate activism as a national security threat would continue: in 2020, *The Guardian* reported that a DHS intelligence assessment had listed Valve Turner Michael Foster and Sam Jessup, who filmed Foster's action, with white supremacist terrorists like Dylan Roof as possible sources of extremist violence.[195]

The implications of such administrative slander are obvious: dissent against the ravages of fossil fuels becomes presumptively illegitimate, and peaceful environmental protest is seen as an acceptable target of the government's national security powers. Big Oil couldn't ask for a better enforcer.

As chilling as these threats are, it's important to note that, up to now, the federal government has not charged the Valve Turners with anything. DHS can shout "eco-terrorism" all it wants, but, in this case, there's been lots of smoke and no fire, despite the efforts of industry and its congressional representatives. This is not to suggest that climate activists should be complacent. The federal government has come down hard on nonviolent environmentalism before, and it is actively engaged in prosecuting and persecuting members of the movement (we'll review this repression in Chapter 3). But a favorite tactic of the police state is to smear its enemies and to threaten them with severe punishment in the hopes that they'll

194 Charlie Passut, "DOJ Vows to Prosecute Protesters Who Damage Pipelines," *NGI's Daily Gas Price Index* (Nov. 14, 2017), https://www.naturalgasintel.com/articles/112447-doj-vows-to-prosecute-protesters-who-damage-pipelines.

195 Adam Federman, "Revealed: US listed climate activist group as 'extremists' alongside mass killers," *The Guardian* (Jan. 13, 2020), https://www.theguardian.com/environment/2020/jan/13/us-listed-climate-activist-group-ex-tremists.

turn tail and run. So far, the story of the Valve Turners has instead served as a testament to the power in standing firm.

This has much to do with the fact that, flipping the federal government's script, the Valve Turners went to court to put the government and industry on trial. Rather than accept their role as criminals, the activists sought to show that the real crimes of the climate age are being perpetrated in boardrooms and agency head-quarters. They amassed evidence of injury and inaction and of the need for civic intervention. As their trial dates approached, they doubled down on their necessity defense theory.

For some in the group, the strategy would prove enormously successful. For others, the campaign to justify their protest would end with the stroke of a judge's pen.

Washington

Ken Ward's case was the first to go trial and the last to be resolved. The story of his tortuous prosecution demonstrates just how advantageous the state's position is in a criminal case, and how it can exploit its power to control a defendant's life.

Ward had turned a valve on the TransMountain pipeline in Anacortes, Washington, the latest in a string of climate direct actions he'd undertaken that had elegantly combined potent symbolism with immediate impact. Ward was the one who, along with Jay O'Hara, had piloted the lobster boat *Henry David T.* into the path of coal ships in Massachusetts. In that case, the prose-cutor had dropped charges and joined the activists in their call for global warming regulation. This time, things went a little differently.

In October, the Washington state district attorney's office pressed felony charges of sabotage and burglary and a misdemeanor charge of trespass, with a total maximum punishment of twenty years in prison and $41,000 in fines. (Defense attorneys launched a successful effort to have charges dropped against Lindsey Grayzel, a filmmaker who was arrested on the scene along with cinematographer Carl Davis, based largely on the fact that prosecuting journalists for doing their job violates the First Amendment.) At the "omnibus" hearing on December 2, 2016, where pre-trial matters were sorted out, the defense team indicated its intent to rely on the necessity defense, and offered a preliminary list of experts on climate science and civil disobedience. The prosecution then responded with a motion *in limine* similar to the one in Minnesota, the first move to bar the necessity defense at trial.

To accomplish this goal, the state argued that "[t]he harm sought to be avoided (global warming) could not realistically be minimized by the defendant's actions." This was an attack on the efficacy element of the defense. The state also asserted that "[t]he harm to privacy interests of the landowner and the pipeline owner greatly outweighs any potential benefit to the environment," which would debunk Ward's argument about his "choice of evils." Finally, the state claimed that "[t]here are clearly many other legal alternatives to attempt to influence global warming, including lawful protest, legislative action or driving an electric vehicle,"[196] which would make the activists' turn to civil disobedience unreasonable.

---

196   State's Response to Defense of Necessity and Defense Witnesses at 2-3, *Washington v. Ward*, No. 16-1-01001-5 (Skagit Cty. Sup. Ct., Wash. Jan. 24, 2017).

These were well-worn arguments, and the best response was to stick to the facts. The defense team—the Civil Liberties Defense Center, Climate Defense Project, and Seattle attorney Ralph Hurvitz—answered with a description of Ward's four decades of climate activism in the mainstream environmental movement, describing how, with greenhouse gas emissions on the rise, "Mr. Ward came to understand that the issue of climate change would require other than incremental changes to arrest global climate degradation." The attorneys also emphasized that the proper test at this pre-trial stage was simply whether or not Ward's case met a "preponderance of the evidence" standard: whether the facts showed that it was more likely than not that his actions were necessary. Ultimately, this meant that, if Ward offered enough preliminary proof, it was the job of the jury—not the judge—to evaluate the reasonableness of his actions.[197]

The Washington team had some favorable law to lean on. As discussed in the previous Valve Turners section, the necessity defense differs from state to state, and seemingly minor variations in court precedent can have a major impact. Luckily for Ward, there was some good Washington law on the thorny "legal alternatives" element, which requires necessity defendants to show that they had no options besides breaking the law. The state Court of Appeals had decided a case in 2005 in which, considering whether a man barred from having a firearm was nonetheless justified in carrying a gun because his previous assailants were still at large, it ruled that a necessity defendant had simply to show "that he had

197 Response to the State's Motion to Preclude Necessity Defense and to Strike Witnesses at 3-7, *Washington v. Ward* (Jan. 23 2017).

actually tried the alternative or had no time to try it, or that a history of futile attempts revealed the illusionary benefits of the alternative."[198] Ward could prove that and then some: climate change was here, and the political process—"a history of futile attempts" if there ever was one—hadn't worked.

Unfortunately, Judge Michael E. Rickert of the Skagit County Superior Court saw things differently. On January 24, 2017—more than three months after the protest action—the court held a hearing on the necessity defense. Arguing first, the state prosecutor claimed that "a single action in our little tiny county" couldn't do anything to avert global warming—the existence of which, he noted, was a matter of controversy, because we just "don't know" what's happening anywhere beyond northwest Washington. He pointed to a camera in the room and said, "This is all part of a show."[199]

It was the defense's turn. Judge Rickert invited Ralph Hurvitz to the podium, and told him that "I immediately liked you because that is one novel approach to life and to the necessity defense"— something he hadn't seen succeed in twenty-five years on the bench.[200] He listened as Mr. Hurvitz outlined the elements of the defense and the ways in which Ward satisfied them. He heard that this was a question for the jury, which decides the facts of a case.

Then, without citing any case law, Judge Rickert opined that the defense didn't apply. Necessity was more properly suited to

---

198   *State v. Parker,* 127 Wn. App. 352, 355 (2005).

199   Motion Hearing Verbatim Report of Proceedings at 7, *Washington v. Ward* (Jan. 24, 2017).

200   *Id.* at 14.

cases of "immediate harm," he said. But that wasn't the situation here: there was no immediacy to

> this particular threatened harm, which is climatic change, global warming, whatever. I don't know what everybody's beliefs are on that. But I know there's tremendous controversy over the fact whether it even exists and even if people believe that it does or doesn't, the extent of what we are doing to ourselves, our climate, and our planet. There's great controversy over our political leaders. A person may feel hamstrung and bound because there's no reasonable legal alternative because the voting process didn't work. Someone I guess could surmise they need to take action into their own hands and break the law in order to fix a mighty wrong being perpetrated by one of our leaders somewhere. I know the logical extreme is utilizing this defense. In a situation like this would be, I think would be some crazy results.[201]

This was a shocking acquiescence to the forces of climate denial. Ignoring the facts in Ward's offer of proof—which contained ample evidence of the existence and extremes of climate change and promised to support this account with expert testimony at trial— Judge Rickert simply decided that the matter was too controversial to merit further discussion.

He also concluded, again without any evidence, that there might still be useful legal alternatives for Ward to pursue. Mr. Hurvitz riposted that the defense had expert witnesses on this question. The judge speculated that there might be other experts out there who would disagree with their assessment—ignoring the fact that the purpose of a trial is to test contrasting bodies of

201 *Id.* at 15.

evidence. As to the all-important point that it was up to the jury to assess whether or not Ward had met the requirements of the necessity defense, Judge Rickert balked at the idea:

> It would be like the Scopes monkey trial. I mean all [of a] sudden that trial was the debate of whether or not [there was] a divine beginning, or we all came from monkeys. That happened in 1926 and is still one of the most famous trials in American history next to OJ Simpson. But I don't see bringing in a jury for a matter of weeks to debate a Burglary case and a Sabotage case, because the thing that they would have to get to is they would have to come to a conclusion in order to prevail on this necessity defense that, in fact, global warming is out there, and global warming is harmful, and that Mr. Ward is the frontline warrior and is going to take care of it. So the trial would become whether or not—the trial would focus on the existence and the severity of the climatic change, and that's not what we are here to do. That's not what superior court is here to do. That's for the legislative arena, not for the judicial arena to debate that. I don't think there's a judge in the world, including Al Gore, if he were a judge, who would give the necessity defense in this situation because it doesn't fit on any of the four corners. So I would grant the motion in limine. This is not a case for the necessity defense; although it would be interesting.[202]

Just like that, Ward's best argument was tossed out. There would be no climate necessity defense at trial.

This was an inauspicious but not altogether unexpected start to the Valve Turners' courtroom battles. As discussed earlier, the political necessity defense has long been a tool for political activists, but

202 *Id.* at 16.

many judges still pretend it doesn't exist. Time and again, they reject it prior to trial on the idea that this is not what courts are for. No political necessity defendant walks into a pre-trial hearing with good odds.

Still, the show had to go on. Ward's trial began the following week—the state meanwhile dropped the trespass charge, leaving only felony burglary and sabotage—but there wasn't much to argue over. Ward admitted that he had entered the TransMountain Pipeline control site and turned a valve. He even showed a video of his action. (Interestingly, testimony from a prosecution witness revealed that the line was not in operation that day, and so Ward had not really turned anything off. But his warning to the company did result in another line being shut down, and so, as desired, there was a pause in the flow of tar sands oil to Washington state.) The only thing up for debate, really, was Ward's "state of mind": why he'd done what he'd done. Deprived of evidence and experts to substantiate his motivations, and barred from making the legal argument that his actions were necessary—the jurors were never even informed that such a defense existed—Ward was left to rely on the strength of his own convictions, and his ability to convey them to a group of twelve regular people.

Sometimes that's enough.

In his opening statement, Mr. Hurvitz emphasized the seriousness of the problem that had motivated Ward: "The planet is at a crossroads. We're not talking here about a social issue; we're talking about survival."[203] When it was his turn to testify, Ward spoke at length about his transformation from mainstream

203 Verbatim Report of Proceedings, Vol. 1 at 105, *Washington v. Ward* (Jan. 30, 31, and Feb. 1, 2017).

environmentalist to climate radical, citing the work of former government climate scientist James Hansen, whom he'd wanted to call as an expert. He also explained several exhibits that showed the historical rise in atmospheric concentrations of carbon dioxide, what Skagit County would look like in 2050 with five feet of flooding, and the letter to President Obama that he and the other Valve Turners had sent prior to their protest. The prosecutor strenuously objected to all this talk about climate change. Judge Rickert allowed much of it to go forward, though he did restrict bits about Ward's experience with civil disobedience. "We're not talking about, like, a matter of opinion here," Ward told the jury. "And neither are we talking about sort of one of a range of issues. The very conditions that make our society possible are threatened here and we need to act appropriately."[204]

In their closing statements, the lead attorneys presented starkly different ideas about civil disobedience. The prosecutor went for a knockout punch, echoing the federal government's propaganda about the threat of environmental extremism: "When you break the law to accomplish a greater goal, how is that different from other organizations such as terrorist groups?"[205] Mr. Hurvitz, for his part, closed with an analogy to the Boston Tea Party, another group of dissidents who interfered with corporate property in the name of higher ideals.

Trial adjourned for jury deliberation around three o'clock on the afternoon of the second day. The next morning, everyone returned to court. And waited. Then waited some more.

204 *Id.*, Vol. 2 at 186.
205 *Id.*, Vol. 2 at 208-9.

Around 1:30, the jury sent a note saying that they could not reach a decision. Judge Rickert called them in and asked whether they had tried their best. They nodded. Then the judge grabbed his gavel, said there was a hung jury, and declared a mistrial.[206]

Ken Ward was free.

The Valve Turners and their supporters were ecstatic. Somehow, with all the best cards taken from the deck, climate civil disobedience had won in court. This was not a result most judges and lawyers would have expected. Generally, defendants who confess to their alleged crimes—and who have been blocked from introducing most of their evidence and witnesses—are found guilty. But Ward found a way to convey moral urgency on the stand. He has a knack for making climate change science comprehensible.

In the end, the jurors probably felt uncomfortable convicting someone who had so obviously acted out of principle, and who caused no damage in the process. This was a major endorsement of the Valve Turners' theory of change. If you act out of principle, and if you communicate effectively, ordinary people who walked into the courthouse with no particular feelings on global warming might nonetheless endorse a radical vision of what reasonable climate politics looks like.

But juries are famously inscrutable: you never quite know what motivates a verdict, and one group of twelve people might reach an entirely different conclusion from another. Knowing this, the state prosecutor decided to test his luck and try Ward again. Because the first jury had failed to reach a decision, the door was open for

---

206 *Id.*, Vol. 2 at 254.

another prosecution. The slate was wiped clean and the process began all over again.

Meanwhile, the new administration was doing everything it could to stymie the efforts of people like the Valve Turners. On the same day that Ward's first trial began, President Trump signed an executive order resurrecting the Keystone XL pipeline. In February, Rex Tillerson was confirmed as secretary of state. Scott Pruitt was confirmed as head of the Environmental Protection Agency.

In May, Ward's case resumed. Once again, the prosecution moved to block the necessity defense, and once again Judge Rickert granted the motion.[207] Once again, Ward defended himself with one hand tied behind his back and hoped for the best.

Things did not go quite as well in round two. On June 7, the jury announced that they had found Ward guilty of burglary, but that they had failed to reach a decision on the sabotage charge.[208] Not the desired outcome, to be sure, but still rather remarkable: another jury had refused to fully support the prosecution's case, despite Ward describing in detail how he had done what he was charged with. Jurors who spoke to Ward and his supporters after the trial said that they had sought a legal way to acquit him but that they couldn't find one.[209]

207 "Judge Denies Climate Activist's Necessity Defense, Restricting Right to Defend Protest at Trial," *Climate Defense Project* (May 10, 2017), https://climatedefenseproject.org/judge-denies-climate-activists-necessity-defense-restricting-right-defend-protest-trial/.

208 "After Court Restricts Constitutional Right to Defense, Climate Activist Receives Split Verdict for Pipeline Protest," *Climate Defense Project* (June 7, 2017), https://climatedefenseproject.org/12205-2/.

209 Tim Faulkner, "R.I. Native Guilty on 1 Charge; Hung Jury on Sabotage," *EcoRI News* (June 12, 2017), https://www.ecori.org/renewable-energy/2017/6/10/ward-guilty-on-one-charge-hung-jury-on-sabotage-in-valve-turner-trial; Sara Bernard, "Split Decision: Valve-Turner and Climate Activist Ken Ward

It's worth pausing on that fact. The jurors did not want to convict Ward, but they felt bound by the law to do so. The necessity defense exists for precisely this type of situation. It provides, in the words of Judge Safer-Espinoza in *People v. Gray,* "an essential safety valve to law enforcement in a democratic society."[210] Had the jurors known of this safety valve, it seems, they would have used it. This appears to be the general trend of political necessity cases: although comprehensive data is hard to come by, evidence from the first wave of political necessity trials in the 1970s and 1980s suggests that juries acquitted by reason of necessity more often than not.[211] But Judge Rickert, basing his ruling on what he thought a reasonable jury would conclude, had found this result implausible. This mismatch between judge and jury is yet another example of the gap between those who administer the law and those who live under it.

Later that month, Ward was sentenced to time served, thirty days of community service, and six months of community supervision (a type of probation). He and his legal team announced that they were filing an appeal based on the double denial of the necessity defense.[212]

The meaning of this first set of trials was ambiguous. On the one hand, the prosecution and the judiciary had teamed up to suppress

Convicted On One Count," *Seattle Weekly* (June 7, 2017), https://www.seattleweekly.com/news/split-decision-valve-turner-and-climate-activist-ken-ward-convicted-on-one-count/.

210   *People v. Gray,* 571 N.Y.S.2d 851, 866 (N.Y. Crim. Ct. 1991).

211   *Id.* at 871; Bernard D. Lambek, "Necessity and International Law: Arguments for the Legality of Civil Disobedience," *Yale Law and Policy Review* 5 (1986), 472-492, 473.

212   "Sentence for "Valve-Turner" Climate Activist Ken Ward: No More Jail Time," *Climate Direct Action* (June 23, 2017), available at https://climatedefenseproject.org/sentence-valve-turner-climate-activist-ken-ward-no-jail-time/.

discussion of climate change in the courtroom, and an activist had received a criminal sentence. On the other hand, jurors had proven amenable to the notion that global warming demands immediate, drastic action, and—three times out of four over the course of two trials—they had refused to convict, even though the judge had told them only to consider the immediate facts before them.

The indeterminacy of this situation—momentum shifting between the powers that be and climate advocates desperate for a public awakening—mirrored that of society at large. A fossil plutocracy, now firmly ensconced in the White House, had inspired ever greater climate resistance. The middle ground—moderate regulations, market-driven reforms, plodding political lobbying— had given way to explicit confrontation, and some of this drama's chief settings were small county courthouses in the American west.

North Dakota

Michael Foster's experience in the North Dakota courts was rather different from Ken Ward's in Washington. For one thing, Foster and his co-defendant Sam Jessup, who'd been filming Foster's action, were much further from their base of support on the West Coast, making it difficult to pack the court with friendly faces and to draw energy from fellow activists. For another, the state government was coming off a nearly year-long war against the anti-DAPL resistance at Standing Rock, during which the most violent, racist, and corrupt aspects of the police, prosecutors, and courts had become evident: authorities maimed nonviolent protesters, caged Indigenous activists, and contracted with mercenaries to spy on organizers. Although Foster and Jessup went to trial in Cavalier, hundreds of miles north of Standing Rock, they and people like them—hard-core environmentalists who targeted industry infrastructure—were likely not favorites of the majority-white and decidedly conservative population of the region.

To Foster's credit, he did not let this situation intimidate him. In the months leading up to trial, he kept up a busy schedule of lecturing and trainings, speaking to youth groups and explaining the rationale behind valve turning. He sat for a long profile in *Seattle Met*, which examined everything from a childhood spent alongside oil refineries in Deer Park, Texas to the way in which his dedication to a low-carbon lifestyle and climate organizing had torn his family apart.[213] And he pressed for a necessity defense to explain his conduct to a jury.

The law of necessity in North Dakota is much less favorable than in Washington; in fact, it hardly exists. A provision in the criminal code allows for the defense of "justification,"[214] but the state Supreme Court has called it "gibberish."[215] Necessity defenses have occasionally been offered in the state, but there is no firm law on what its elements are and how it should be proven. Count this as a lesson in the intricacies of our federalist legal system: no two state necessity defenses ever look the same.

Cavalier sits in Pembina County, a home of the Ojibwe people and one of the world's centers of sugar beet production. Nearly seven thousand people are spread over more than one thousand square

---

213 Kathryn Robinson, "Michael Foster Is Defiant," *Seattle Met* (June 5, 2017), https://www.seattlemet.com/news-and-city-life/2017/06/michael-foster-is-defiant.

214 N.D.C.C. § 12.1-05-01.

215 *State v. Hass*, 268 N.W.2d 456, 461 (N.D. 1978).

miles. The Keystone Pipeline, which Foster turned off, runs along the county's western edge, sitting about four feet above the ground and carrying tar sands oil from Canada down to refineries in Nebraska. The controversial Keystone XL project is a proposed expansion of this line, aimed at increasing capacity from around 600,000 to 830,000 barrels per day. Even without the expansion, the pipeline is a major contributor to total U.S. greenhouse gas emissions.[216]

But no one besides the defense wanted to talk about that at Foster's trial. Just like their counterparts in Minnesota and Washington, the North Dakota prosecutors filed a motion *in limine* in September 2017 to bar the necessity defense. The state's motion favorably cited Judge Rickert's comments in Ken Ward's Washington case that the dangers of climate change are uncertain, and mimicked the judge's argument that the Valve Turners illegitimately sought "to turn this into a trial on global warming." "The valve-turners' motive for breaking the law," the motion read, "is simply not relevant."[217]

Foster's attorney Mike Hoffman, with the assistance of the Civil Liberties Defense Center and Climate Defense Project, punched back with a thirty-page memorandum that described the constitutional right to present a defense and offered ample proof of the harms of climate change and tar sands oil. The argument also focused on the particular dangers of the Keystone pipeline that Foster had shut off. This was an important focus: between 2010 and

---

216 Jonathan L. Ramseur, et al., "Oil Sands and the Keystone XL Pipeline: Background and Selected Environmental Issues," *Congressional Research Service* R42611 (2014), 9.

217 Brief in Support of Motion in Limine at 4, *North Dakota v. Foster,* No. 34-2016-CR-00187 (Northeast Jud. Dist. Ct. Pembina Cty., N.D. Sep. 19, 2016).

2016, the pipeline spilled at least thirty-five times, including one incident in April 2016 that dumped seventeen thousand gallons of oil in South Dakota, and which the pipeline company, TransCanada, didn't even discover until a passerby notified it.[218] Spills in 2017 and 2019 each released another four hundred thousand gallons of oil.[219]

Nevertheless, the courts once again sided with the state. Judge Laurie A. Fontaine of the Northeast Judicial District Court of Pembina County referenced Foster's own evidence of the futility of legal efforts to address global warming—lobbying, litigation, the Clean Power Plan, the Paris Agreement—to conclude that legal alternatives were in fact available. And she ruled that the dangers from the pipeline were neither imminent nor capable of being avoided by civil disobedience.[220] The jury would not hear anything about necessity.

Renowned climate scientist James Hansen, who had prepared to testify in Ward's case and who had already traveled to Cavalier to appear at Foster's trial, held a press conference with Foster to denounce the judge's decision. Hansen had helped to make global warming front-page news when he testified to Congress in 1988 on the link between fossil fuels and rising temperatures.[221] As his

218 Defense Response to State's Motion in Limine to Exclude the Necessity Defense, *North Dakota v. Foster*, (Sep. 27, 2016); Alan Neuhauser, "Keystone Leak Worse Than Thought,' *U.S. News & World Report* (Apr. 8, 2016), https://www.usnews.com/news/articles/2016-04-08/keystone-pipeline-leak-worse-than-thought.

219 Hannah Knowles, "Keystone Pipeline leaks 383,000 gallons of oil in second big spill in two years," *Washington Post* (Nov. 1, 2019), https://www.washingtonpost.com/climate-environment/2019/10/31/keystone-pipeline-leaks-gallons-oil-second-big-spill-two-years/.

220 Memoranda Decision and Order Granting Motion in Limine, *North Dakota v. Foster* (Sep. 29, 2016).

221 Philip Shabecoff, "Global Warming Has Begun, Expert Tells Senate," *The New*

warnings went unheeded, Hansen had transformed from a staid government scientist to an activist getting arrested outside the White House.[222] In Cavalier, he told reporters that, by barring the jury from hearing about climate change, the court "is giving priority to the rights of big business over the public, and over young people in particular. Governments were instituted to protect people, not corporations."[223]

The same week, Foster published an op-ed in *Newsweek*, describing his constant frustration over the failure to acknowledge the scale of the climate crisis, a failure that included the state's suppression of his evidence. "The prosecution's position is more than tactical," he wrote. "It reflects a larger societal trauma response, which tends to paralyze and silence us before climate threats. Not naming the climate elephant in the courtroom mirrors our larger discourse on extreme weather and other climate-related disruptions."[224]

Indeed, Hurricane Harvey had just ravaged Houston, where Foster grew up, and the scope of the damage wrought by Hurricane Maria in Puerto Rico and elsewhere in the Caribbean was coming

York Times (June 24, 1988), https://www.nytimes.com/1988/06/24/us/global-warming-has-begun-expert-tells-senate.html.

222 Jeff Goodell, "NASA Scientist Hansen Arrested at Tar Sands Protest–A Grim Sign of the Times," *Rolling Stone* (Aug. 31, 2011), https://www.rollingstone.com/politics/politics-news/nasa-scientist-hansen-arrested-at-tar-sands-protest-a-grim-sign-of-the-times-102929/.

223 Jessica Corbett, "Barred From Testifying for 'Valve Turners,' Renowned Climate Scientist Speaks Out," *Common Dreams* (Oct. 5, 2017), https://www.commondreams.org/news/2017/10/05/barred-testifying-valve-turners-renowned-climate-scientist-speaks-out.

224 Michael Foster, "Why I Turned Off the Keystone Pipeline and Face 22 Years in Jail," *Newsweek* (Oct. 3, 2017), https://www.newsweek.com/why-i-turned-keystone-pipeline-and-face-22-years-jail-676841.

to light. The mismatch between reality and judicial discourse was impossible to ignore.

None of this mattered in the Pembina County Courthouse, where, as in Ward's case, Foster, Jessup, and Hoffman did their best against an opponent with all the advantages. The defendants spoke about their backgrounds and their motivations, though they were limited by the limits on evidence. In his closing statement, the prosecutor compared the Valve Turners to the Unabomber and to radicals seeking to impose Sharia law on the United States, a moment of Islamophobia reminiscent of the private security firm TigerSwan's claim that the Water Protectors at Standing Rock used a "jihadist insurgency model."[225] In the end, the jury convicted both Foster and Jessup of felony conspiracy to commit criminal mischief and misdemeanor trespass. Foster was also convicted of felony criminal mischief and acquitted of reckless endangerment.

Foster was remarkably composed about the outcome.

"I'm feeling so relieved and peaceful right now, because I've been wondering for a year how this would all play out, and now I don't have to wonder," he told a reporter for *High Plains Reader*. "I'm grateful to the jury for wrestling with this for several hours. I'm kind of disgusted with myself and my coastal elitism," he added. "I can just imagine how I look and sound, some of my attitudes—and there's a part of me that thinks I may relocate to a place like North Dakota to do some climate work."[226]

225 Aileen Brown, Will Parrish, and Alice Speri, "Leaked Documents Reveal Counterterrorism Tactics Used at Standing Rock to 'Defeat Pipeline Insurgencies,'" *The Intercept* (May 27, 2017), https://theintercept.com/2017/05/27/leaked-documents-reveal-security-firms-counterterrorism-tactics-at-standing-rock-to-defeat-pipeline-insurgencies/.

226 C. S. Hagen, "A valve turner's trial: mostly guilty," *High Plains Reader* (Oct.

Foster—who had always expected that he would serve time for his action—was ultimately sentenced to a year of prison, with two additional years suspended. He ended up serving five months in the Missouri River Correctional Facility near Bismarck. Jessup, who was represented by William Kirschner at trial, received a two year suspended sentence to be served as probation.

Facing the least hospitable legal system of any of the Valve Turners, and wishing to put the case behind him after prison, Foster elected not to appeal the denial of his necessity defense. He did, however, challenge the evidentiary basis of the criminal mischief charges, arguing that the State had not properly proved an element of its case: that he had intentionally caused $10,000 in damages to TransCanada. In January 2019, the Supreme Court of North Dakota ruled that Foster himself had proven this element by expressing a desire to do "something big," and because he was part of a large, coordinated action against multinational corporations.[227]

So the convictions stood. Like the trial judge, the state's highest court had used Foster's own words against him. With the impeccable logic of the state, it was the fact of resistance itself—not the harms caused or avoided, or the culpability of those targeted, or even the purpose of the action—that constituted the crime.

Montana

You know the script by now. The prosecutor, hearing that an environmental extremist is planning to offer some harebrained legal

6, 2017), https://hpr1.com/index.php/feature/news/a-valve-turners-trial-mostly-guilty/.

227 *North Dakota v. Foster*, 2019 ND 28 at 7 (Jan. 15, 2019).

theory, petitions the court to limit the scope of trial. The defense attorney responds with a long brief bursting with scientific opinions and legal citations. The judge, wary of her overtaxed court calendar, issues a brief decision that cuts the activist down to size. The jury, never knowing that there is an entire body of law covering the precise situation that they are tasked with resolving, convicts the activist.

That's pretty much what happened with Leonard Higgins, the Valve Turner in Montana, though the order of things was a little different. In Montana, the defense is required to make the first move, and Higgins and his attorneys filed a brief that detailed his political and spiritual awakening after retiring from thirty-one years as an Oregon state employee. Higgins—mild-mannered, tightly cropped white beard, and with the voice of a veteran bedtime raconteur—had in recent years cofounded his local 350.org group, sued the Oregon Department of Motor Vehicles for permitting a "megaload" of mining equipment destined for the tar sands oil fields, and helped to block oil trains. Still, warming rose unabated, and so he shut off a pipeline.[228]

Higgins had a great expert up his sleeve: Steve Running, professor of ecology at the University of Montana and a member of the Intergovernmental Panel on Climate Change that won the Nobel Prize in 2007. Higgins also asked the court to bring in Erica Chenoweth, a scholar on civil disobedience and social movements from the University of Denver. These experts were part of a growing roster of climatologists, social scientists, and oil industry analysts

---

228 Defendant's Memorandum on Necessity, *Montana v. Higgins*, DC-16-018, (12th Jud. Dist. Ct., Mont. Mar. 13, 2017).

who—after decades of studying climate change, the government's failure to address it, and the power of nonviolent civil resistance— were willing to travel the country and testify on behalf of activists in climate protest cases. They took no fees for their testimony or their preparation of scientific evidence, in contrast to the usual practice of five-figure payouts for expert witnesses. And they were taking a professional risk: especially in the hard sciences, there persists a cultural bias against scientists involving themselves in politics.

Testifying as an expert witness—and, if you're an attorney, preparing an expert—takes a lot of work. You prepare academic resumés and publication records to demonstrate requisite knowl- edge on a topic. You go through lengthy practice sessions to figure out the line of questioning at trial. You testify at pre-trial hearings or submit witness reports to inform a judge's weighing of evi- dence. And in climate necessity cases, you often find out a day or two before jury selection that all this work has been for naught: the judge doesn't want to hear what you have to say. If you're James Hansen, you might protest this rejection with a speech on the courtroom steps.

As Washington and North Dakota had gone, so went Montana. The state's necessity defense is codified in a statutory provision that provides for the defense of "compulsion." Unlike traditional necessity defenses, Montana's compulsion defense focuses on harm to the individual who broke the law, rather than on more general harms to others or to society.[229] The prosecution, rehears- ing a now-common argument, warned in its pre-trial briefing

---

229 Mont. Ann. Code § 45-2-212.

that Higgins's necessity argument could be used by terrorists.[230] Judge Daniel A. Boucher of the Twelfth Judicial District Court in Chouteau County agreed with the state's position, writing in his order denying the necessity defense that "Higgins cringes from the individual responsibility that historically accompanies protest and social change. It is clear from his memorandum that he expects to attract publicity through his trial, and in turn, to place U.S. energy policy on trial."[231] After an emergency petition to the state Supreme Court was denied,[232] Higgins was told to report to the courthouse in Fort Benton—an early fur trade outpost on the Missouri River—shortly before Thanksgiving 2017.

Once again, the jurors—who were selected after a *voir dire* (questioning) process that focused on preferences for elk or bird hunting—were treated to a rather odd trial. In his opening statement, Herman Watson IV, Higgins's local attorney practicing out a family law firm in Bozeman, acknowledged that his client had cut a chain, entered the Spectra site, and turned the valve. The state then called two sheriff's deputies and a pipeline operations manager who described the incident exactly as the Valve Turners' website, social media streams, and public lectures did. The only live issues were what Higgins had been trying to accomplish, and what the pipeline company had suffered as a result.

The prosecutor went to great lengths to elicit testimony showing that Higgins had caused more than $1,500 in damages, as

---

230 State's Reply to Defense Response Re: Defense of Necessity and Defense Witnesses, *Montana v. Higgins* (Mar. 31, 2017).

231 Order Denying Defendant's Defense of Necessity at 2, *Montana v. Higgins* (Apr. 11, 2017).

232 Order, *Montana v. Higgins*, DC-16-018, (Mont. S. Ct. May 30, 2017).

required by Montana's criminal mischief statute (Higgins was also charged with trespass). Both sides agreed that the replacement costs for the valve cover and the chain added up to about one thousand dollars. But the state, aided by testimony and records from Spectra employees, also wanted to hit Higgins with the hourly wages for workers who inspected the damage and made repairs, even though they charged no overtime and were working within their regular duties.

When its turn came, the defense did get to call one expert witness: Anthony Ingraffea of Cornell University, who appeared via video link. A civil and environmental engineer who knows pipeline safety procedures backwards and forwards—he helped write guidelines for the American Pipeline Institute—Ingraffea would come to form a key part of the growing climate necessity brain trust. In Fort Benton, during an examination by Higgins's other trial attorney, Lauren Regan of the Civil Liberties Defense Center, Ingraffea said that the Valve Turner actions posed no threat of a spill: their methods had correctly accounted for how pipelines decrease their flow in response to manual shut-off, and advanced computer sensor systems prevented any unexpected result.[233] Ingraffea's testimony made it clear that, despite the hysterics of the pipeline industry and the national security state, shutting down the pipelines was much safer for the public than their continued operation.

Next on the stand was Higgins. He talked about his childhood in Oregon's Willamette Valley, picking beans during the summer

233 Transcript of Trial, vol. 2, *Montana v. Higgins*, (12th Jud. Dist. Ct., Mont. Nov. 21, 2017).

and learning about civic duty from his tight-knit farming community. His three decades as a government employee and his success as a homeowner and father would seem to make him a model citizen, but Higgins expressed some regret over the direction of his life.

"I look back and I really felt that I have got sucked into what all of us call the American dream," he told the jury. "I mean I kind of got pulled off the community and family . . . [I wanted] to atone and try to make up for just paying attention to my own comfort and success."[234] This moral unease led directly to the Valve Turners' action: "the fact that all five of us are older professionals, we felt thought [*sic*] that us risking our freedom would more fairly demonstrate the problem than just talking about the facts."[235]

The prosecutor and the judge didn't make things easy for Higgins. When the defense tried to enter a visual exhibit that showed the warming projections that had motivated Higgins's turn to activism, the prosecutor moved to exclude it, and the judge agreed. Then, on cross-examination, the prosecutor pressed Higgins for the names of individuals who had helped prepare his action. Higgins, to his credit, stuck to naming just the other Valve Turners, who were already facing prosecution.

Finally, before Higgins was dismissed, the judge asked some strange questions:

Q. Mr. Higgins, we seem to have lost something here. You are charged with criminal trespass. Your lawyer said you intend to plead guilty. Did you trespass on property owned by Spectra/Enbridge?

---

234 Transcript of Trial, vol. 3 at 9, *Montana v. Higgins* (Nov. 22, 2017).

235 *Id.* at 17.

A. Yes, I did.

Q. And I think your testimony was that you did this not for you, but for your children and grandchildren?

A. Yes, your Honor.

Q. So at no point did you feel your life was being directly threatened by Spectra or Enbridge; is that right?

A. So like so many people, my happiness depends on them. Happiness is my least happy child, like any other of my children, my well being depends on their well being.[236]

To anyone privy to the pre-trial maneuvers, the meaning of this inquiry was clear: Montana's compulsion defense only excuses conduct intended to avoid direct physical harm to the defendant. Higgins's concern for his children would be off-point. But to the jury, who were listening to the exchange, this would not have made any sense; they had never heard compulsion or necessity mentioned in court. In fact, the whole point of the judge's pre-trial order was to exclude such questions from trial. Now—without any opportunity for the defense to develop evidence or to make an argument—Judge Boucher was raising the issue from the dead, only to do the state's job from the bench by trying to show that the defense could not satisfy its elements. Any juror—any "reasonable juror"—would surely have concluded that Higgins's case was missing something.

Higgins was convicted on both counts.

Four months later, the judge laid down a sentence of three years' deferred imprisonment, meaning that Higgins wouldn't have to serve any time in jail, although he did have to pay $3,755.47 to Spectra (now merged with Enbridge) (the state had sought over

236 *Id.* at 25-26.

$25,000).[237] Already a year and a half removed from the action, Higgins's legal journey then slowed to a glacial pace. Delays in producing a trial transcript triggered a series of extended deadlines on the appeals calendar. As Higgins awaited a final resolution, fires ravaged California and destroyed a town called Paradise, and a new congresswoman named Alexandria Ocasio-Cortez—who'd been inspired to run for office during her time at Standing Rock[238]—introduced a resolution for a Green New Deal.

Finally, the defense filed their appellate brief with the Montana Supreme Court in February 2019. It was a mix of high-minded principle and legal technicality. Higgins had acted morally and justifiably, his lawyers argued, and the court had mismanaged his case. They pointed out Judge Boucher's failure to "state, either in writing or on the record, the court's findings of fact and conclusions of law," as required when rejecting evidence; his improper speculation on Higgins's desire to attract publicity; his prejudicing of the jury by independently raising the necessity and compulsion issue at trial; and his limiting of Higgins's testimony on how climate change had inspired his action. These errors were compounded, the defense said, by the fact that the judge had given the state great latitude in introducing questionable work orders and payroll receipts from Spectra, and in counting pipeline workers' normal salary and mileage in the restitution amount. One side had gotten all the benefits of judicial discretion.[239]

237 Sentencing, *Montana v. Higgins* (March 20, 2018).

238 Rebecca Solnit, "Standing Rock inspired Ocasio-Cortez to run. That's the power of protest," *The Guardian* (Jan. 14, 2019), https://www.theguardian.com/commentisfree/2019/jan/14/standing-rock-ocasio-cortez-protest-climate-activism.

239 Opening Brief of Appellant, *Montana v. Higgins*, (Mont. S. Ct. Feb. 12, 2019).

The state requested and was granted an extension for their reply, which wasn't submitted until November. The brief relied in part on the old prosecutorial chestnut studied in the next section, *United States v. Schoon*, which purports to draw a distinction between "direct" and "indirect" civil disobedience. Short version: pretty much all civil disobedience is "indirect," and so no one gets the necessity defense.[240]

A final decision from the court didn't come until March 2020. As anticipated, it sided with the state on all questions. Higgins wasn't entitled to a necessity defense, the high court ruled, and the restitution award was reasonable.[241] To be fair to the judges, most of the law was on the state's side: even the defense had had to cite *United States v. Schoon* as the most persuasive federal necessity decision for Montana state courts.

But things had changed since the first round of briefing in early 2017. Not only was there ever-greater evidence of the ravages of climate change and of the government's failure to address them. There had also been major advances in the climate necessity defense, and, for the first time, legal precedent to allow someone like Higgins to make his case to a jury.

This sea change in the law of climate protest originated one state to the east, in the Minnesota trial of Emily Johnston and Annette Klapstein. The Montana Supreme Court may have chosen to ignore it, but other judges did not. Within the space of a year and a half, the climate necessity defense would go from fool's errand to

240 Brief of Appellee, *Montana v. Higgins,* 2020 MT 52 (Nov. 13, 2019).

241 *Montana v. Higgins,* 2020 MT 52 (2020).

doctrine cited in casebooks, and, outside Fort Benton at least, activists would suddenly have some good law on their side.

In the next Valve Turners section we'll turn to the Minnesota case to see how this change played out, and how these cases might finally make an impact on the teetering edifice of fossil law.

CHAPTER 3

Guardians at the Sea Walls

What this book has been calling "fossil law"—the global network of rules and regulations that, paired with physical infrastructure, move oil, gas, and coal from the earth to the air—was established to provide cheap and reliable energy. It has depended upon the consent and complicity of producers and consumers alike, and there is a great deal of responsibility to be passed around for the mess in which we find ourselves. Needless to say, the burden of blame grows greater as you move up the economic ladder, and, broadly speaking, Indigenous peoples, racial minorities, the working class, and the young will have less to account for in the final reckoning of the climate crisis than older and more affluent white people in the North Atlantic.

That's one way to describe our addiction to fossil fuels. But qualification number one: the fossil fuel system wasn't simply "established." A market-focused story of how we came to rely on carbon-burning energy—the story that people naturally flock to a superior product—ignores the enormous influence that governments and corporations have played in promoting, even

compelling, the use of fossil fuels. Our review of the legal infrastructure of extraction and consumption in the last chapter
revealed that there's no such thing as a natural market for oil, gas,
and coal: it's propped up by an elaborate system of subsidies, privileges, and favorable regulations.

Qualification number two: this story is not in the past. It's ongoing. In fact, as the fossil fuel system confronts the twin challenges of
climate change and popular resistance, its assertion of dominance
has become ever more flagrant. We're still living through an age of
resource wars, only now much of the conflict is centered on enforcing the use of fossil fuels rather than on simply controlling their
flow.

The use of coercive force, whether through state-sanctioned
violence, criminal prosecution, or industry lawsuits, is an essential element in the legal system's relation to the climate crisis. Too
often, lawyers and academics consider environmental law to be
simply a matter of government regulation, the topic of Chapter 1.
But we cannot understand the dominance of the fossil fuel system—and we cannot hope to dismantle it—without also confronting the system's fundamental reliance on legal violence. The Valve
Turners' court battles are just one example of how industry and
state respond when their power is challenged.

The focus of this chapter is the criminal legal system, where
the union between law, state power, and fossil fuels is most overt.
The analysis begins by looking at how, in the United States, police
forces started targeting radical environmentalists in the post-9/11
era, a campaign that laid the groundwork for the response to the

first wave of mass climate mobilizations during the Keystone XL controversy. Two case studies then illustrate the state of criminal fossil law today.

First, the struggle against the Dakota Access Pipeline at Standing Rock shows how the repression of dissent and the violation of Indigenous rights are a necessary condition of the fossil fuel system's ongoing operation. In the aftermath of Standing Rock, a wave of protest-suppressing legislation has spread across the country, strengthening the hand of the state as it supports the build-out of new fossil fuel infrastructure.

Next we turn to the Peruvian Amazon, where a study of resistance to oil drilling will illuminate the global alliance between fossil fuel corporations and sovereign states. Though this book focuses on climate law in the United States, there is an urgent need for instruction and inspiration from beyond our borders, where many of the best advances in the field are taking place. As such, a recent case emerging from a conflict in Bagua, Peru serves as a source of cautionary hope, suggesting a better path forward for courts as they deal with questions of Indigenous sovereignty, environmental well-being, and economic development.

Judicial opinions and statutes do not just exist on paper. For advocates eager for a healthier and more equitable world, one of the most pressing tasks is to transform the legal system from an agent of fossil fuel domination to one of climate justice liberation. Let's see how that transformation might take place, starting with today's dire situation and moving toward some models of a possible future.

The Other Environmental Law

Perform a simple thought experiment. Assume that the government heeded the warnings of climate scientists in the 1960s and that fossil fuels were deemed a danger to the public. Imagine armed officers arresting engineers at pipeline routes and mercenaries surveilling the movements of oil executives. Imagine counter-terrorism intelligence reports citing gas company stock prospectuses as evidence of threats to the social order. Picture neighbors of oil refineries calling 911 and seeing plant managers hauled off in cuffs.

This is not a state of affairs we should desire: the use of state violence is a crude instrument for climate justice, and one more likely to exacerbate conflicts than to resolve them. But the unlikeliness of the image emphasizes the absurdity of its obverse, which is our reality: sovereign power exercised in the interest of climate criminals.

We can identify several antecedents to this situation. As discussed in Chapter 2, the exertion of colonial and police power made it possible for the modern fossil fuel system to develop in the first place. Violations of the legal rights of Indigenous people, poor people, and communities of color—and the assault and prosecution of those who resist—have always gone hand-in-hand with the development of new energy reserves. As the fragile structure of environmental and administrative law begins to fracture—fossil fuel companies encountering greater legal resistance to their exploitation of permits and regulatory processes, climate justice advocates exposing the system's inability to confront catastrophe—the once mundane business of infrastructure expansion has become a more naked assertion of force.

The Green Scare represents the high-water mark of the government's persecution of environmental activists. Beginning in the 1990s, the federal government began targeting groups associated with the animal rights movement and the Earth First! school of ecotage. Focused primarily on political activity in the Pacific Northwest, the FBI and Justice Department were emboldened after the September 11 attacks and the resulting Patriot Act to target activists engaged in direct action against logging companies, real estate developers, and other environmental bad actors. They used strategies developed in the COINTELPRO program of the 1960s and 1970s, which surveilled, entrapped, and murdered leaders of the civil rights, Black Power, and Puerto Rican nationalist movements, among others.[242] In 2006, Congress passed an updated law called the Animal Enterprise Terrorism Act, which defined nonviolent acts like freeing mink from slaughter farms as acts of terror punishable by up to twenty years in prison.[243] In 2008, the FBI asserted that "eco-terrorists and animal rights extremists are one of the most serious domestic terrorism threats in the U.S. today."[244]

From 2001 to 2019, seventy environmentalists and animal rights activists were charged with federal crimes stemming from Green Scare surveillance and infiltration.[245] Daniel McGowan, for example, was punished under terrorism sentencing enhancements

242 Will Potter, *Green is the New Red* (San Francisco: City Lights Books, 2011).

243 Pub. L. No. 109-374, 120 Stat. 2652 (2006), codified at 18 U.S.C. § 43.

244 "Putting Intel to Work Against ELF and ALF Terrorists," *FBI.gov* (June 30, 2008), https://archives.fbi.gov/archives/news/stories/2008/june/eco-terror_063008.

245 Alleen Brown, "The Green Scare: How a Movement That Never Killed Anyone Became the FBI's No. 1 Domestic Terrorism Threat," *The Intercept* (March 23, 2019), https://theintercept.com/2019/03/23/ecoterrorism-fbi-animal-rights/.

for helping to burn down two lumber mills and sent to federal prison for five and a half years.[246] Laura Gazzola, a member of the Stop Huntington Animal Cruelty organization who engaged in speech and organizing activities but was never charged with any direct action or property damage, was sentenced to four and a half years.[247]

That this police response was out of all correspondence to the nature of the activists' actions—no one in the targeted movements had ever hurt anyone—did not seem to matter to the legal system. During the same period, the FBI was regularly entrapping young Muslims in nonexistent terrorism schemes.[248] "National security" was the by-word of the day, and any threat to business as usual—including threats to the profits of environmentally destructive companies—was deemed worthy of the harshest punishment.

As resistance to fossil fuels accelerated in the campaign against the TransCanada Keystone XL Pipeline—a two thousand-mile line that would carry tar sands oil to the Gulf Coast for refining and export—the government had a playbook to draw from. In 2011, over one thousand protesters were arrested in a series of demonstrations in front of the White House after the State Department issued an environmental impact statement finding that the pipeline posed no serious ecological risk. This was the largest act of climate civil disobedience the country had ever seen. Over the

---

246 Anna Merlan, "Daniel McGowan: The FBI's Least Wanted," *The Village Voice* (Sep. 25, 2013), https://www.villagevoice.com/2013/09/25/daniel-mcgowan-the-fbis-least-wanted/.

247 Potter, *Green is the New Red*, 153.

248 Peter Aldhous, "How the FBI Invents Terror Plots to Catch Wannabe Jihadis," *BuzzFeed News* (Nov. 17, 2015), https://www.buzzfeednews.com/article/pe-teraldhous/fbi-entrapment.

coming years, the Tar Sands Blockade coalition staged a series of protests, sit-ins, and equipment lockdowns along the route of the Keystone XL's Texas extension, and solidarity actions cropped up across the United States. In response, TransCanada hired off-duty police officers to patrol the route and to surveil activists in their homes. The company also presented the FBI with a list of potential charges that could be brought against activists. In 2013, when demonstrators hung a glitter-covered banner in the headquarters of one of TransCanada's contractors, they were charged with a "terrorism hoax." The FBI—which, relying on its old strategies for justifying repression, had described Keystone XL as "vital to the security and economy of the United States"—was later forced to admit that it had violated its own procedures in coordinating with local police departments and in cultivating movement informants.[249]

The fight against Keystone XL marked the arrival of the climate justice movement as a major force in U.S. politics, and it also signaled the type of overt and covert governmental reaction that would be brought to bear against nonviolent climate dissent. As fossil fuel companies continue to expand infrastructure in the hopes of locking in multi-decade profits before regulation strands their reserves—and as state and federal governments issue approvals for these projects despite incontrovertible evidence of their harm— the climate justice movement has entered into increasingly direct confrontation with the criminal legal system. This was seen most clearly in a remote corner of the northern plains less than a year after the Paris climate talks and in the waning days of the Obama

---

249 Ted Hamilton, "The Virtues of Uncertainty: Lessons from the Legal Battles Over the Keystone XL Pipeline," *Vermont Journal of Environmental Law* 18 (2016), 222-286.

administration, when fossil law's business as usual hit another unexpected obstacle.

Standing Rock and the Maintenance of the Colonial Legal Order

The issues and values at stake in the Standing Rock conflict extended well beyond global warming. As described in the first part of the Valve Turners narrative, the government-backed effort to construct the Dakota Access Pipeline (DAPL) through unceded Oceti Sakowin territory followed over a century and a half of treaty-breaking and administrative oppression by the United States government. To focus on the legal side of things, the federal government is still bound by the 1868 Fort Laramie Treaty, which recognized thirty-two million acres in present-day South Dakota as a permanent "Great Sioux Reservation," with additional protections for surrounding hunting areas. The Sioux have the right to refuse entry to any intruders in this area. But despite the fact that such treaties are the "supreme law of the land,"[250] the United States has continually invaded, flooded, and pillaged the territory—a fact recognized by the Supreme Court itself in *United States v. Sioux Indian Nation*, when it ordered payment of $106 million in return for the federal government's illegal seizure of the Black Hills. The tribes have refused to accept this monetary compensation for the unceded land.[251]

---

250 U.S. Const., Art. VI.

251 448 U.S. 371 (1980). In describing the government's dealings with the Oceti Sakowin, the Supreme Court cited a Court of Claims opinion: "A more ripe and rank case of dishonorable dealings will never, in all probability, be found in our history." *Id.* at 388, *(quoting United States v. Sioux Nation,* 207 Ct. Cl. 234, 241). On refusal of the compensation, *see* Estes, *Our History is the Future.*

As with many conflicts whose climate significance has now come to the fore, the Oceti Sakowin sovereignty battle originally had little to do with greenhouse gases. Indeed, the fact that fossil fuel conflicts are often overlaid on top of long-running struggles for political, cultural, and environmental justice is a sign of the intimate relation between fossil capital and imperial power. As documented by Lower Brule Sioux historian Nick Estes in *Our History Is the Future*, groups such as the Society of American Indians worked throughout the first half of the twentieth century to resist federal administration and enforce treaty rights.[252] In the 1940s, several tribes lobbied and protested against the disastrous Pick-Sloan dam project that inundated Indigenous lands and displaced thousands of people.[253] In the 1970s, the International Indian Treaty Council engaged in international diplomacy, most often in solidarity with formerly colonized peoples, as it sought U.N. recognition of American Indian tribes as a sovereign states.[254]

Most relevant to the criminal law focus of this chapter, the U.S. government tried nearly 150 Oceti Sakowin activists for their role in the bloody standoff at Wounded Knee in 1973, in which members of the American Indian Movement, backed by traditional chiefs, asserted sovereignty over the site of the infamous 1890 massacre of two hundred Oceti Sakowin. The defendants and Wounded Knee Legal Defense/Offense Committee used the opportunity to instruct courts and the public on the long history of U.S. injustices against the nation, noting correctly that, under the terms of

252 *Id.* at 208-222.

253 *Id.* at 133-167.

254 *Id.* at 202-3, 232-245.

the Fort Laramie Treaty, the U.S. federal courts had no jurisdiction over alleged criminal acts at the site in question. They also exposed rampant illegality in the FBI's surveillance methods and the prosecution's withholding of key evidence. A large roster of expert witnesses, including historian Roxanne Dunbar-Ortiz and activist scholar Vine Deloria, Jr., spoke about the persistence of Indigenous resistance and the legal basis of the Sioux sovereignty claims. In the end, charges against nearly all of the defendants were dismissed,[255] a sign of the political gains that can be won from a robust legal response to government repression.

When a version of this history replayed itself in 2016 at Standing Rock, a new crime had been added to the list of injustices visited upon the Oceti Sakowin: the climate-wrecking consequences of oil pipelines. The Water Protectors at the Oceti Sakowin camp thus allied themselves with the international climate justice movement as they fought against a pipeline that would violate their sovereignty, destroy valuable ecological, cultural, and religious resources, and exacerbate the global climate catastrophe.

The response by the North Dakota state government was swift and terrifying. Police arrived in military gear to combat unarmed protesters, shutting off roads to and from the reservation. In repeated instances of excessive force, they lobbed tear gas and fired water hoses. After police confiscated personal and culturally sensitive belongings, items were returned covered in urine. The police attacked journalists and racially profiled protesters at the

255 John William Sayer, *Ghost Dancing the Law: The Wounded Knee Trials* (Harvard University Press, 2000); Roxanne Dunbar-Ortiz, *The Great Sioux Nation: Sitting in Judgment on America* (New York: American Indian Treaty Council Information Center, 1977).

Kirkwood Mall in Bismarck, North Dakota. After one particularly violent attack on Water Protectors, the police forced arrestees into dog cages, singling out Indigenous protesters for strip searches.[256]

Of the nearly fifteen thousand Water Protectors and supporters who visited the camp over the four months of heightened conflict between protesters and police, 837 found themselves facing criminal charges in North Dakota. Charges included felony civil disorder and criminal mischief. 393 cases were dismissed, 336 were resolved by guilty plea or pretrial diversion, forty-two ended in acquittal, and twenty-six in conviction at trial—statistics that testify to the tremendous work of lawyers at the Water Protector Legal Collective, who, building from a scrappy legal aid tent at the camps, established an efficient and effective legal wing for the movement in the face of severe financial and logistical obstacles.[257]

Two of these cases are worth examining in detail. Red Fawn Fallis, a member of the Oglala Lakota who served as a medic at Standing Rock, was arrested during an early morning raid on one of the camps. The police who tackled her seemed to have picked her out of the crowd; as it later emerged, an FBI informant who infiltrated the camp had developed a romantic relationship with Fallis and given her a gun. The gun apparently went off when Fallis was tackled, and she was charged with "discharge of a firearm in relation to a felony crime of violence," which carries a penalty of up to life in prison. Prior to trial, Fallis's defense team attempted to bring the nature of this subterfuge to light, and also sought to raise

256 Estes, *Our History is the Future*, 3-5, 53-54, 55-56.

257 "ND State Criminal Cases." *Water Protector Legal Collective* (Jan. 23, 2020), https://waterprotectorlegal.org/nd-state-criminal-defense/.

the issues of Oceti Sakowin sovereignty and the police relationship with private mercenaries. But the federal judge deemed such questions irrelevant. Facing limited options to defend herself, or to discuss the highly relevant matter of the illegality of the pipeline and the government's actions, Fallis pled guilty in 2018 to felony disorder and possession of a firearm by a felon, and was sentenced to fifty-seven months of incarceration.[258] She is one of five Water Protectors who were sent to federal prison.[259]

In February 2017, Chase Iron Eyes, an attorney with the Lakota People's Law Project, was arrested along with dozens of others as they tried to establish a new protest camp. Charged with trespassing, Iron Eyes asserted a necessity defense—the same one used by the Valve Turners—based on the fact that DAPL posed a serious threat to the people and environment of Standing Rock. The defense's extensive court filings described surveillance of Iron Eyes by private security operatives and pointed out that, as an enrolled member of the Standing Rock Sioux, he was incapable of trespassing on unceded treaty land. Facing the need to turn over documentation related to the private security operations at Standing Rock, the state offered Iron Eyes a plea deal with no prison time, which he accepted.[260]

---

258 Will Parish, "Standing Rock Activist Accused of Firing Gun Registered to FBI Informant Is Sentenced to Nearly Five Years in Prison," *The Intercept* (July 13, 2018), https://theintercept.com/2018/07/13/standing-rock-red-fawn-fallis-sentencing/; C.S. Hagen, "Infiltrated: No-DAPL Activist Hoodwinked by Paid FBI Informant, Defense Says," *High Plains Reader* (Jan. 11, 2018), https://hpr1.com/index.php/feature/news/infiltrated-no-dapl-activist-hoodwinked-by-paid-fbi-informant-defense-says.

259 "NoDAPL Political Prisoners," *NoDAPL Political Prisoners* (2020), https://www.nodaplpoliticalprisoners.org/.

260 *Indian Country Today* Editorial Team, "North Dakota Prosecutors Drop All Serious Charges Against Chase Iron Eyes," *High Plains Reader* (Aug. 22, 2018),

Fallis and Iron Eyes's legal teams cited collusion between the pipeline company, North Dakota law enforcement, and TigerSwan, a company that bills itself as "a modern consultancy for global risk management and mitigation."[261] As documented by *The Intercept*, TigerSwan began to infiltrate the Standing Rock camps in September 2016 and provided the company and police with reports of their spying efforts and with strategies for undermining the nonviolent movement. Describing Standing Rock as a movement that used "the jihadist insurgency model," TigerSwan flew drones over protests, listened in on phone conversations, and used dogs to attack demonstrators. As revealed by its reports, its entire approach to the protest was pervaded by anti-Indigenous racism and a counterterrorism attitude to dissent. Even though it lacked a license to operate in North Dakota, the company worked closely with police to single out activist targets and with the pipeline company to build evidence for a lawsuit against climate justice advocates and organizations.[262]

Such anti-environmentalist alliances of government and private industry have grown in recent years, from the coordination between pipeline companies and Texas and Oklahoma state police

https://hprl.com/index.php/feature/news/north-dakota-prosecutors-drop-all-serious-charges-against-chase-iron-eyes/; Opposition the State's Motion in Limine, *North Dakota v. Iron Eyes*, No. 30-2017-CR-00223 (N.D. South Cent. Jud. Ct. Aug. 7, 2017).

261 Home page, *Tigerswan.com* (2020), https://www.tigerswan.com/.

262 Alleen Brown, Will Parrish, and Alice Speri, "Leaked Documents Reveal Counterterrorism Tactics Used at Standing Rock to 'Defeat Pipeline Insurgencies'"; Alleen Brown, Will Parrish, and Alice Speri, "Dakota Access Pipeline Company Paid Mercenaries to Build Conspiracy Lawsuit Against Environmentalists," *The Intercept* (Nov. 15, 2017), https://theintercept.com/2017/11/15/dakota-access-pipeline-dapl-tigerswan-energy-transfer-partners-rico-lawsuit/.

during the battle against the Gulf Coast Pipeline[263] to the whole-sale co-opting of the Coos County Sheriff's Office in Oregon, where Pembina Pipeline Corporation, seeking to build a natural gas export facility at Jordan Cove, purchased crowd-control equipment and funded the million-dollar budget of a special police unit devoted to surveilling and infiltrating activist groups.[264] The American Petroleum Institute, the fossil fuel industry's chief lobby group, has noted that it "work[s] with" the FBI and the Department of Justice.[265] In many areas where battles over extraction take place, there's no daylight between the fossil fuel industry, private security contractors, and law enforcement.

After the intense police violence at Standing Rock, and after the Trump administration fast-tracked regulatory approvals, DAPL began operating. The state-backed fossil fuel system had won another—perhaps temporary—victory in its campaign to compel consumption of its products, consequences be damned.[266]

263 Adam Federman, "Undercover Agents Infiltrated Tar Sands Resistance Camp to Break up Planned Protest," *Earth Island Journal* (Aug. 12, 2013), https://www.earthisland.org/journal/index.php/articles/entry/undercover_agents_infiltrated_tar_sands_resistance_camp_to_break_up_planned/.

264 Will Parrish and Alleen Brown, "Paid by the Pipeline: A Canadian Energy Company Bought an Oregon Sheriff's Unit," *The Intercept* (Feb. 12, 2020), https://theintercept.com/2020/02/12/jordan-cove-oregon-pembina-pipeline/.

265 Alexander C. Kaufman, "Environmentalists Say They're Averting Climate Disaster. Conservatives Say It's Terrorism," *Huffington Post* (Feb. 21, 2018), https://www.huffpost.com/entry/pipeline-environmentalist-terrorism_n_5a85c2ede4b0058d55672250?guccounter=1.

266 Legal challenges finally succeeded in 2020—four years after the resistance at Standing Rock began—when the federal district court for the District of Columbia ruled that the Army Corps of Engineers had acted improperly in not preparing a full environmental impact statement for DAPL. The court ordered the pipeline drained of oil as the Corps prepared this analysis. *Cheyenne River Sioux Tribe*, No. CV 16-1534 (D.D.C. July 6, 2020). Given the possibility of a successful appeal or the Corps's re-approval of the project, the future of the pipeline remained unclear.

As in so many such battles, victory was contingent upon rebuffing legal challenges based on environmental and Indian law. But, in the face of unprecedented resistance from Native Americans and their allies, DAPL also had to rely upon the full force of the state's criminal enforcement powers.

The consequences of such enforcement are terrible. For those hoping to understand the nature of the fossil fuel system today, they also provide an important lesson. Fossil law has a powerful police force. Anyone who resists that force is a potential suspect.

Climate Law's Police Phase

The physical imprint of fossil fuel infrastructure on our land is enormous and growing. The confrontation at Standing Rock was significant not only for the nature of the opposition that it engendered but for what the oil industry and its allies learned from the experience. In the past four years, government and private enterprise have grown more sophisticated in their approach to building pipelines and shipping fuel. Anticipating resistance to these projects, they secure political support from the highest state authorities while simultaneously targeting grassroots activists with laws that ban protests against "critical infrastructure" (pipelines, refineries, and ports) and with frivolous lawsuits that drain resisters' money and time. Not long ago, the fossil fuel system's business as usual was secured by a lax regulatory environment and a lack of public scrutiny. Now, that business is enforced by a more public campaign of coercion.

Some recent examples of fossil law's enforcement: in British Columbia, the oil giant Kinder Morgan has met with stiff opposition from First Nations and climate advocates over its plans to expand the Trans Mountain Pipeline, which carries tar sands oil from Alberta to a planned export terminal on the Pacific Coast. Protests culminated in 2018, when hundreds were arrested attempting to stop pipeline construction near Burnaby Mountain. In a remarkably harsh ruling, the province's highest court granted an injunction in favor of the company, ordering protests to stay at least five meters away from construction zones.[267] But as protesters defied the order and mobilizations flared across the country, and after another court found that that required consultations with affected Indigenous groups had been insufficient, the future of the project seemed in doubt. Prime Minister Justin Trudeau's federal government saved the day, buying the pipeline and winning full regulatory approval a year later. This was a glaring instance of state support for an industry under popular assault, and an attempt to guarantee the exploitation of tar sands fields for decades to come.[268] In early 2020, the pipeline cleared another major hurdle when the Canadian Federal Court of Appeals ruled that further consultations with First Nations had been sufficient.[269]

---

267   Order Made After Application, *Trans Mountain Pipeline ULC and Mivasair et al.*, No. S-183541 (Supreme Court of British Columbia June 1, 2018); Chris Campbell, "Injunction upheld covering protests at Burnaby Trans Mountain site," *Burnaby Now* (Feb. 22, 2019), https://www.burnabynow.com/news/injunction-upheld-covering-protests-at-burnaby-trans-mountain-sites-1.23642506.

268   Ian Austen, "Canadian Court Halts Expansion of Trans Mountain Oil Pipeline," *New York Times* (Aug. 30, 2018), https://www.nytimes.com/2018/08/30/world/canada/alberta-oil-pipeline-trudeau.html; Ian Austen, "Canada Approves Expansion of Controversial Trans Mountain Pipeline," *New York Times* (June 18, 2019), https://www.nytimes.com/2019/06/18/world/canada/trudeau-trans-mountain-pipeline.html.

269   Merrit Kennedy, "Canadian Court Clears the Way for Trans Mountain Pipeline Expansion," *NPR* (Feb. 5, 2020), https://www.npr.org/2020/02/05/803002446/canadian-court-clears-the-way-for-trans-mountain-pipeline-expansion.

In Virginia and West Virginia, dozens of protesters have been arrested since 2018 as they attempt to stop the natural gas Mountain Valley pipeline. Tree-sits and construction blockades have been successful in slowing construction,[270] even as court challenges to the pipeline's FERC permit have failed.[271] (The Supreme Court decided in 2020 that the Forest Service had properly allowed the pipeline company to tunnel under the Appalachian Trail.)[272]

In Louisiana, the L'eau Est La Vie camp was established in 2017 to stop the Bayou Bridge Pipeline, the terminus of DAPL. Led by Indigenous women, the resisters repeatedly disrupted construction through sensitive wetlands in the Atchafalaya Basin, home to the Atakapa-Ishak people, among others.[273] Lawsuits by environmentalists and local landowners documented many instances of inadequate environmental review by the Army Corps of Engineers as well as the pipeline company's failure to follow proper eminent domain procedures. Despite a court injunction that ordered a temporary halt to construction, the company proceeded with its plans, ultimately finishing the pipeline and paying a total of $450 to property owners whose lands it had illegally invaded.[274]

---

270 Michael Sainato, "Through Snow and Rain, Tree Sitters Continue to Fight a Gas Pipeline," *The American Prospect* (Dec. 23, 2019), https://prospect.org/environment/through-snow-rain-tree-sitters-fight-gas-pipeline/.

271 *Appalachian Voice et al. v. FERC*, No. 17-1271 (D.C.C. Feb. 19, 2019).

272 *United States Forest Service v. Cowpasture River Preservation Association*, 590 US _ (2020).

273 Anya Kamenetz, "The Fight to Stop the Dakota Access Pipeline Continues—in the Bayous of Louisiana," *The Nation* (Sep. 6, 2018), https://www.thenation.com/article/archive/the-fight-to-stop-the-dakota-access-pipeline-continues-in-the-bayous-of-louisiana/; Maia Winkler and Mary Lovell, "Bayou Bridge Pipeline Meets Resistance from the L'eau Est La Vie Camp," *Teen Vogue* (Oct. 16, 2018), https://www.teenvogue.com/story/bayou-bridge-pipeline-meets-resistance.

274 Matthew D. Ross, "Fresh down the Pipeline: An Analysis of the Fifth

Perhaps the biggest legal story out of L'eau Est La Vie was the state's aggressive pursuit of activists. In May 2018, Louisiana amended one of its laws to introduce new penalties for interfering with the "critical infrastructure" of the oil and gas industries. Under Act 692, pipelines and construction sites were added to the definition of "critical infrastructure," and "unauthorized entry of" and "damage to" fossil fuel company land and facilities became felonies punishable by up to five years of hard labor.[275] Previously, such conduct would have merited minor misdemeanor charges.

The state quickly applied this new legal weapon. Activist Anna White Hat was arrested at an anti-Bayou Bridge protest, charged with "unlawful entry of critical infrastructure," and forced to post a $21,000 bond. As Sara Sneath of ProPublica has noted, White Hat's judge had also imposed the $450 fine on the pipeline company for illegally intruding on private land—essentially the same crime, but with drastically different consequences.[276] White Hat and several other activists and organizations later sued the state in a case brought by the Center for Constitutional Rights and New Orleans movement attorney Bill Quigley, pointing out that Louisiana has 125,000 miles of pipelines: for standing almost anywhere

Circuit's Decision in Atchafalaya Basinkeeper v. United States Army Corps of Engineers," *Tulane Law Review* 93, no. 4 (April 2019): 1057–1078; Julie Dermansky, "Bayou Bridge Pipeline Construction Mess Poses Major Risk to Atchafalaya Basin," *Desmog Blog* (Oct. 10, 2019), https://www.desmogblog.com/2019/10/10/bayou-bridge-pipeline-construction-mess-poses-major-risk-atchafalaya-basin.

275 Act 692 2018 Session Louisiana Legislature, amending RS 14:61(B)(1)(C), and (D), and enacting (B)(3) and RS 16:61.1.

276 Sara Sneath, "Louisiana Pioneers New Ways to Suppress Environmental Activism," *truthdig* (Feb. 13, 2020), https://www.truthdig.com/articles/louisiana-pioneers-new-ways-to-suppress-environmental-activism/.

in the state, a person could be condemned to five years of forced servitude.[277]

In the same summer of 2018, three protesters kayaking through the basin were blown to shore by fan boats operated by private security officers who had been hired by the police. Having touched land, the protesters were charged with "unlawful entry." (They are now suing for violation of their First Amendment rights.)[278] As of February 2020, fifteen people had been charged under the newly amended law.[279]

Louisiana's effort to criminalize anti-fossil fuel activism falls into a pattern of other "critical infrastructure" bills that have flowered across the country. Originating in the American Legislative Exchange Council—a right-wing lobbying group supported by the oil, gas, and coal industries—these laws have mandated drastic penalties for interfering with fossil fuel business operations.[280] As of 2020, at least fifteen bills similar to Louisiana's have been enacted across the country.[281] Sneath notes that the roots of this

277 Complaint, *White Hat et al. v. Landry,* No. 19-CV-00322 (M.D. La. May 22, 2019). The lawsuit alleges that the law is overly broad and vague and that it prohibits protected First Amendment activity.

278 "Three Louisiana Water Protectors Sue For Wrongful Arrest During Bayou Bridge Pipeline Protests," *Roderick & Solange MacArthur Justice Center* (Aug. 9, 2019), https://www.macarthurjustice.org/three-louisiana-water-protectors-sue-for-wrongful-arrest-during-bayou-bridge-pipeline-protests/.

279 Sneath, "Louisiana Pioneers New Ways to Suppress Environmental Activism."

280 Alleen Brown "Ohio and Iowa Are the Latest of Eight States to Consider Anti-Protest Bills Aimed at Pipeline Opponents", *The Intercept* (Feb. 2, 2018), https://theintercept.com/2018/02/02/ohio-iowa-pipeline-protest-critical-infrastructure-bills/.

281 Connor Gibson, "State Bills to Criminalize Peaceful Protest of Oil & Gas 'Critical Infrastructure,'" *PolluterWatch* (updated Apr. 21, 2021), https://polluterwatch.org/state-bills-criminalize-peaceful-protest-oil-gas-critical-infrastructure-pipelines/; "US Protest Law Tracker," *International Center for Not-for-Profit Law* (updated Sep. 7, 2021), https://www.icnl.org/usprotestlawtracker/.

industry-led legislative campaign stretch back to 2003, when—in the midst of the post-9/11 Green Scare—executives and their political allies saw an opportunity to align state and industry by defining anti-corporate direct action as violent extremism.[282] Conservative legislators have recently sought to pass anti-protest laws targeting pro-Palestinian boycotts, labor strikes, and highway demonstrations—a tactic often used by the Movement for Black Lives—but have had most success with critical infrastructure bills.[283]

This campaign picked up steam after Standing Rock, as the fossil fuel system sought new ways to scare activists away from similar mobilizations. In North Dakota, the sponsor of that state's ALEC-modeled bill mentioned Michael Foster's Valve Turner action as the inspiration for her legislation.[284] Prosecutors have begun to use these new powers: in Houston in 2019, thirty-one activists who dangled from the Fred Hartman Bridge to block oil tankers were each hit with a federal obstruction of critical infrastructure charge carrying up to two years in prison.[285] (A grand jury failed to indict the protesters on the new felony charges, issuing misdemeanors instead.)[286] The Trump administration proposed a new federal ver-

282 Sneath, "Louisiana Pioneers New Ways to Suppress Environmental Activism."

283 Maggie Ellinger-Locke, "Anti-Protest Legislation is Threatening Our Climate," *Greenpeace* (May 3, 2019), https://www.greenpeace.org/usa/anti-protest-legislation-is-threatening-our-climate/.

284 "US Protest Law Tracker," *International Center for Not-for-Profit Law.*

285 Mose Buchele, "Activists Say New Laws To Protect Critical Infrastructure Aim To Silence Them," *NPR* (Sep. 25, 2019), https://www.npr.org/2019/09/25/763530303/activists-say-new-laws-to-protect-critical-infrastructure-aim-to-silence-them.

286 Ryan Schleeter, "Grand Jury Refuses Felonies for Greenpeace Activists and Others Charged in Houston Oil Industry Protest," *Greenpeace* (Mar. 4, 2020), https://www.greenpeace.org/usa/news/grand-jury-refuses-felonies-for-greenpeace-activists-and-others-charged-in-houston-oil-industry-protest/.

sion of such a law in 2019: anyone who "imped[ed] the operation of" an interstate pipeline could face twenty years in prison.[287]

One of the scarier aspects of this wave of repressive lawmaking is that it targets anti-fossil fuel activism generally, not just specific protest actions. For example, Oklahoma House Bill 1123, which served as the template for ALEC's model legislation, allows for up to a million dollars in fines for an organization "found to be a conspirator with persons" who have trespassed on or damaged critical infrastructure.[288] Indiana's SB 471, enacted in 2019, imposes a penalty of up to $100,000 for similar conduct—which could include words of encouragement, donating funds, or cheering from the sidelines.[289] In response to an ACLU lawsuit based on such concerns, South Dakota was forced to agree that it wouldn't enforce a new "riot boosting" law that could have applied to almost any form of protest support.[290]

As industry-backed state legislators continue to promote and refine these provisions, First Amendment activities like speech, assembly, and organizing will fall under special suspicion if they address the fossil fuel system. Even if many of these laws ultimately

---

287 Alleen Brown, "Trump Administration Asks Congress to Make Disrupting Pipeline Construction a Crime Punishable by 20 Years in Prison," *The Intercept* (June 5, 2019), https://theintercept.com/2019/06/05/pipeline-protests-proposed-legislation-phmsa-alec/.

288 H.B. 1123, 2017 Leg., 56th Sess. (Ok. 2017), cited in Jenna Ruddock, "Coming down the Pipeline: First Amendment Challenges to State-Level Critical Infrastructure Trespass Laws," *American University Law Review* 69, no. 2 (2019), 665-701, 680.

289 "US Protest Law Tracker," *International Center for Not-for-Profit Law.*

290 Vera Eidelman, "South Dakota Governor Caves on Attempted Efforts to Silence Pipeline Protesters," *American Civil Liberties Union* (Oct. 24, 2019), https://www.aclu.org/news/free-speech/south-dakota-governor-caves-on-attempted-efforts-to-silence-pipeline-protesters/?fbclid=IwAR2127foWCX-wQuN_JyeiwbvKTnnjEOtmtqqrsNFNAFP3wEOBt9ZKkJidkrI.

fall prey to their obvious constitutional deficiencies—it's illegal for the government to target speech based on its political content,[291] and laws must be narrowly drawn so as to give people a fair warning of when they are committing a crime[292]—their main goal is to impose a chilling effect on climate dissidents. Climate justice activists are now routinely asking their attorneys whether standard direct actions will lead to felony charges and whether support work like fundraising and posting on social media will leave them open to prosecution.

A related legal risk for activists involves the use of "strategic lawsuits against public participation," or SLAPPs. These are industry-led efforts to silence dissent using the tools of the private law, usually involving claims such as defamation, interference with business activity, or even racketeering—a charge originally designed to suppress organized crime conspiracies. The substance of these lawsuits is often legally laughable, but the point is not to succeed in court; it's to saddle activists with lawyers' fees and hearing dates, perhaps forcing a settlement and scaring people from threatening corporate bottom lines. This is an old tactic: in 1969, a group of white-owned businesses in Claiborne County, Mississippi sued the NAACP for organizing a boycott in response to racial discrimination, arguing that the social justice campaign had hurt their earnings. The Supreme Court ultimately ruled against the businesses, finding that a boycott is a protected First Amendment activity.[293]

291 *Police Department of the City of Chicago v. Mosley*, 408 U.S. 92 (1972).

292 *Broadrick v. Oklahoma*, 413 U.S. 601 (1973).

293 *NAACP v. Claiborne Hardware Co.*, 458 U.S. 886 (1982).

This precedent hasn't stopped fossil fuel companies from going after environmental activists. In 2017, Energy Transfer Partners, operator of DAPL, sued Greenpeace, Earth First!, and a suite of individual activists—described by the company as "putative not-for-profits and rogue eco-terrorist groups"—for harming the pipeline's construction and reputation (the firm representing Energy Transfer Partners is led by one of Donald Trump's lawyers). The complaint described the anti-DAPL movement as a violent network of paid professional saboteurs whose primary interest is not environmental protection or social justice but rather anti-business zealotry, self-enrichment, and even drug trafficking. The company asked for at least $900 million in damages.[294] In 2019, the federal district court of North Dakota dismissed the lawsuit, noting its "hyperbole" and lack of substantiation.[295] Four days later, the company re-filed in state court.[296]

This type of private industry legal abuse is on the rise and, as in the case of enhanced criminal punishment for dissent, there are troubling signs that the legal system is moving in a reactionary direction. Many of the "critical infrastructure" bills discussed above open the door to SLAPP-like actions, and in 2019 the Fifth Circuit Court of Appeals went against years of free speech precedent by ruling that a Black Lives Matter organizer could be liable

294 Complaint at 2, *Energy Transfer Partners v. Greenpeace et al.*, No. 1:17-cv-00173-BRW (D.N.D. Feb. 14, 2019.

295 *Energy Transfer Partners v. Greenpeace* at 7.

296 Blake Nicholson, "Dakota Access developer sues Greenpeace in state court," *Associated Press* (Feb. 23, 2019), https://apnews.com/c86795a2c7a64cb1b5c-1f7e42c649dba.

for injuries that a police officer suffered at a demonstration under a theory of "negligent protest."[297]

We can view this wave of repression—climate law's police phase—as the latest in a series, stretching from the deportations and speech bans of the Red Scare to the abuses of COINTELPRO and the more recent pressure on immigrant rights advocates.[298] Such a perspective makes clear that the climate justice movement's legal strategy must grapple not only with the laws of global warming, but also with the laws of a warming world—a world in which entrenched fossil interests will not give up without a fight. For now, these interests enjoy the near-universal support of state power.

The use of criminal penalties against climate activists can coexist with official state policies to reduce warming. As Joel Wainwright and Geoff Mann note in *Climate Leviathan*, most governments tolerate staid Earth Day-style environmental protest so long as it steers clear of confronting established interests. But when activists target nodes of economic power like Wall Street or the closed negotiating halls of the Paris climate talks, the police clamp down.[299] As protesters get better at actually disrupting business as usual—whether in the massive coal mine occupations in Germany[300] or in the London business district and transit shut-

---

297   *Doe v. Mckesson*, 945 F.3d 818 (5th Cir. 2019).

298   "U.S. Current Trend: Targeting of Immigrant Rights Activists," *International Center for Not-for-Profit Law* (January 2019), https://www.icnl.org/our-work/us-program/immigrant-rights-activists.

299   Joel Wainwright and Geoff Mann, *Climate Leviathan* (New York: Verso, 2018), 157-172.

300   Jessica Corbett, "Thousands of Activists Stage Protests at Three German Coal Mines to Demand Bolder Climate Policies," *Common Dreams* (Nov. 30, 2019), https://www.commondreams.org/news/2019/11/30/thousands-activists-stage-protests-three-german-coal-mines-demand-bolder-climate.

downs pulled off by Extinction Rebellion in 2019[301]—official legal rhetoric shifts from talk of emissions credits and carbon capture to warnings of terrorist violence and heightened security measures.

This raises the stakes of climate activism, to be sure. But as our detour through the history of oil, gas, and coal made clear, the stakes have always been high for people on the wrong end of the expanding fossil fuel system. By virtue of the greenhouse effect, the vast majority of the world's population now finds itself grouped into a community of interest with these original resisters of mines, pipelines, and refineries: mostly poor people, often black, brown, or Indigenous, and frequently living in areas of past and present colonial invasion. It's important to underscore the fact that fossil fuel workers belong in this community, too: after years of working to give us the energy we all use, they are now doubly vulnerable to uncertainties of transition.

This is not to promote a facile universalism that defines us as all equally effected by, or even equally responsible for, the climate crisis. Such conceptual slippage gives rise to the idea of the Anthropocene epoch, which, for all its usefulness in rendering visible the effect of human action on Earth systems, incorrectly identifies a species-wide human actor as its author. Certain people and groups are far more vulnerable to catastrophe, and certain people and groups have much more to answer for and much more to sacrifice in the years ahead. But considering ourselves as members of a united front, however sharply differentiated, does help to view the conflicts at Standing Rock and Bayou Bridge more clearly. These

301 Alex Marshall, "Arrest Us, Please! Extinction Rebellion's Path to Success," *The New York Times* (Oct. 8, 2019), https://www.nytimes.com/2019/10/08/world/europe/extinction-rebellion-london-greta.html.

aren't just regional struggles involving overzealous police and unfortunately located victims. They are the frontlines of a planetary fight for power. Some might be able to sit out the fight, at least for a while. But everyone's future is at stake.

To emphasize this point, it's worth turning to an oil conflict outside the United States. Fossil law is global, and so is the resistance to it. At a time when U.S. regulators and courts bring up the rearguard of progressive climate action, it's important to learn from legal activists abroad. A judicial struggle over extraction and dissent in Peru offers a tantalizing hint of how the law—up to this point mostly an abettor of industry abuse—might serve the cause of global climate justice.

Defense of the Right to Life

The western part of the Amazon rainforest has long been a site of colonial violence, from the abortive invasions of the Incans and the Spanish to the abuses of the rubber trade in the late nineteenth and earlier twentieth centuries. In the past several decades, as colonists from the coasts and mountains have ventured deeper into Indigenous territory, U.S. oil companies have bought up drilling rights and caused a series of ecological disasters. In the most infamous example, Texaco deliberately dumped sixteen billion tons of toxic wastewater in a large forested area in Ecuador from the 1960s to the 1980s—the levels of contaminants were two hundred times higher than those allowed under U.S. law—poisoning thousands of people and destroying extensive ecosystems.[302] In 2011, an

---

302 Rex Wyler, "Chevron's Amazon Chernobyl Case Moves to Canada," *Intercontinental Cry* (Sep. 9, 2017), https://intercontinentalcry.org/chevrons-amazon-chernobyl-case-moves-canada/.

Ecuadorian court ordered Chevron, which had bought Texaco, to pay $9.5 billion dollars in damages. The company has refused to abide by the ruling: instead, portraying itself as a victim, it has used hundreds of attorneys to fight the penalty in U.S. courts, launched smear campaigns against activists, and even brought a billion-dollar lawsuit against the plaintiffs' U.S. lawyer, Steven Donziger, who Chevron successfully had disbarred and placed under house arrest for failing to turn over his phone and laptop (the judge in that case appointed one of Chevron's law firms to act as Donziger's prosecutor after the government refused to participate).[303]

The exploitation of the western Amazon continues. In 2008, the Peruvian government began lifting environmental regulations and expediting oil exploration permits as part of a free trade agreement with the United States designed to increase the development of Amazonian oil reserves by U.S. firms. In the northern part of the country's rainforest, members of the Awajún and Wampi nations, which form part of the Jíbaro language family, began blocking oil company personnel from entering their territories, eventually setting up a highway blockade near the city of Bagua. The Amazonians had the law on their side. According to Convention 169 of the International Labour Organization, which Peru has adopted as domestic law, the state is required to consult with Indigenous communities over any resource development on their land. Indeed,

---

303 Sharon Lerner, "How the Environmental Lawyer Who Won a Massive Judgment Against Chevron Lost Everything," *The Intercept* (Jan. 29, 2020), https://theintercept.com/2020/01/29/chevron-ecuador-lawsuit-steven-donziger/.

Peruvian courts would later find the government's permitting actions illegal.[304]

But, as we've learned, the letter of the law often means little when the fossil fuel system encounters direct resistance. On June 5, 2009, police tear-gassed and stormed the Bagua blockade. Battles between the police and Awajún, Wampi, and mestizo protesters broke out across the area, and by the end of the conflict twenty-three policemen and ten civilians were dead, with many more missing. Instead of conducting a wide-ranging investigation into the use of force by the police—which U.S. diplomats had encouraged, as later revealed in cables released by WikiLeaks[305]—the government decided to prosecute a group of fifty-three defendants, many of them Indigenous, for crimes ranging from homicide to public disturbance. Those charged included Albert Pizango, leader of the pan-Amazonian group AIDESEP, who was not even in Bagua at the time.[306]

304 S. James Anaya, *Report of the Special Rapporteur on the situation of human rights and fundamental freedoms of indigenous people: Observations on the situation of the indigenous peoples of the Amazon region and the events of 5 June and the following days in Bagua and Utcubamba provinces, Peru,* United Nations Human Rights Council, A/HRC/12/34/Add.8, 5 (2009). A useful resource for U.S. audiences curious about the conflict is the 2016 documentary *When Two Worlds Collide,* directed by Heidi Brandenburg and Matthew Orzel.

305 "On Fifth Anniversary of Peru FTA Bagua Massacre of Indigenous Protestors, State Department Cables Published on Wikileaks Reveal U.S. Role," *Amazon Watch* (June 9, 2014), https://amazonwatch.org/news/2014/0609-state-department-cables-published-on-wikileaks-reveal-us-role-in-bagua-massacre.

306 *La sentencia del Caso Baguazo y sus aportes a la justicia intercultural,* Juan Miguel Jugo Viera, ed. (Lima: CNDH, 2017); Antonio Peña Jumpa, "A 7 años del conflicto de Bagua: La sentencia sobre los hechos de la "Curva del Diablo" y su legitimidad," *ius360.com* (Oct. 13, 2016), https://ius360.com/columnas/7-anos-del-conflicto-de-bagua-la-sentencia-sobre-los-hechos-de-la-curva-del-diablo-y-su-legitimidad/.

The trial was grueling. Over seven years, the state put many of the defendants in pre-trial detention—often in extreme conditions at high-altitude prisons that were especially taxing for rainforest residents—scheduled irregular hearings hundreds of miles from defendants' homes, and failed to provide interpreters for the many witnesses and defendants who didn't speak Spanish.[307] It seemed as though the Bagua case would follow the pattern typical to Peru and other Latin American countries, where environmentalists and Indigenous activists are frequently arrested, convicted, and murdered for their defense against extractive invasions.[308]

The 392-page decision issued by the Superior Court of Amazonas in 2016 was thus a jolt to the fossil fuel system. Amid an extensive discussion of the political and economic issues leading to the Bagua blockade, and with a withering dismissal of the state's shoddy evidence-gathering and flimsy accusations, a panel led by Judge Gonzalo Zabarburú Saavedra argued that the court's role was to minimize conflict and to correct historical injustices. Rather than using the power of punishment to exacerbate tensions between a development-hungry central government and besieged Amazonians, the judges wrote, the courts should embrace an ethic of "legal pluralism" in which "[w]e understand law as part of a cultural phenomenon and not as an ensemble of prescriptions or particular rules of conduct."[309]

307 *Bagua: entendiendo al Derecho en un contexto culturalmente complejo,* Gustavo Zambrano, ed. (Lima: PUCP, 2017).

308 *Defenders of the Earth: Global killings of land and environmental defenders in 2016* (Washington, DC: Global Witness, 2017).

309 Sentencia: Expediente No. 00194-2009 [0163-2013] (Corte Superior de Justicia de Amazonas: Sala Penal de Apelaciones Transitoria y Liquidadora de Bagua, Sep. 22, 2017), 83.

The court's analysis of the prosecution's case centered on the history of colonialism in the Peruvian Amazon and cited international and domestic law—including Convention 169 and the United Nations Declaration on the Rights of Indigenous Peoples—that protects Indigenous peoples' right to consult on extractive projects and to preserve the integrity of their territory. It also devoted many pages to a study of the Awajún and Wampi attitudes toward nature, emphasizing that legal pluralism required heightened attention to how such attitudes shape conceptions of legal and illegal behavior. Much of this discussion was filtered through the writings of non-Indigenous anthropologists and was framed as part of a Western effort to make the state more responsive to the diversity of its citizenry, rather than as the recognition of legitimate alternatives to the state's governance.[310] But, whereas U.S. courts have at best mentioned such matters in passing and at worst excluded them from consideration when ruling on the simple "facts" of a case—at Standing Rock, for example, federal courts have mostly dismissed claims based on Indigenous sovereignty, culture, and history in favor of more technical environmental law disputes— the Amazonas court actually relied upon Indigenous rights and attitudes in reaching its verdict.

"This is why our duty in reaching this sentence," the panel wrote, "is to be cautious, because not respecting their cosmovision of the earth in their understanding of norms is like violating their right to life, because this involves their existence, their culture, and their way of life ... [P]rotest directed toward defense of lands, if we

310 *Id.* at 120-154.

wish to assimilate it to our form of seeing life and culture, is equivalent to the defense of the right to life."[311]

Finding that the state had failed to prove its case and that the protests at Bagua were justified, the court acquitted all fifty-three defendants. In 2020, the Peruvian Supreme Court of Justice affirmed the ruling.[312]

According to Peruvian legal scholars, two trends accounted for the political and conceptual advances of the Bagua decision. First, the Peruvian judiciary had several years prior embarked on an institutional mission of addressing "intercultural justice," seeking to redress the country's long history of colonial oppression and to curb the often pro-development, anti-Indigenous practices of the prosecutors and police. Second, the defendants and their lawyers successfully used the years-long trial to focus the judges' attention on issues of cultural difference and environmental protection. Mirroring the national debate over the significance of the violence at Bagua, this courtroom conversation used the language and concepts of the law to reach a resolution on the politics of development in the Amazon.[313]

---

311 *Id.* at 146. It's worth noting that Amazonian attitudes toward oil drilling are not monolithic; many Awajún and Wampi in fact support it. See Barbara J. Fraser, "Peruvian court: indigenous communities must be consulted before drilling," *National Catholic Reporter* (Apr. 5, 2017), https://www.ncronline.org/blogs/world/eco-catholic/peruvian-court-indigenous-communities-must-be-consulted-drilling.

312 "Baguazo: absuelven a 53 indígenas por los sucesos en la Curva del Diablo," *La Républica* (Jan. 31, 2020), https://larepublica.pe/politica/2020/01/31/baguazo-absuelven-a-53-indigenas-por-los-sucesos-en-la-curva-del-diablo/.

313 Wilfredo Ardito Vega, "Las múltiples dimensiones de una sentencia avanzada," in *La sentencia del Caso Baguazo*, 9-25; *Bagua: entendiendo al Derecho en un contexto culturalmente complejo*, Gustavo Zambrano, ed.

What lessons does the Bagua decision hold for the law of climate change? For one thing, it shows that courts need not always facilitate the state's defense of industry and suppression of dissent. Juan Carlos Ruiz Molleda, one of Peru's leading human rights attorneys, has called the ruling "an historic milestone in the recognition of protest rights in our country."[314] We can imagine how this milestone might be exported back to the nation responsible for much of the violence at Bagua. Rather than closing their ears to arguments about Indigenous rights and government criminality, judges in North Dakota and Louisiana could choose to recognize the applicability of international and Native American treaties ("the supreme law of the land") and the well-founded legal justifications for civil disobedience. Instead of a univocal imposition of fossil law via prosecutors, police, and the courts, the legal system might be disaggregated to rebuke, via strategic lawyering and responsible judging, the state's violence on behalf of industry.

The Bagua decision also suggests that courts might awaken from their ideological slumber to do justice not only to persecuted earth defenders but also to the principles and values for which they fight. The Amazonas court used the idea of legal pluralism to confront the Peruvian criminal legal system's complicity with colonial violence. If we depart from the decision's rather measured tone and extend its premises beyond the modest ambition of recognizing diverse perspectives within a centralized legal regime, we might imagine a radical judicial practice that diffuses state power in favor of Indigenous peoples and their own varied visions of territorial

---

314 "Aportes de la sentencia del caso El Baguazo al reconocimiento del derecho a la protesta," in *La sentencia del Caso Baguazo*, 61-90.

governance and stewardship. Such a practice would also promote environmental protection as a paramount value, showing how any discrete legal conflict over development and resistance necessarily involves questions beyond the narrow concerns about economics and state power present in much of our written law. Courts decisions in this aspirational climate justice vein would not only use acquittals to push back on the use of criminal fossil law; they would also employ reasoning and principles that embody the ethical mandates of our era of global warming.

So how do we get from here to there? If there's one thing to be learned from the resistance to criminal fossil law, it's that the struggle for climate justice is not just about protecting the environment: it's about protecting rights to land, livelihoods, and liberty, too. The next chapter examines court cases that take this conjunction into account, confronting climate change with a variety of existing legal principles—namely constitutional and human rights—as well as cutting-edge ideas like the atmospheric trust doctrine and the rights of nature. If we have any chance of avoiding the worst effects of global warming, principles like these will form the core of the new climate law.

The Valve Turners Part 3: "Our Sympathies Start to Overwhelm Us"

Minnesota

Emily Johnston and Annette Klapstein were the last of the Valve Turners to stand trial. They had a long wait: along with Ben Joldersma and Steve Liptay, who had supported and documented the action at Enbridge Lines 4 and 67 in Minnesota, they watched court deadlines come and go, saw their fellow Valve Turners convicted, and witnessed the atmospheric concentration of carbon tick up five points before they got their turn before a jury.[315] They would not get a verdict until two days shy of the second anniversary of their protest.

Court delays, painful as they are, can have a strategic benefit. The trials in Washington, North Dakota, and Montana—where the climate necessity defense was denied in each instance— were instructive for the legal team. Its initial filing in Minnesota,

---

315 "Trends in Atmospheric Carbon Dioxide," *Global Monitoring Laboratory, Earth System Research Laboratories, National Oceanic and Atmopsheric Administration* (2020), https://www.esrl.noaa.gov/gmd/ccgg/trends/graph.html.

the Defense Response to State's Memorandum in Opposition to Affirmative Defense of Necessity, excerpted in the first part of the Valve Turners narrative, leaned heavily on climate doom and gloom. The weight of the arguments and evidence dealt with the special circumstances of the global emergency, hoping to balance any doubts about the law of necessity with the urgency of the facts. This was all morally and legally compelling. But the judges in the first three trials had brushed away the warming crisis like a crumb from their court papers. Perhaps a new tack was needed.

The Minnesota defense lawyers—Lauren Regan of the Civil Liberties Defense Center as coordinating attorney, Tim Phillips of Minneapolis as local counsel, and Kelsey Skaggs of Climate Defense Project appearing in-state for her organization—backed up the opening brief cited above with affidavits from four expert witnesses who had agreed to testify at trial. James Hansen, the renowned climate scientist, described the ecological and social crisis that would ensue from unchecked warming, and stated that, in his expert opinion, Johnston and Klapstein had acted reasonably to deal with an imminent threat.[316] Bill McKibben, perhaps the country's most high-profile climate activist and the co-founder of 350. org, concluded from his thirty years of study and organizing that civil disobedience was necessary to break through political inertia on the issue.[317] Martin Gilens, a political scientist at Princeton, summarized his research showing that economic elites such as fossil

---

316 Declaration of James E. Hansen in Support of Defendants' February 3, 2017 Motion, *Minnesota v. Klapstein*, No. 15-CR-16-413 (9th Jud. Dist. Ct., Clearwater Cty. Minn. Aug. 14, 2017).

317 Declaration of William McKibben in Support of Defendants' February 3, 2017 Motion, *Minnesota v. Klapstein* (March 20, 2017).

fuel companies and executives have outsized influence on government action, whereas "the preferences of the average American appear to have only a minuscule, near-zero, statistically non-significant impact upon public policy."[318] Tom Hastings, an expert on peace and conflict studies at Portland State University, described how, in the face of government inaction, nonviolent disobedience had been integral to the success of the women's suffrage, labor, civil rights, and migrant workers' rights movements.[319]

Given that most of these affidavits had been on the docket for months, Judge Robert D. Tiffany may already have been primed to accept the reasonableness of the defendants' testimony when the Clearwater County District Court finally convened a pre-trial hearing on August 15, 2017. The four defendants gathered to have their theory of necessity tested in the Bagley, Minnesota courthouse, close to the headwaters of the Mississippi River. For two hours, they took turns on the stand as Tim Phillips walked them through their activist biographies, covering familiar ground: a sudden and scary encounter with the scope and severity of the climate crisis, followed by a fever of self-education in science and political organizing, then frustrated efforts at legislative lobbying, petition drives, and public outreach. Finally, the turn to civil disobedience, including the Shell No! campaign in Seattle that had led to the oil giant's abandonment of its Arctic drilling scheme and had served as a lesson in the fruits of direct action. Each defendant was articulate and cogent in her description of why the Valve Turners' action was

318 Declaration of Martin Gilens in Support of Defendants' February 3, 2017 Motion at 2, *Minnesota v. Klapstein* (March 4, 2017).

319 Declaration of Tom Hastings in Support of Defendants' February 3, 2017 Motion, *Minnesota v. Klapstein* (March 20, 2017).

necessary. The prosecutor did his best to undermine their moral urgency, attempting to show hypocrisy (they'd traveled to court by car), lack of immediacy (no baby was attached to the pipeline in need of rescue), and futility (the oil has kept flowing). None of these blows hit the mark.[320]

Legal argument isn't just about content; it's about how you package content to make a compelling case. After the pre-trial hearing, each side had a chance to make their arguments in a new way through a supplemental brief. Trusting that the dangers of climate change had been sufficiently illustrated by the February filing, the expert submissions, and the defendants' hearing testimony, the defense attorneys decided to give the judge a more traditional reason to rule in their favor. Here is what they wrote on the first page of their second filing: "This brief clarifies the central issue before the Court at this pre-trial stage: the constitutional right of Defendants to present their evidence of necessity. Having satisfied their initial burden of making a prima facie showing on each element of the necessity defense, Defendants must now be allowed to present evidence, call experts, and testify as to their motivations."[321]

Note the shift in emphasis away from the climate crisis and toward procedural rights, an issue that hadn't appeared until page thirty-one of the first defense brief. This shift served two purposes. First, it put Judge Tiffany in the judicial comfort zone of due process. The Sixth Amendment of the U.S. Constitution, Supreme Court precedent on defendants' rights, Minnesota cases that require a jury

---

320 Transcript of Contested Omnibus Hearing, *Minnesota v. Klapstein* (Aug. 15, 2017).

321 Defense Supplemental Brief on the Affirmative Defense of Necessity at 1, *Minnesota v. Klapstein* (Sept. 11, 2017).

to hear evidence that meets a basic standard of admissibility: this is all material that a Clearwater County judge is happy to chew on, and anxious to get right lest an appeals court overturn him. On the other hand, the field of climate law is so underdeveloped that a lower court judge would often rather err on the side of abstention than risk a potentially controversial ruling on the relevance of climate science.

Second, the focus on constitutional rights signaled confidence in the defense's evidentiary record. We don't need to parse facts right now, the brief asserted: we've met our initial burden, and we don't need to convince you that global warming is real. That's for the jury to decide. Let's get on to the trial.

There was some good law for the defense team to work with. The Minnesota Supreme Court has held that defendants must be "afforded a meaningful opportunity to present a complete defense."[322] The U.S. Supreme Court has ruled that due process requires the capacity to present the defense's "version of the facts."[323] The defense brief was careful to distinguish the evidentiary standard for *presenting* a necessity defense in the first place— what the First Circuit of Appeals has called an "entry-level burden of producing competent evidence"[324]—from the standard for a *jury instruction*, which a judge issues after the close of evidence and which requires an "'underlying evidentiary foundation' as to each element of the defense," according to the Eighth Circuit.[325]

322 *State v. Richards,* 495 N.W.2d 187, 191 (Minn. 1992).

323 *Washington v. Texas,* 388 U.S. 14, 19 (1967).

324 *United States v. Maxwell,* 254 F.3d 21, 29 (1st Cir. 2001).

325 *United States v. Kabat,* 797 F.2d 580, 591 (8th Cir.1986), *quoting United States v. Goss,* 650 F.2d 1336, 1345 (5th Cir. 1981).

In other words, the pre-trial test is an easy one for defendants to pass. Once all witnesses, testimony, and exhibits have been presented at trial, the judge can still decide that it's not appropriate to give the jury the option of acquitting by reason of necessity. Luckily for the Minnesota defendants, there was a rare state case that directly addressed this issue. In 1984, the Minnesota Supreme Court held that a group of anti-war protesters who had staged a demonstration at the headquarters of defense contractor Honeywell Corporation had the right to at least show their evidence to a jury. The court called the use of prosecutorial motions *in limine*—the main tactic by which the state prevents political defendants from presenting their theory of a case—"questionable," and stressed that the jury, not the judge, has the right to evaluate the sufficiency of evidence.[326]

The defense brief crisply summarized this precedent, and for extra points noted that, since October 2016, the fate of the climate had grown even more dire. It also pointed out that, contrary to the state's suggestions at the pre-trial hearing, the pipeline that Johnston and Klapstein had targeted was anything but safe. Enbridge, the pipeline operator, had seen forty-nine spills in Minnesota since 2002, as well as an explosion in 2007 that killed two people. But the defense's conclusion noted that "the question before the Court is not whether Defendants should be acquitted by reason of necessity. Rather, it is whether they have made a preliminary showing entitling them to make that argument before a jury."[327]

---

326 *State v. Brechon*, 352 N.W.2d 745, 748 (Minn. 1984).

327 Defense Supplemental Brief at 7, *Minnesota v. Klapstein* (Sep. 11, 2017).

The prosecution took a different approach. Its filing was admirably concise. Focusing on the question of imminence, the body of the motion was composed almost entirely of four excerpts from the pre-trial hearing transcript where the prosecutor examined the defendants:

Cross examination of Ms. Klapstein

MR. HANSON: Um, but there was no natural catastrophe happening right there? There no oil spill happening right there?

MS. KLAPSTEIN: No, there was not.

Cross examination of Ms. Johnston

MR. HANSON: Did you see any individuals in imminent danger?

MS. JOHNSTON: Ah, no, I did not.

Cross examination of Mr. Joldersma

MR. HANSON: Was there anyone in immediate peril at that site?

MR. JOLDERSMA: No.

Cross examination of Mr. Liptay

MR. HANSON: Okay. Did you observe anyone in immediate danger at the site?

MR. LIPTAY: No.[328]

---

328 State's Supplemental Brief Regarding Defense's Necessity Defense at 2, *Minnesota v. Klapstein* (Sept. 15, 2017).

This was good lawyering: isolate the issue, and have the other side make your case for you. Of course, it was also rather preposterous. The defense's case had nothing to do with whether or not anyone was in danger at the pipeline site. The prosecution was relying on the old trick of scale that has proven so effective in defeating other climate legal efforts: global warming is happening everywhere, so it's happening nowhere. The time to act is always, so the time to act is never. The protesters were protecting all of us, so they were protecting no one. The law simply doesn't apply.

Judge Tiffany sat on the briefs for a month. In the meantime, Michael Foster went to trial in North Dakota, deprived of his necessity defense, and was convicted of two felonies and a misdemeanor.

On October 11, 2017, a year to the day after the Valve Turners' action, Judge Tiffany issued his order: the defendants would be allowed to present their necessity defense at trial.

This was a momentous ruling. Only two previous climate necessity defenses had ever gone before a jury (see The Valve Turners, Part 1), and this was the first time that a judge had issued a written opinion allowing the defense—a fact of great importance in our precedent-dependent legal system. Stories on the case appeared in local, progressive, and climate media,[329] noting that Judge Tiffany had described how the necessity defense applies only

329 The Associated Press, "Minnesota judge allows 'necessity defense' in pipeline case," *MPR News* (Oct. 17, 2017), https://www.mprnews.org/story/2017/10/17/minnesota-judge-allows-necessity-defense-in-pipeline-case; "Minnesota Judge to Allow "Necessity Defense" at Trial of Climate Activists," *Democracy Now!* (Oct. 18, 2017), https://www.democracynow.org/2017/10/18/headlines/minnesota_judge_to_allow_necessity_defense_at_trial_of_climate_activists; Phil McKenna, "Judge Allows 'Necessity' Defense by Climate Activists in Oil Pipeline Protest," *Inside Climate News* (Oct. 16, 2017), https://insideclimatenews.org/news/16102017/climate-change-activists-arrest-pipeline-shutdown-necessity-defense.

in "emergency situations" and that "Minnesota's standard for the necessity defense is high."[330]

This was a major victory for the Valve Turners, to be sure. After three straight defeats in which judges had blocked the most important evidence from trial, the group now had a concrete legal breakthrough that could be cited by future protesters. But just as remarkable as the opinion's effect was its brevity: Judge Tiffany devoted only two short paragraphs to the question of necessity, and used nearly all of that space to cite the controlling law. He provided no comment on the defense's evidence, nor on the reasoning that had led to his decision. The words "climate," "warming," and "civil disobedience" were entirely absent from the ruling. And here is how the order ended: "The Court's grant is not unlimited and the Court expects any evidence in support of the defense of necessity to be focused, direct, and presented in a non-cumulative manner. The State of Minnesota may object at trial on the above or other lawful grounds."[331]

For an attorney reading between the lines, the meaning of these sentences was clear: Judge Tiffany felt bound to allow the defense's theory of the case based on the quantity of evidence presented, but there was no guarantee that the jury would get a necessity instruction. The judge had effectively encouraged the prosecution to be aggressive in its challenges to testimony and evidence. This was not going to be some freewheeling symposium on global warming and political corruption.

---

330 Order and Memorandum at 5, *Minnesota v. Klapstein* (Oct 11, 2017), *quoting State v. Johnson*, 289 Minn. 196, 199 (1971).

331 *Id.* at 6.

There were two ways to interpret the order's style. On the one hand, the biggest climate necessity ruling to date had regrettably failed to mention the warming crisis, demonstrating, even in a moment of victory, the legal system's reluctance to deal with the issue. On the other hand, the opinion's restriction to matters of evidentiary standards and due process indicated that the defense team's strategy of shifting the emphasis had worked: they had gotten the judge to rule in their favor without even mentioning the major issue at hand. This suggested that, with some favorable state precedent and a bit of luck, the law of climate change might be built with unlikely materials.

Both readings had some truth to them. Over the course of the following two years, the climate necessity defense would grow incrementally from the oblique approval of Judge Tiffany's opinion to emphatic endorsements by state supreme courts. Even as the cloud of climate change grew ever darker, its shadow would finally begin to creep up the courthouse steps.

The Prosecution Takes a Break

Only three days after the Minnesota Valve Turners won the right to present the necessity defense at trial, a district court in Spokane, Washington made a similar ruling.[332] The case stemmed from an action that occurred the month before the Valve Turners' action, when George Taylor, a pastor and member of Veterans for Peace, had helped to block train tracks that carried crude oil through the

---

332 Mitch Ryals, "Spokane judge OK's necessity defense for climate change lawbreaker," *Inlander* (Oct. 18, 2017), https://www.inlander.com/Bloglander/archives/2017/10/18/spokane-judge-oks-necessity-defense-for-climate-change-lawbreaker.

city. After reviewing pre-trial evidence very similar to that seen in the Valve Turner cases, Judge Debra R. Hayes concluded that Taylor had met his burden of proof and was entitled to the necessity defense. Unlike Judge Tiffany's decision in Minnesota, Judge Hayes's opinion, which was issued nearly five months after her initial ruling allowing the defense, discussed at length Taylor's evidence on climate change and the dangers of oil transport by rail, and correctly noted that many political necessity defenses had succeed in the past.[333] Following this initial victory, the state appealed, beginning a long series of reversals and re-reversals.[334] In a similar fashion, the nationwide climate necessity movement, which had metastasized since the Valve Turners' action, experienced a flurry of setbacks and advances.

On the losing side of the ledger, Valve Turner Leonard Higgins was convicted in November 2017 after his necessity defense was denied. In Minneapolis, a group of activists who had staged a stadium banner-drop to advocate divestment from the Dakota Access Pipeline were barred from presenting necessity evidence. Anti-fracking protesters at the Port of Olympia, Washington, opponents of the Enbridge Line 3 tar sands pipeline in Wisconsin and in Minnesota, and resisters of the Spectra Algonquin Incremental Market pipeline in Cortlandt, New York would all see their climate necessity defenses denied over the next fifteen months.[335]

But there was good news, too. An odd and inspiring case came out of Boston, where thirteen defendants—including Al

---

333 Findings of Fact and Conclusions of Law at 5-8, *Washington v. Taylor*, No 6Z0117975 (Dist. Ct. Spokane Cty., Wash. Mar. 13, 2018).

334 See "Climate Necessity Defense Case Guide," *Climate Defense Project*.

335 *Id.*

Gore's daughter Karenna, a dedicated climate activist, and Tim DeChristopher, who had served nearly two years in federal prison after attempting the first high-profile climate necessity case in 2009—faced charges after interfering with the construction of the West Roxbury Lateral Pipeline. With the help of a large legal team, the activists used the pre-trial discovery process to reveal the pipeline company's lack of a safety plan for potential explosions. The judge had signaled her willingness to let the defendants mount a climate necessity defense when, on the eve of trial in March 2018, the state reduced the charges to civil infractions, a move that deprived the activists of the opportunity to present their case to a jury. At the resulting civil hearing, the judge acquitted the entire group. In response to a request by the defense attorneys, she noted that her decision was by reason of necessity. This was, in some ways, the first courtroom victory for the climate necessity defense, although the defendants never put on a proper defense and no jury considered their evidence.[336]

Something similar happened in North Dakota five months later in the case of Chase Iron Eyes, discussed in Chapter 3. North Dakota prosecutors had singled Iron Eyes out as a leader of the Standing Rock movement. His attorneys mounted an aggressive defense that included the necessity theory and used the pre-trial discovery process to produce evidence of the state's collusion with

336 *Id.*; Carolyn Kormann, "Sometimes Fighting Climate Change Means Breaking the Law," *The New Yorker* (Apr. 3, 2018), https://www.newyorker.com/tech/annals-of-technology/sometimes-fighting-climate-change-means-breaking-the-law.

private mercenaries. Shortly before trial, the state reduced its charges and let Iron Eyes walk free.[337]

This peculiar pattern repeated itself again in May 2019, in a case involving protesters from the Michigan Poor People's Campaign. The activists had been arrested at the state Department of Environmental Quality as they demonstrated against the agency's myriad failures to protect the public, including the Flint lead pipe scandal, the permitting of the Enbridge Line 5 pipeline, and a deal that allowed Nestle to siphon off large quantities of public water. The defense filed a necessity memorandum based on this array of environmental harms. As the judge was considering the issue, the prosecutor decided to drop the charges.[338]

Though it's impossible to definitively ascertain prosecutors' motives in these cases, the evidence suggests that the aggressive tactics of defense attorneys, combined with the growing momentum of the climate necessity defense, led the states to surrender rather than face the prospect of embarrassing defeats at trial. Only a year and a half prior, a climate necessity case seemed a sure win for any state's attorney: no judicial opinion had ever recognized the theory, and no defendant had ever walked free because of it. But in the wake of Judge Tiffany's opinion and the ruling in the Taylor case—and with uncomfortable information about how the

337 *Indian Country Today* Editorial Team, "North Dakota Prosecutors Drop All Serious Charges against Chase Iron Eyes"; Opposition to the State's Motion in Limine, *North Dakota v. Iron Eyes*, No. 30-2017-CR-00223 (N.D. South Cent. Jud. Ct. Aug. 7, 2017).

338 Defendants' Joint Memorandum of Law in Support of Necessity Defense, *Michigan v. Alpert*, No. 18—6143-SM (Ingham Cir. Ct., Mich. May 10, 2019); "Michigan Prosecutor Dismisses Charges Against Poor People's Campaign Activists," *Climate Defense Project* (May 10, 2019), https://climatedefense-project.org/michigan-prosecutor-dismisses-charges-against-poor-peoples-campaign-activists/.

government protects fossil fuel companies coming to light—three high-profile climate necessity cases ended with a prosecutorial white flag. Gratifying as these results were for the defendants and movements involved, they were, from the state's point of view, preferable to a clear courtroom resolution.[339]

Unfortunately for the advocates of fossil law, such a resolution was not long in coming.

An "Unusually Strong" Argument

Although prosecutors generally aren't allowed to appeal an acquittal—this is the famous rule against "double jeopardy"—they are sometimes allowed to appeal an adverse pre-trial ruling. After Judge Tiffany handed down his groundbreaking decision in *Minnesota v. Klapstein*, the state did just that, filing a motion with a higher court to get the order overturned. In their appeal, the prosecutors argued that allowing the necessity defense to go forward would have a "critical impact" on its case because it would substantially lower the chances of securing a conviction. This premise might strike you as odd: after all, the point of due process rights is to make the prosecutor's job harder. Unfortunately, our courts tend to give a lot of leeway to the policy goals of conviction and confinement, and so there are many mechanisms, from motions *in limine* to appeals based on "critical impact," that give the state a chance to erode their opponents' advantages.

---

339 *See* Alex Marquardt, "How climate protesters are defending their civil disobedience–and winning in court," *Fast Company* (Nov. 12, 2018), https://www.fastcompany.com/90266249/how-climate-protesters-are-defending-their-civil-disobedience-and-winning-in-court.

In late 2017, the Valve Turners' Minnesota legal team settled into another round of briefing. A first attempt to have the prosecution's appeal dismissed was rebuffed by the Minnesota Court of Appeals, which asked both sides to submit longer arguments. The prosecutor responded with a brief that argued that the necessity defense would "unnecessarily confuse the jury and conflate the issue regarding the Respondents' [defendants'] culpability." The brief went on to attack the activists' evidence in much the same way that the prosecutor had done in the court below: using selective quotes from the pre-trial hearing, it argued that there was no imminent threat at the site of the protest, that the defendants had failed to avail themselves of legal alternatives by not appealing to the legislatures of Minnesota and Canada to turn off the pipeline, and that they had failed to avert the harm because they could not demonstrate how much carbon was prevented from entering the atmosphere. [340] Again, this was good lawyering, but it was also a little too sneaky.

The Valve Turners had always made the case that the Enbridge pipeline posed a threat to the entire planet, not just to hypothetical individuals present on the morning of October 11. Their long track records of legal activism had demonstrated the need for lawbreaking, so minor examples of other tacks they could have taken were unconvincing. And the intended effect of their action was to spur political change to address global warming as a whole, not just to incrementally lower carbon dioxide concentrations. But the state's brief pressed the idea that, given such broad questions of social

---

340 Appellant's Pretrial Appeal Brief and Addendum at 7, *Minnesota v, Klapstein*, No. A17-1649 (Minn. Ct. App., Nov. 17, 2017).

good and political efficacy, the political necessity defense should not exist in the first place, and certainly should not be heard here.

The defendants had to respond with some rather counterintuitive arguments. If, at the pre-trial stage, they had basically admitted that they had done what the prosecutor claimed, they now had to show that, even with the necessity defense, the state had a good chance of convicting them, because this would show that there was no "critical impact" on the state's case. Their brief thus acknowledged the prosecution's "smoking-gun" evidence, noted that the state could still object to any and all evidence at trial, and even cited a related Iowa pipeline protest case in which, despite a similar showing, activists had been convicted by a jury. For good measure, and because this was the first time that the Court of Appeals had considered the matter, the defense lawyers included fourteen pages that summarized the Valve Turners' evidence on each element of the defense: the severity and imminence of climate change (including choice quotes from the federal government and *Massachusetts v. EPA*), the lack of legal alternatives (focused on the activists' own experience and the testimony of experts), and the efficacy of civil disobedience (featuring expert testimony and the successful Shell No! campaign against Arctic drilling).[341]

The stakes were high as the Court of Appeals considered these briefs, and not just for the four defendants. Appeals court decisions have far greater precedential value than trial court orders. As the rising tide of climate necessity defenses across the country demonstrated, there was growing impatience with the political

---

341 Respondents' Pretrial Appeal Brief and Addendum, *Minnesota v. Klapstein* (Nov. 26, 2017).

and legal establishments' inability to address climate change. An appellate decision allowing a group of climate civil disobedients to make their case at trial would signal that this impatience had penetrated to the heart of the judiciary and that the fossil fuel industry's social license might be in danger of expiring. On the other hand, a reversal would suggest that Judge Tiffany's decision had been an anomaly, and would give prosecutors an all-important precedent to work from in their efforts to suppress the defense.

So the industry's allies intervened. In November 2017, the Minnesota Chamber of Commerce filed an amicus—or "friend of the court"—brief, a tool used by interested parties to present their view of the case. The Chamber of Commerce brief was full of predictable hyperbole about the purported danger of the activists' pipeline sabotage, but the real heart of the argument was the existing balance of climate power. "This case concerns whether Minnesota will encourage political protesters to commit criminal acts to advance their policy agenda," the Chamber wrote. "[T]he outcome of this appeal will have profound ramifications for business and public safety across the state." The brief went on to warn that "chaos would ensue" if protesters were allowed to justify their civil disobedience in court, and painted a nightmare scenario of emboldened activism: "Imagine those seeking to avert a health crisis asserting that it is necessary to destroy fast-food fryers; those protesting wealth inequality asserting that it is necessary to steal; or those advocating for the homeless asserting that breaking and entering is necessary."[342]

342 Brief and Addendum of *Amicus Curiae* The Minnesota Chamber of Commerce Supporting Appellant The State of Minnesota at 1-2, 13, 14, *Minnesota v, Klapstein* (Nov. 27, 2017).

For all its bombast, the Chamber's arguments represented an important clarification of the political issues at stake. Unlike the Valve Turner cases in Washington, North Dakota, and Montana, where trial judges had endorsed dubious notions about the unreliability of climate science and the twisted personal motives of the defendants, the briefing in Minnesota centered on crucial questions about the function of the court system and the place of political economic issues in the law. The Chamber was even offering a picture of what a just society's criminal legal system might look like if such cases were allowed to proceed: its last two examples, at least, would be lauded by many legal activists.

A perspective from the other side was needed, then. In early December, an amicus brief was filed by the Society of American Law Teachers, the nation's largest independent association of legal academics, along with over 100 individual law professors, including leading constitutional and environmental law theorists. Authored by Alex Marquardt of Climate Defense Project, with lead signatory Bill Quigley, a renowned activist defense attorney, constitutional lawyer, and professor at Loyola University New Orleans School of Law, the brief forcefully argued for the place of political protest cases in the court system and for the strength of the defendants' necessity case. The professors asserted that "there is an incontrovertible public interest in the debate and exchange of political ideas, and courts, as fact-finding forums, are essential to the vindication of that interest." To justify the point, they noted that, in the U.S. legal tradition, courts have served as an important part of the First Amendment "marketplace of ideas." This was especially the case in the debate over global warming: "As rigorous fact-finding forums in which principled rules of evidence govern the validity of the truth-seeking process, courts are much-needed sites of argumentation on politicized and urgent civilizational issues such as the impending climate emergency."

Contrary to what the prosecution and the Chamber of Commerce claimed, the professors argued that political necessity defenses actually further the values of free speech, self-government, and the prevention of abuse of power because concerned citizens get to explain their conduct to a jury of their peers. In a system in which prosecutors enjoy enormous power to decide what charges to issue and what plea deals to offer, they stressed, the preservation of due process rights is essential. The professors closed by noting that "the argument for necessity evidence in climate civil disobedience cases is unusually strong" because the threat of global warming is so clear-cut, climate activists suffer from an unusual degree of state and industry repression (see Chapter 3), and the right to a healthy environment is a basic principle of the law (see Chapter 4). "Nonviolent civil disobedience is part of the American democratic tradition," the professors wrote. "The four individuals named above stand in the shoes of the American freedom fighters, the abolitionists, the suffragettes, the civil rights campaigners of the 1960s, and the antiwar protesters that followed. Criminal trials in which protesters have explained and argued their views are an integral part of that tradition."[343]

Four months later, the Minnesota Court of Appeals ruled in the Valve Turners' favor.

The majority's opinion was relatively restricted in its scope. It considered simply whether the prosecution had made a compelling

---

343 Brief of Law Professors and Legal Education Organizations as *Amicus Curiae* in Support of Respondents at 4, 6, 16, 27, *Minnesota v, Klapstein* (Dec. 4, 2017).

case that it would suffer a "critical impact" from the presentation of the necessity defense, and decided that it would not. The final lines from the trial court's order, which had warned that all evidence would still be subject to scrutiny, were crucial to the Court of Appeals' conclusion: "the effect of the district court's order in this matter is so conditioned by and dependent upon the resolution of issues and objections not yet before it," the court found, that it made no sense to speculate about how the state's case would be affected.[344]

The decision was a milestone, to be sure. This was the first time that an appellate court had sanctioned the use of the climate necessity defense. But the state decided to give it one last shot and filed a petition for discretionary review at the Minnesota Supreme Court (with no right to appeal the loss, the prosecution had to ask the court to take the case). On July 17, 2018, in a one-sentence order, the state's highest court denied the petition, sending the case back to Clearwater County.[345]

With this ruling in hand, Emily Johnston, Annette Klapstein, and Ben Joldersma, could breathe a big sigh of relief (the other defendant, Steve Liptay, who had recorded the action, had had his charges dismissed in the meantime). The prosecution had gambled and lost big. A state's highest court had now effectively ruled that the type of pre-trial case made by the Valve Turners and other climate necessity defendants was sufficient for a jury trial. Going forward, it would be much harder for prosecutors to assert that such a theory was outside the bounds of the law.

344 Unpublished Opinion at 7, *Minnesota v. Klapstein* (April 23, 2018).

345 Order, *Minnesota v. Klapstein*, No. A17-1649 (Minn. S. Ct. July 17, 2018).

Still, the decision was limited in its immediate impact. The Court of Appeals and the Supreme Court had not actually reviewed and approved a climate necessity defense. They had just decided that the prosecution had to go through with the trial as Judge Tiffany had ordered. The Valve Turners were still waiting for the ultimate legal victory: acquittal by a jury of their peers.

On to trial, then.

The Definition of Damage

Having waited nearly two years, Johnston, Klapstein, and Joldersma were eager to get themselves and their experts into a courtroom. But there was still one minor hurdle: a pre-trial and settlement conference on September 27, at which attorneys for both sides would hash out the witnesses and exhibits they planned to present and at which Judge Tiffany would make some initial decisions about how to organize the trial. Such conferences are usually pretty technical, and there was no reason to expect that this one would make any significant difference in how the defendants would present their case. After all, they had just emerged victorious from a nearly year-long battle over their right to argue necessity.

So the court's resulting order on October 3 came as a shock. Judge Tiffany spent the bulk of the order dealing with routine matters: the process for selecting jurors, a rule forbidding attorneys from using witnesses' first names, reserving a seat for the courtroom sketch artist. But appearing in the middle, in two short lines of text, was an enormously consequential ruling: the judge had decided to grant the state's motions *in limine* to bar expert testimony on climate change and legal alternatives.

The Valve Turners and their attorneys were flummoxed. Was the judge reversing his own decision to grant the necessity defense after the state Court of Appeals and the Supreme Court had just affirmed him?

A short memorandum was attached to the order, and it only confused matters. Judge Tiffany summarized the rules of evidence in Minnesota, noting that expert testimony must pass a "helpfulness" test: that is, it must help the jury resolve a central question in the case. He wrote:

> Defendants indicate that their expert Witnesses will discuss climate change. But this expert testimony on climate change fails the helpfulness test. The effects of climate change, in particular in Minnesota, are "within the knowledge and experience of a lay jury and the testimony of the expert[s] will not add to the precision or depth of the jury's ability to reach conclusions" about climate change. See *State v. Helterbridle*, 301 N.W.2d 545, 547 (Minn. 1980); see also Minn. R. Evid. 403.

> Defendants also indicated that their expert witnesses will discuss the lack of alternatives to civil disobedience in the political process. Expert testimony on civil disobedience fails the helpfulness test. As citizens who participate in the political democratic process, the jury is in the best position to determine the effectiveness of the political process. In this matter, the jury is "in as good a position to reach a decision as the expert[s]" and any expert testimony "would be of little assistance to the jury and should not be admitted." See *State v. Saldana*, 324 N.W.2d 227, 229 (Minn. 1982).[346]

---

346 Order Following Pretrial/Settlement Conference at 10, *Minnesota v. Klapstein* (9th Jud. Dist. Ct. Oct. 3, 2018).

Expert witnesses were not needed, Judge Tiffany had decided, because understanding climate change and the political process requires no expertise.

For anyone paying attention to the case history and other climate necessity trials, this conclusion was astounding. Ken Ward's court in Washington had ruled that global warming was so far beyond the reach of even an experienced judge that no criminal trial could possibly deal with it. Months of litigation and sharply divided judicial opinions had dealt with the question of legal alternatives with no clear consensus. Capable as ordinary jurors are, it certainly seemed that specialized knowledge on these topics would be useful.

Excluding experts was one thing. What followed was even worse: "In any case," Judge Tiffany's order read, "in the current matter the Defendants cannot, as a matter of law, rely on civil disobedience and a lack of legal alternatives to prove the necessity defense."[347]

But this was the defense's entire case. Without expert testimony and without mentioning legal alternatives and civil disobedience, there was simply no way of arguing that turning the valves had been necessary. How could Judge Tiffany have approved the necessity defense a year prior only to dismiss its entire substance now?

The judge did not address this contradiction. Instead, he justified his conclusion by relying on the worst case in the political necessity literature, *United States v. Schoon*, decided by the federal Ninth Circuit of Appeals in 1991 (the court amended the opinion in

347 *Id.* at 4.

1992). In that case, activists were charged with obstruction and failure to obey police orders after they spilled fake blood in a Tucson
IRS office to protest the U.S. government's involvement in the civil
war in El Salvador. A lower court had barred the necessity defense
prior to trial, and the defendants appealed to the Ninth Circuit.

Judge Boochever, writing for the court, based his decision to
uphold the lower court on a distinction between "indirect" and
"direct" civil disobedience. "Indirect civil disobedience," he wrote,
"involves violating a law or interfering with a government policy
that is not, itself, the object of protest. Direct civil disobedience, on
the other hand, involves protesting the existence of a law by breaking that law or by preventing the execution of that law in a specific
instance in which a particularized harm would otherwise follow."
Indirect civil disobedience, according to Judge Boochever, included
most types of activism that make their way into political necessity
cases: street protests, occupations of congressional offices, interference with military infrastructure. In these instances, civil disobedients are typically charged with trespass or disorderly conduct,
laws that have little do with the political issue at stake. On the other
hand, for example, those who staged lunch counter sit-ins as part
of the civil rights movement were charged under segregation statutes, meaning that they were directly violating a law that they considered objectionable.[348]

The direct/indirect distinction was intended to systematize
the element-by-element analysis applied to any political necessity
defense. In the view of the Ninth Circuit, indirect civil disobedience
could never target a legitimate imminent harm (government policy

348 971 F.2d 193, 196.

is by its very nature not a legal injury), it could never be efficacious (the protest itself will not fix the problem), and it could never lack for legal alternatives (you always have some viable option besides breaking the law).

This might sound straightforward. But the argument simply does not stand up to scrutiny.

For one thing, the court's focus on government policy is misleading. Protesters are rarely concerned only with unjust state action: what motivates them are the *effects* of such action. For example, climate protesters are worried about the enormous social and environmental consequences of climate change and so, in order to address these, they have to target the government's failures on the matter. But government policy itself is not their primary concern. Even in the case before the Ninth Circuit in *Schoon*, the IRS protesters were not fundamentally focused on U.S. foreign funding; they were worried about people being killed in El Salvador as a result of that funding. So the harm element is a bit more complicated than the court assumed.

As for Judge Boochever's second point, it is unclear why direct civil disobedience should be more causally effective than indirect civil disobedience. In both instances, policy change is required to realize the promise of the protest. Lunch counters were not directly desegregated by sit-ins; they were desegregated by court orders, municipal ordinances, and federal legislation. The same goes for protests in which activists are arrested for trespass or disorderly conduct. The theory of change remains the same.

Finally, the court's legal alternative argument is simply bunk. Some hypothetical legal course of action exists in any civil disobedience situation. Even an activist targeting Jim Crow could have petitioned Congress or written a strongly worded letter to Bull Connor rather than break the law. The point is not whether such options exist; it is whether they're viable.[349]

Perhaps the most risible aspect of the indirect/direct civil disobedience distinction is the effort by federal judges to carve out the civil rights movement as the sole instance of legally acceptable direct action. Making room for this one type of legitimate political necessity is clearly a recognition that to do otherwise—to describe even the lunch counter sit-ins as illegitimate—would rob the law of any moral force. But this distinction, too, collapses with a harder look. At least three thousand arrestees at civil rights actions were charged with trespass and disorderly conduct, not with violation of a segregation ordinance.[350] Were their protests futile acts of "indirect" civil disobedience? Is there *any* type of protest for which the *Schoon* opinion would allow a necessity defense?

In fact, Judge Boochever did offer one hypothetical. Unfortunately for those who cite him, it supports precisely the type of case that the Valve Turners brought. "If a city council passed an ordinance requiring immediate infusion of a suspected carcinogen into the drinking water," the judge wrote, "physically blocking the delivery of the substance would constitute direct civil disobedience: protestors would be preventing the execution of a law in a

---

349 For detailed critiques of *Schoon*, see William P. Quigley, "The Necessity Defense in Civil Disobedience Cases: Bring in the Jury"; James L. Cavallaro, Jr., "The Demise of the Political Necessity Defense: Indirect Civil Disobedience and *United States v. Schoon*," *California Law Review* 81 (1993), 351-385; and Lance N. Long and Ted Hamilton, "The Climate Necessity Defense: Proof and Judicial Error in Climate Protest Cases."

350 John Alan Cohan, "Civil Disobedience and the Necessity Defense," *Pierce Law Review* 6 (2007), 111-175, 116.

specific instance in which a particularized harm—contamination of the water supply—would otherwise follow."[351]

Substitute "atmosphere" for "drinking water" and "climate" for "water supply," and you've got the classic case of anti-fossil fuel direct action. Especially when a climate activist is charged with a law that makes damage to a pipeline a criminal offense—as was the case with the Minnesota statute that protects the transmission of poisonous fuels—the symmetry could not be neater. Climate activists are directly targeting a harm that is protected by a specific law; they are charged under that specific law and their action ameliorated the harm. Thus, their lawbreaking is necessary.[352]

Despite its glaring flaws of logic and historical analysis, *Schoon* shows up in any decently researched prosecution brief. At the last moment, it had reared its ugly head in *Minnesota v. Klapstein*, too. With five days to go before trial, and with a large team of supporters and volunteers on site and expert witnesses on the way, the defense attorneys scrambled to respond to Judge Tiffany's confounding order.

Working late into the night, the lawyers wrote a motion that strenuously objected to the due process violation represented by undermining the defense's entire case on the eve of trial. Expert witnesses are supposed to be admitted whenever their testimony will shed special light on a central question, the motion argued. This was the case with the legal alternatives element, and it was

---

351   *Schoon*, 971 F.2d at 196.

352   The defense made this point in a final supplemental motion on the first day of trial, in the hope of preserving the issue for appeal. Memorandum on *State v. Rein, United States v. Schoon,* and Pretrial Standard for Admitting Necessity Evidence, *Minnesota v. Klapstein* (Oct. 8, 2018).

certainly the case with climate change, as well: the lawyers cited opinion research showing that only about half of Clearwater County residents believed that climate change is currently affecting the weather. Clearly expert knowledge on the issue was needed. For good measure, the lawyers attacked Judge Tiffany's reliance on *Schoon*, pointing out both the problems in that case and the fact that, in his initial decision allowing the necessity defense, the judge had not even mentioned it.[353]

The lawyers filed their motion a day after Judge Tiffany's order. The next day, the judge ruled against them. In response to the defense argument regarding the need for expert testimony on climate change, he simply concluded that "[t]his data indicates that a jury will have general knowledge of climate change but does not share the same beliefs as Defendants."[354]

Even as the odds seemed to shift decisively in the state's favor, yet another unexpected pre-trial development muddied the waters. At the September 27 conference, the prosecutor had announced that he was dropping the trespass charges. Emily Johnston was now facing only a felony charge of criminal damage to a pipeline, and Annette Klapstein and Ben Joldersma were charged with felony aiding and abetting.

The reason for the prosecutor's decision remain mysterious. Perhaps, as often happens, he hoped to streamline the case and to focus the jury's attention on the chief issue: interference with pipeline operations. Perhaps he figured that a felony conviction would

353 Motion to Reconsider Pretrial Rulings, *Minnesota v. Klapstein* (Oct. 4, 2018).

354 Order Following Defendant's Motion to Reconsider at 4, *Minnesota v. Klapstein* (Oct. 4, 2018).

be punishment enough—the charge carried a maximum of ten years in prison—and he did not want to pile on any lesser misdemeanors. Or perhaps he felt a pang of conscience, and wished to open a narrow window of opportunity for the defense. Whatever the motive, this move would end up determining the outcome at trial.

Proceedings commenced at 8:37 on the morning of Monday, October 8, 2018, variously celebrated as Indigenous Peoples Day and Columbus Day. As the defendants, lawyers, and supporters gathered at the Bagley courthouse, the Intergovernmental Panel on Climate Change released a special report. Scientists had concluded that the world had already warmed by one degree Celsius, and, at current rates of warming, was very likely to reach 1.5 degrees between 2030 and 2052. Noting that the Paris Agreement had set a goal of two degrees warming with an "aspiration" of 1.5, the report stated that effects like sea level rise, drought, and extreme weather would be significantly worse at the higher target. Even the dangerous world of 1.5 degree warming would be possible only with a 40 percent reduction in 2010 CO_2 emissions by 2030 and with net-zero emissions by 2050. Accomplishing this "would require rapid and far-reaching transitions in energy, land, urban and infrastructure (including transport and buildings), and industrial systems ... These systems transitions are unprecedented in terms of scale, but not necessarily in terms of speed, and imply deep emissions reductions in all sectors."[355]

355 Intergovernmental Panel on Climate Change. "Summary for Policymakers," 6, 8-9, 17.

With this context in mind, jury selection was the first item on the agenda in Bagley: a long process of *voir dire*, in which attorneys for both sides asked the jury pool about their personal backgrounds, their experiences with the judicial system, and any reasons why they might not be impartial in the coming trial. For all the cynicism that our criminal legal institutions inspire, jurors' earnest participation is a rare point of pride. Almost without exception, the people called to serve in Minnesota were honest in their answers, upfront about their biases, and committed to sacrificing work and child care duties to do the job asked of them. Lauren Regan, conducting *voir dire* for the defense, focused on the prospective jurors' thoughts on climate change and civil disobedience. Several members of the pool worked in the energy industries or had family and friends who did so, and many lived alongside pipelines. Just like the residents of Standing Rock with whom the Valve Turners had acted in solidarity, this community sat on the frontlines of the fight for climate justice. But it was also a decidedly conservative crowd: many expressed doubt about global warming and its causes, and the majority indicated that they did not think it was proper to violate the law to advance a moral cause.[356]

The next morning, after twelve jurors and two alternates had been selected, Regan noted to Judge Tiffany that the previous day's discussion had made it "quite evident that, unlike the Court's prior rulings regarding the common knowledge of the jury pool . . . there was a fairly evident lack of knowledge or information about the actual facts and science of climate change . . . it appeared that maybe there were two out of fifty-five people who actually had an

---

356   Trial Transcript at 90-102, *Minnesota v. Klapstein* (Oct. 8-9, 2018).

understanding of ninety-nine percent of the scientific consensus in the world regarding climate change."[357] The point of her comment was not to cast aspersions on the jury; it was to refute the judge's conclusion that expert testimony on climate change would not be "helpful." Regan requested that the climate scientist James Hansen, who had already submitted his credentials and declaration, be allowed to testify. The prosecutor argued that "[p]utting a scientific stamp on that would be misleading to the jury." The judge decided to withhold ruling on the matter until the defense actually moved to put Hansen on the stand.[358]

It was now time for opening statements. The prosecutor essentially recounted the events of October 11, 2016, confident that the defendants' own admissions would do his job for him. Regan had a different task: she had to frame the same facts within the Valve Turners' political and ethical commitments, hoping to prime the jury for an eventual argument on necessity.

Here's how Regan began:

> Good morning ladies and gentlemen. In this case, our clients, Emily Johnston, Annette Klapstein, and Ben Joldersma, believe what people around the world believe, that they have a moral duty to care for the world we live in. To care and protect the land, the water. To protect their children, including children and grandchildren that are not yet born. Our clients also believe what ninety-nine percent of scientists in the world believe. That if we do not take action now to protect people and the planet from the serious harms caused by global warming, it will soon be

357 *Id.* at 182-3.
358 *Id.* at 184.

too late to do anything to turn back events that have been in progress since the industrial revolution.

Regan went on to stress that the activists were not targeting oil industry workers. In fact, they had devoted their lives to a cause that would replace the dangerous work of fossil fuel extraction with labor in a clean economy. She pointed out that, had all the pipeline shut down that day remained inoperative, U.S. emissions would have gone down by 15 percent. And she tried to draw the sting from one of the prosecutors' main claims—that the defendants had endangered the community by placing their hands on pipeline infrastructure—by previewing the anticipated testimony of Anthony Ingraffea, the pipeline expert from Leonard Higgins's trial in Montana. His testimony, at least in theory, had survived the judge's pre-trial rulings on civil disobedience and climate change, and would prove that the valve-turning had been safe.[359]

The state's first witness was the sheriff of Clearwater County. Under examination by the prosecutor, he described how his office received reports of intrusion at the valve site for Enbridge Lines 4 and 67 on the morning of October 11. His testimony served as the basis for the prosecutor to introduce several exhibits, among them the bolt cutters used by Johnston and Klapstein, photographs of the scene, and the video that they live-streamed that morning.

Next, Enbridge's local supervisor took the stand. He described his team's response to the Valve Turners' call: how they implemented shut-down procedures and checked the rest of the line for any problems. On cross-examination, Regan asked a routine but crucial question: "When you shut down the pipeline for

359 *Id.* at 198, 201-2, 204.

maintenance or the other reasons, does it cause damage to the pipeline?"

"If it's done correctly," the supervisor responded, "it doesn't cause damage."[360]

That was it for the state. Its case was straightforward: Johnston had shut off the valve, so she was guilty of damaging the pipeline. The others were guilty of helping.

Lawyers make lots of routine motions throughout the course of a case: motions to compel discovery, motions to dismiss charges, motions to delay a proceeding. Some of these are granted, many of them are not: the point is to never let an opportunity for a small victory slip by, and the duty to a client requires pushing every reasonable advantage. Often, such maneuvers also preserve a record for appeal: unless you make a note of a potential issue at the appropriate time, a higher court will refuse to review it.

At the close of the state's evidence, Tim Phillips, the Valve Turners' Minnesota counsel, made one of these routine motions. He asked Judge Tiffany for a judgment of acquittal. This is a fairly typical request, and very seldom granted. The defense asks the court to rule in its favor before it puts on any evidence, on the theory that no reasonable juror could convict based on what the prosecutor has already presented. Remember: a defendant does not have to prove anything at trial. The prosecution has to make its case beyond a reasonable doubt. That is a high bar to clear, and it is worth at least asking a judge to rule that the state has failed to do so.

Phillips justified his motion this way: the statute under which Emily Johnston was charged, criminal damage to a pipeline, has

360 *Id.* at 230.

a specific definition for "pipeline": "an aboveground pipeline, a belowground pipeline housed in an underground structure, and any equipment, facility, or building located in this state that is used to transport natural or synthetic gas, crude petroleum or petroleum fuels or oil or their derivatives, or hazardous liquids, to or within a distribution, refining, manufacturing, or storage facility that is located inside or outside of this state. Pipeline does not include service lines."

Note that "chain" and "padlock" do not appear in that definition. According to the witness testimony and the defendants' video, these were the only things that were damaged in the Minnesota Valve Turner action. What's more, Enbridge's own supervisor had just said on the stand that the pipeline itself does not suffer harm during a shut-down. So, according to the letter of the law, none of the charges could be supported.[361]

The prosecutor did not have a compelling response. Judge Tiffany considered the question for a moment.

Then, as the defense counsel prepared to mount their case, the judge announced that "[t]here is not damage to a pipeline. The State has failed to present evidence, even when I construe that in a light most favorable to the State, to show that a reasonably minded jury could find the Defendant Johnston guilty of committing damage." He then dismissed all charges against the three activists.[362]

It took a few moments for these words to sink in. Without even taking the stand, the Minnesota Valve Turners had just been acquitted. Word slowly spread from counsel table to the public seats and

---

361 *Id.* at 245-6 and Minn. Stat. 609.6055(1)(c).

362 Transcript at 251-2, *Minnesota v. Klapstein* (Oct. 8-9, 2018).

the hallways outside, and in short order an impromptu celebration spilled onto the courthouse steps.

After two hard years of pressing the climate necessity defense, the last group of Valve Turners to stand trial were free. They never got the chance to make the case they wanted, but aggressive lawyering, a bit of luck, and an unexpected prosecutorial maneuver—why *did* the state ever drop those trespass charges?—had snatched victory from the jaws of defeat.

And so the campaign for the climate necessity defense rolled on, by fits and starts.

The Campaign Expands

But there was still one Valve Turner case in progress: *Washington v. Ward*. The case had been making its way up the appellate ladder ever since Ken Ward's conviction on felony sabotage in his second trial in June 2017. Though Ken was the first Valve Turner to go to trial, he would have to wait the longest for a final result.

Even as they worked on the Montana and Minnesota cases, the defense team prepared and filed an appeal in Washington five months after Ward was convicted. Recall from Part 2 of the Valve Turner narrative that there was plenty to object to in the way the case had been handled. Judge Rickert had declined to allow expert testimony on climate change because he thought there was "tremendous controversy over the fact whether it even exists," and he didn't want to see the "Scopes monkey trial" of global warming.[363] Even after the first jury had failed to convict and Ward's attorneys

---

363 Motion Hearing Verbatim Report of Proceedings at 16, *Washington v. Ward*, No. 16-1-01001-5 (Skagit Cty. Sup. Ct., Wash. Jan. 24, 2017).

had provided more proofs of the existence of climate change and the effectiveness of civil disobedience, the judge had stuck by his decision.

As they had done in Minnesota, the Valve Turner lawyers pressed hard on the issue of constitutional rights. In their brief to the Washington Court of Appeals, they reviewed the strength of Ward's evidence and argued that Judge Rickert's comments were not only inappropriate but also legally problematic: if indeed climate change is a matter of great controversy, then it is just the sort of factual matter that a jury is entitled to consider. Likewise, a court cannot substitute its own judgment on that issue or on the question of whether protesters have reasonable legal alternatives: as soon as there is a real factual conflict, you must have a trial to test the evidence. Doing otherwise—robbing the jury of its function as fact-finder and barring the defendant from making his case—violates the process rights of the Sixth Amendment.

To show the existence of this conflict, one part of the appellate brief reiterated Ward's necessity argument, stressing that the political nature of the case made no difference to the question of whether or not the basic elements of the defense were met. Washington law was favorable in this regard: the state necessity defense considers whether or not a defendant was "reasonable" in thinking that committing a crime was necessary, and the defendant only needs to show the absence of "reasonable" legal alternatives—not the absence of any and all alternatives, no matter how futile.[364] There is also no requirement that a defendant show immi-

364 *State v. Parker*, 127 Wn. App. 352 (2005).

nent physical harm to his person, which proved to be a problem in Leonard Higgins's case in Montana.

The other major theme that the defense lawyers presented had to do with the standard of review. This is a technical matter that has enormous influence over the fate of an appeal. Judges on appeal do not simply re-litigate a case: generally, they're deferential to their lower courts, cognizant of the fact that judges have to make split-second decisions and that second-guessing every ruling would make the work of trial courts impossible. So evidentiary rulings of the type that Judge Rickert made when he excluded Ken's expert testimony are usually judged under an "abuse of discretion" standard. This means that a trial judge's evidentiary decisions will only be overruled if they are patently unreasonable, based on bad law, or premised on facts outside the record. Prosecutors love the abuse of discretion standard. It makes it highly likely that a lower court's decisions will be preserved.

But a special set of trial court decisions are reviewed differently: those that deal with constitutional rights. In these matters, appellate courts employ a *de novo,* or "fresh look," standard. They consider constitutional questions as though they're posed for the first time, giving defense attorneys wider amplitude to ask for a reversal.

If you're thinking like a lawyer, you've already identified the basic question that governs these standards: how do we know when we're dealing with a normal evidentiary ruling versus one with constitutional stakes? The Valve Turner lawyers argued that excluding Ward's evidence had violated his Sixth Amendment rights, and so asked for *de novo* review. The state claimed that Judge

Rickert's rulings were routine matters of trial management, and so pushed for the abuse of discretion standard. The fate of Ward's necessity defense hinged on this threshold distinction.

Every attorney knows that it makes a huge difference which judge reviews your case. For all the judiciary's postures of impartiality, no two judges are alike: some are well-known fans of defense rights, while others are notorious for their pro-police zealotry. It was a rare bit of luck for the Valve Turner team, then, when their appeal landed before Judge David S. Mann of the Washington Court of Appeals' Division One in Seattle. Mann, who had only been on the court for about a year, had worked as a geophysicist before law school. After earning a certificate in environmental law at Lewis & Clark, one of the best schools in the field, he worked in private practice on environmental, land-use, and property matters. According to his official online profile, he spent his leisure time rescuing dogs, running trails, and backpacking.[365] This was probably not a guy who would cringe at seeing climate change on his docket.

Judge Mann's decision was a long time in coming. A full fifteen months passed between the time the state filed their response brief and the issuance of the Court of Appeals ruling on April 8, 2019. When it came, it was close to the ideal climate necessity opinion that activists had been working toward for years.

Three things made Judge Mann's opinion a massive leap forward for the movement. First, it engaged directly and in detail with Ken Ward's evidence, linking his proffered expert testimony and personal history to each element of the defense. This provided

---

365 "Judge David S. Mann," *Washington Courts* (2020), https://www.courts. wa.gov/appellate_trial_courts/bios/?fa=atc_bios.display&folderid=div1&-fileID=mann.

a roadmap for advocates and judges to evaluate climate necessity defenses in the future. It affirmed that, if a basic standard of proof had been met, this type of theory should be treated no differently from traditional necessity defenses.

Second, Judge Mann applied *de novo* review to Judge Rickert's trial court evidentiary decisions. Those decisions, the appellate court decided, had violated Ken Ward's constitutional right to present a defense. Judge Mann wrote that the Sixth Amendment guaranteed the right to present a well-argued theory, even in a case involving controversial political matters—shutting the door on the prosecutorial argument that, whether or not an activist's necessity defense is fully articulated, a trial judge can still choose to exclude it in the interest of running a simple trial.

Crucial to Judge Mann's ruling on this point was the idea of reasonableness in Washington's necessity defense. "Ward presented sufficient evidence that he reasonably believed the crimes he committed were necessary to minimize the harms that he perceived," the judge wrote. "Ward's offer of proof included evidence of how past acts of civil disobedience have been successful, evidence of previous climate activism campaigns, and evidence of his own personal successes in effectuating change through civil disobedience. Specifically, Ward offered evidence that he has been working with environmental issues for more than forty years but that the majority of his efforts failed to achieve effective results." Because there was sufficient evidence at the pre-trial stage, "[w]hether Ward's beliefs were reasonable was a question for the jury."[366]

366 *Washington v. Ward*, 438 P.3d 588, 594 (Wash. Ct. App. 2019), *review denied*, 193 Wash. 2d 1031, 447 P.3d 161 (2019).

Finally, Judge Mann's opinion instantly became the most powerful precedent in the climate necessity playbook because it was published in an official court reporter series. This solemnizes a court decision as good law that can be cited with authority in future briefs and opinions. Many appellate decisions are not approved for publication: the opinion in *Minnesota v. Klapstein*, for example, is unpublished, making its status as precedent weaker. With *Washington v. Ward* now on the books, climate advocates had a precedent that directly engaged with the elements of the climate necessity defense and squarely addressed defendants' right to present it.

But the prosecution did not give up. Instead, it filed a petition for further review with the state's highest court, focusing again on the standard of review question. The state thought Judge Mann had been wrong to skip straight to the *de novo* standard rather than give Judge Rickert the benefit of the doubt on his evidentiary rulings.[367] The defense team pointed out in a response that the Court of Appeals opinion had given these decisions their required latitude, but that the rulings were so off-base—they utterly failed to give Ward's evidence a fair shake—that a constitutional question had been properly triggered.[368]

The Washington Supreme Court agreed. In September 2019, it denied the state's petition.[369] This made the climate necessity defense a matter of established state law, with a published appellate opinion providing the standard by which all future attempts

---

367 Petition for Review, *Washington v. Ward*, No. 97182-0 (Wash. S. Ct. May 8, 2019).

368 Answer to Petition for Review, *Washington v. Ward* (June 7, 2019).

369 Order, *Washington v. Ward*, No. 97182-0 (Sep. 4, 2019).

could be measured. In short order, the case would start appearing in law school classrooms as an illustration of the elements of common law necessity defense and of the way in which the courts deal with political protest.

If you were the state's attorney, you might very well have given up at this point. You had twice succeeded in barring Ward's climate necessity from trial, only to have juries deadlock on three out of four charges. The Court of Appeals had issued an opinion that vindicated the defense's theory of the case and provided an important weapon for future litigants, and the state Supreme Court had upheld it. Ward had already served time in pre-trial detention and performed community service. Even if he were ultimately convicted in a third trial, he likely would not face any more punishment.

Nonetheless, with the result of the second trial overturned, the window was open for the state to prosecute again, and it did so. Ward and his defense team were put on notice to prepare for a third round. It was a prospect that was in one sense exciting, as the stage was set for a jury trial featuring a full suite of necessity evidence and testimony, but it was also a bit exhausting: the Valve Turner action was now more than three years past, and defendants and supporters alike were eager to move on to new campaigns.

In the end, unexpected circumstances intervened. The prosecutor moved to delay the initial February 2020 trial date to May. In early March, the novel coronavirus began spreading across the United States, with Seattle as one of the first hotspots. Courts were shut down and all trials postponed indefinitely, including Ward's. A tentative date was finally set for early 2021, even as the pandemic peaked. After months of soul-searching, Ward decided that it would be imprudent to ask attorneys, witnesses, and supporters to travel and gather for his defense. In December 2020, he accepted a plea offer from the state that required him to plead guilty to misdemeanor trespass and imposed no jail time.[370]

"Our Sympathies Start to Overwhelm Us"

In and around the time of the Washington appellate victory, other climate necessity cases were making their way through the courts. In Minnesota, a group of Catholic Workers had taken inspiration from the Valve Turners and turned valves on Enbridge Lines 3 and 4, which carry tar sands oil from Alberta. Their action was part of a broad, Indigenous-led campaign against the expansion of Line 3; many activists had been arrested in lockdowns on construction equipment, and the police were actively surveilling organizers.[371] The so-called "Four Necessity" Valve Turners—acting in the long Catholic Worker tradition of civil disobedience against war and environmental injustice—were denied the bulk of their necessity defense by a trial court in August 2019, although they were allowed to present a "limited" justification argument without the benefit of expert testimony. They were convicted of misdemeanor charges in July 2021.[372]

One of the most significant climate necessity trials occurred in February 2019 in Portland, Oregon, where a group of Extinction

---

370 Judgment and Sentence, *Washington v. Ward*, No. 16-1-01001-5 (Skagit Cty. Sup. Ct., Wash. Dec. 9, 2020).

371 Will Parrish and Alleen Brown, "How Police, Private Security, and Energy Companies Are Preparing for a New Pipeline Standoff," *The Intercept* (Jan. 30, 2019), https://theintercept.com/2019/01/30/enbridge-line-3-pipeline-minnesota/.

372 Climate Necessity Defense Case Guide," *Climate Defense Project*.

Rebellion activists (including Valve Turner Ken Ward) blockaded and built a garden on railroad tracks used to transport tar sands oil. The defense team, led by Lauren Regan and Cooper Brinson of the Civil Liberties Defense Center, asserted a "choice of evils" defense, which in Oregon allows defendants to argue that they acted to avert a "public emergency." Based on successful pre-trial briefing, the defense was able to put on a climate expert and an attorney-cum-environmental scientist to speak about the dangers of global warming and the lack of effective legal alternatives to address it. Crucially, the defendants were able to get a jury instruction. In the end, five of the six jurors voted to acquit, resulting in a mistrial. The prosecutor declined to re-file the charges. The trial broke ground as the first in which a climate necessity defense was argued to the end, put before a jury, and resulted in defendants walking free—although it fell short of being the first in which defendants were acquitted by reason of necessity.[373]

Around the same time, another activist who had attempted an action similar to the Valve Turners' was able to put on a climate necessity defense before a Washington state jury, which convicted him of burglary, sabotage, and malicious mischief.[374] Also in Washington, Division Three of the state Court of Appeals overturned the decision allowing George Taylor, the train-blockading pastor mentioned above, to present his necessity defense. Shortly

373 Jake Johnson, "Landmark Win in 'Fight for Habitable Future' as Jury Refuses to Convict Climate Activists Who Presented Necessity Defense," *Common Dreams* (Feb. 28, 2020), https://www.commondreams.org/news/2020/02/28/landmark-win-fight-habitable-future-jury-refuses-convict-climate-activists-who; *see* entry for "*Oregon v. Butler*" in "Climate Necessity Defense Case Guide," *Climate Defense Project*.

374 *See* entry for "*Washington v. Zepeda*" in "Climate Necessity Defense Case Guide," *Climate Defense Project*.

before this book went to press, the Washington Supreme Court stepped in and approved Taylor's necessity defense, creating a crucial precedent for activists.[375]

Meanwhile, climate protesters in France, Switzerland, and Britain were acquitted on various theories of justification.[376] Activists across the world continued to be arrested for their resistance to fossil fuel infrastructure—and, in many regions, were even killed—and lawyers continued to defend them, sometimes taking plea deals, sometimes fighting the factual basis of the charges, sometimes calling the state's bluff and using the courtroom as a forum on climate justice. There were signs that at least some judges were taking note, and that the establishment was worried: in a climate protest case in Britain, a judge told defendants: "This is going to be my last Extinction Rebellion trial for a little while . . . I think they only allow us to do so many of these before our sympathies start to overwhelm us."[377]

The atmospheric concentration of carbon dioxide continued to tick upward: around 415 parts per million by the time the Valve Turner cases entered their fourth year.[378] Fossil fuel companies and their government backers continued to explore new fossil fuel reserves and used force and coercion to expand the network of

375 State *ex rel. Haskell v. Spokane Cty. Dist. Court*, Wash. No. 98719-0 (July 15, 2021). This is the first full opinion from a state's highest court to endorse the climate necessity defense, and it makes clear that the sorts of argument made by defendants like the Valve Turners fit within the traditional doctrine of necessity.

376 "Climate Necessity Defense Case Guide," *Climate Defense Project.*

377 Jeremy Harding, "The Arrestables." *London Review of Books* (Apr. 16, 2020), 18.

378 "Trends in Atmospheric Carbon Dioxide," *Global Monitoring Laboratory, Earth System Research Laboratories, National Oceanic and Atmospheric Administration* (2020), https://www.esrl.noaa.gov/gmd/ccgg/trends/graph.html.

pumps, pipelines, and export terminals that would lock the world's economy to poisonous energy for decades. In early 2020, the worlds' governments were compelled by a pandemic—rather than by cries for justice—to slow economic activity. The atmosphere was offered a brief reprieve at the price of enormous human suffering. This crisis offered a preview of what an ill-designed transition might look like, making clearer than ever that the world's most pressing question was not whether to drastically shift the basis of the world's economy, but when.

Even as the United States government rushed to save the oil industry—in the early days of the pandemic, it leased out space in its Strategic Petroleum Reserve to help companies off-load unsold supply[379]—and even as state legislatures continued to increase penalties for challenging the energy status quo, an oppositional movement grew on the margins of the law. The early successes of the climate necessity defense were amplified through a global network of activists and attorneys who coordinated strategies, shared briefs, and polished each other's ideas. The movement is both political and intellectual at once, striving to advance the work of climate justice advocates on the streets and to jump-start an evolution in our legal system's approach to global warming—a movement facing steep odds, working at the uneasy juncture of authority and revolt.

379 Sheela Tobben and Jennifer A. Dlouhy, "DOE working to lease out 23 MMbbl of Strategic Petroleum Reserve capacity," *World Oil* (Apr. 14, 2020), https://www.worldoil.com/news/2020/4/14/doe-working-to-lease-out-23-mmbbl-of-strategic-petroleum-reserve-capacity.

CHAPTER 4

Climate Legal Activism

The previous chapter showed how the fossil fuel system uses the enforcement apparatus of the criminal legal system to maintain its market dominance and to subdue its opponents. Whether through traditional methods of surveillance and prosecution or through more novel legal tools like critical infrastructure bills, judges and prosecutors tend to deploy their powers against climate justice advocates rather than against those degrading the climate.

The ruling from the Bagua conflict in Peru suggests a different approach: it shows how actors within the legal establishment—criminal defendants, their attorneys, and judges—can ally with social movements to stop the expansion of fossil fuel infrastructure and to model a new climate politics using legal principles like Indigenous rights, environmental protections, and the doctrine of justification.

That's just one court case, of course. By and large, our legal institutions have proven ill-equipped to seriously address climate change. This is due largely to industry capture, as fossil fuel companies dominate political systems around the world and get the laws that they pay for. This is nothing new in the history of the law: legislatures, courts, and attorneys tend to work for those with the most economic power, even as the myriad exceptions to this rule testify to the fact that power is never stable—and that a legal project is indispensable to any liberation effort.

But the problem with the law of climate change goes beyond simply favoring the haves over the have-nots. Global warming presents the law with a foundational crisis, as great as the crises of politics, economics, and culture. Private property rights, rules of standing, and corporate privilege all belong to a worldview born of the middle-class ascendancy of the eighteenth and nineteenth centuries and the Industrial Revolution, a worldview in which ideas like the primacy of individual initiative and the human-natural divide are taken as given, just like the law of gravity and the supply-demand curve. Such assumptions clearly will not do in era of massively distributed guilt and harm, of precarious ecological entanglement, and of unstable background conditions. Something more than tinkering is called for. Just as badly as we need new energy sources, we need new legal ideas.

Fortunately, we have much greater control over human laws than we do over the laws of nature, and—even within the Western tradition—there are plenty of dissident currents, alternative perspectives, and Copernican-shifts-in-the-wings that can help us to change course. Unfortunately, we have so far proven profoundly bad at designing social systems that can deal with rapid technological change and ecological catastrophe.

But there are lawyers on the case. In this chapter, we'll study the legal activism side of the climate justice movement, where new ideas about duties, legal subjectivity, and state control are being developed toward a more equitable and less ecologically disruptive society. We can think of these cases and concepts as "prefigurative law" that builds the legal systems of the future using today's legal tools.[380]

Examples of prefigurative climate law include the human right to a stable climate system, the atmospheric trust doctrine, and the rights of nature. Vastly different and often contradictory to each other, these ideas all originate in the recognition that our legal system is in need of a serious update, if not a total overhaul. In the words of Doug Kysar, professor of environmental law at Yale, proponents of these concepts "would restore the romantic, even illiberal spirit that once animated environmentalism"[381]—and, in many instances, would seek to go beyond environmentalism altogether.

Crucially, climate legal activism treats climate change as a social phenomenon in need of a social solution. If injustice and inequality lie at the root of the global warming crisis, then we cannot rely only on technological fixes or market signals to keep emissions down: we also need to address the societal ills that have produced our environmental malaise. This understanding provides the basis for building climate justice on the foundation of human rights.

In marrying theory to practice, these projects confront the always vexing question of how to balance the prospect of

---

380 This term, adapted from the "prefigurative politics" of radical social movements, is found in Margaret Davies, *Law Unlimited: Materialism, Pluralism, and Legal Theory* (New York: Routledge, 2017), 16 and in Boaventura de Sousa Santos, "Towards a socio-legal theory of indignation," in *Law's Ethical, Global and Theoretical Contexts: Essays in Honor of William Twining,* eds. Upendra Baxi, Christopher McCrudden, and Abdul Paliwala (Cambridge University Press, 2017), 115-142, 138.

381 Kysar, *Regulating from Nowhere,* 230.

immediate results with the promise of dramatic change. For some climate justice advocates, these campaigns of legal reform are irresponsibly idealistic; for others, they are pointlessly devoted to an institution of inherent domination.

These prefigurative climate law efforts are presented here in increasing order of ambition, from expansions of existing doctrines to proposals for new ways of thinking about humanity's place in nature. The bulk of the examples come from outside the United States. Although U.S. environmental law served as the inspiration for many countries' schemes of environmental regulation, it has lagged far behind in crafting legal solutions to the climate crisis. In the coming years, the main sources of progressive climate law will be places like Bogotá and The Hague, not Washington, D.C. Above all, the claims of Indigenous peoples have proven crucial to advancing climate justice in the legal realm, and they will continue to be at the vanguard of the struggle for climate justice. The end of the chapter will summarize the contribution that these new ideas make to the overall goal of a new climate politics and ask what chance they have of turning our ship in the midst of the climate storm.

Keeping the Law Honest

Bleak as our assessment of existing climate law must be, there are certain elements of the current edifice that allow for immediate and sometimes significant progress in lowering emissions. Some of these traditional environmental law strategies were mentioned in Chapter 1: the Sierra Club's Beyond Coal campaign, which leverages assessment and procedural requirements to close down or prevent the construction of hundreds of coal plants; challenges to pipeline companies' use of the power of eminent domain; and lawsuits based on tort law, which would hold fossil fuel companies accountable for harming the health and property of individuals or governmental entities.

Similar cases from other countries have added to the pressure on fossil fuel firms. In one of the first international climate tort cases, for example, in 2015 a homeowner in Huaraz, Peru named Saúl Ananías Luciano Lliuya sued RWE, Germany's largest electricity producer. He alleged that his home, which sits near the banks of Lake Palcacocha in the Andes, was at risk of flooding: run-off from the massive glaciers that loom over Huaraz had increased in recent years, and remedial measures were needed to block the rising waters. He asked a court in Essen, Germany to order the defendant to bear part of these costs, as it had contributed one half-percent of global greenhouse gas emissions.

After a district court dismissed Luciano Lliuya's claim on familiar grounds—causation was hard to prove, and RWE had only contributed a negligible amount to the warming that was eroding Huaraz's glaciers—a higher court reversed the decision. The case is now plodding forward as experts are convened and information is gathered. Its survival to this point is remarkable enough—suggesting that some courts are open to unconventional tort claims on climate—and the lawsuit has drawn international attention for the way it links the vulnerability of low-emitting populations like Peruvian Andeans to the quotidian pollution of places like Germany.[382]

382 Decision, Lliuya v. RWE AG, No. 2 O 285/15 (District Court Essen, Germany Dec. 15, 2015) (unofficial translation by Germanwatch), available at http://climatecasechart.com/non-us-case/lliuya-v-rwe-ag/; "Saúl versus REW—The

A similar case was brought in 2019 by the "climate change spokesman" for a group of Maori communities in New Zealand, alleging that businesses engaged in dairy production, coal mining, electricity production, and oil refining were causing damage to customary fisheries, sites of cultural significance, and public health. The nation's highest court tossed out claims of public nuisance and negligence—finding that the plaintiff was not suffering particularized harm, that direct contributions were difficult to prove, and that the companies were abiding by existing laws—but allowed litigation to proceed on the novel question of whether the defendants had violated a general duty to reduce greenhouse gas emissions in line with internationally recognized targets.[383]

Taking another angle, the environmental law firm ClientEarth filed a complaint against BP for misleading advertising in 2019. Although BP's business relies almost entirely on the sale of fossil fuels, ClientEarth alleged that the company dishonestly touted its commitment to the energy transition through its "Keep Advancing" and "Possibilities Everywhere" ad campaigns, in violation of commercial communications guidelines issued by the Organisation for Economic Co-operation and Development.[384] In targeting the fossil

Huaraz Case," *GermanWatch* (May 8, 2019), https://germanwatch.org/en/huaraz. For international climate law materials, the indispensable resource is the Columbia University Sabin Center on Climate Change Law Non-U.S. Climate Change Litigation Database, available at http://climatecasechart.com/non-us-climate-change-litigation/.

383 *Smith v. Fonterra Co-Operative Group Limited,* [2020] New Zealand High Court 419 (Mar. 6, 2020), available at http://climatecasechart.com/non-us-case/smith-v-fronterra-co-operative-group-limited/.

384 "Complaint against BP in respect of violations of the OECD Guidelines," UK National Contact Point for the OECD Guidelines for Multinational Enterprises, Department for International Trade (Dec. 3, 2019), available at http://climatecasechart.com/non-us-case/complaint-against-bp-in-respect-of-violations-of-the-oecd-guidelines/.

fuel industry's shady marketing practices rather than extraction itself, the case (which is awaiting judgment) resembles the New York fraud action against ExxonMobil discussed in Chapter 1. BP is a good target for this sort of claim: this is the firm that changed its name to "Beyond Petroleum" before reversing course and deciding that oil was good business after all,[385] and its P.R. gurus were responsible for popularizing the idea of the "carbon footprint," which seeks to shift responsibility for global warming from industry heavies to individual consumers.[386]

These cases are all at the frontier of private-law efforts to hold fossil fuel firms to account, and, as courts rely on timeworn arguments to dismiss or diminish them, we should temper our expectation that they will result in any dramatic remedies. But, even in the absence of a historic ruling that changes corporate behavior or drains industry coffers, sustained litigation can have an effect: it sullies the reputation of companies like BP, it scares off investors leery of prolonged court battles, and it goads public authorities to action.

A more direct way of enlisting the power of the state is to cite international climate change agreements in domestic courts. This strategy currently has little prospect of success in the United States, where Congress has refused to ratify warming targets set under the United Nations Framework Convention on Climate Change (discussed in Chapter 1), and where courts routinely ignore the

---

385 Ben Winkley, "Energy Journal: BP No Longer Beyond Petroleum," *Wall Street Journal* (Apr. 3, 2013), https://blogs.wsj.com/marketbeat/2013/04/03/energy-journal-bp-no-longer-beyond-petroleum/.

386 Meehan Crist, "Is it OK to Have a Child?" *London Review of Books* (Mar. 5, 2020), https://www.lrb.co.uk/the-paper/v42/n05/meehan-crist/is-it-ok-to-have-a-child.

constitutional status of treaties. But other countries are, at least on paper, more honest about their commitments, and conventional legal cases have been built upon them. In 2008, for example, a Ukrainian environmental group sued its national government for failing to abide by the Kyoto Protocol targets that it had made legally binding. After an initial victory, an appellate court found that a lack of revenue from pollution funds made compliance impossible.[387]

The Paris Agreement inspired new enthusiasm for this type of case. Outside the United States, many countries touted their commitment to keep warming below two degrees Celsius and promptly made the non-binding treaty either a matter of binding domestic law or the accepted guideline for issuing domestic regulations. It soon became obvious that the "Nationally Determined Contributions" to reducing warming were inadequate, and several lawsuits were launched on the principle that governments had to abide by the original warming target. In New Zealand and the United Kingdom, judges found that the political process was the proper place for climate policymaking, ruling that courts should not interfere with administrative discretion in implementing the Agreement.[388] In France, a group of NGOs and municipal governments used the government's Paris implementation law to sue Total, one of the world's major fossil fuel producers; they alleged

---

387 "Climate change litigation—non-fulfilment by Ukraine of its climate change obligations," *Environment People Law* (2020), http://epl.org.ua/en/law-posts/natsionalne-agentstvo-ekologichnyh-investytsij-dostup-do-informatsiyi-v-natsionalnomu-elektronnomu-reyestri-antropogennyh-vykydiv-2/.

388 *Thomson v. Minister for Climate Change Issues*, [2017] New Zealand High Court 733 (Nov. 2, 2017); *Plan B Earth v. Secretary of State for Business et al.*, C1/2018/1750 (Her Majesty's Court of Appeal, U.K., Jan. 25 2019), available at http://climatecasechart.com/non-us-case/thomson-v-minister-for-climate-change-issues/.

that the company's plan for reducing emissions violated the government's new "duty of vigilance" requirements for meeting Agreement targets. The case is still in its early stages.[389]

So far, the most successful case based on the Paris Agreement has been the effort by environmental groups including Plan B Earth to prevent the U.K. government from building a third runway at Heathrow Airport. The increased air traffic that this runway would allow would make it extremely difficult for the country to meet its Paris commitment of reducing greenhouse gas emissions to 80 percent of 1990 levels by 2050. In a ruling reminiscent of *Massachusetts v. EPA*, the Court of Appeal found that the Paris Agreement, as part of acknowledged national policy, required the government to at least take into account its warming targets when making a decision on Heathrow. The courts refrained from stating what sort of decision such consideration should produce, but, edging closer to the sort of judicial daring we saw in the Bagua decision, the three-judge panel noted that "this is one of those cases in which it would be right for this court to grant a remedy on grounds of 'exceptional public interest' . . . The issue of climate change is a matter of profound national and international importance of great concern to the public."[390] Cloaking this urgency in a modest order that the government scrap its Heathrow plan and start over with its Paris commitments in mind, the court in effect killed the

---

389 *Notre Affaire à Tous et al. v. Total S.A.*, Judicial Tribunal of Nanterre, France (Jan 28., 2020), available at http://climatecasechart.com/non-us-case/notre-affaire-a-tous-and-others-v-france/.

390 *Plan B Earth and others v. Secretary of State for Transport*, [2020] EWCA Civ 214, Court of Appeal, U.K. (Feb. 27, 2020), available at http://climatecasechart.com/non-us-case/plan-b-earth-v-secretary-of-state-for-transport/.

runway—a major, and far too unusual, judicial intervention in favor of the climate.

Climate Rights

Let's move one step up on the ladder of legal activist ambition. If the cases above use relatively traditional environmental law tools to target corporate and government intransigence, the following suite of cases expands the basis upon which courts might rule in favor of climate justice. These cases are built using the fundamental material of the state's legal relation to its subjects and citizens: human and constitutional rights. Here, it is often thought, is the terrain on which the basic conflicts of the day should be decided—and nothing is more basic than the right to be free from climate catastrophe.

Environmental rights have a long pedigree. The 1972 Stockholm Declaration of the United Nations Conference on the Human Environment reviewed the unprecedented impact of economic growth on non-human nature and maintained that "[m]an has the fundamental right to freedom, equality and adequate conditions of life, in an environment of a quality that permits a life of dignity and well-being, and he bears a solemn responsibility to protect and improve the environment for present and future generations." The Declaration also held that "[t]he capacity of the earth to produce vital renewable resources must be maintained and, wherever practicable, restored or improved."[391] The 1982 World Charter for Nature, a resolution of the U.N. General Assembly, was an early effort to articulate the principle of sustainable development, under

---

391 Declaration of the United Nations Conference on the Human Environment, Stockholm Conference, Princ. 1 and 3, U.N. Doc. A/CONF.48/14/rev.1 (adopted June 16, 1972).

the idea that "Nature shall be respected and its essential processes shall not be impaired."[392]

A related project was the Oslo Principles on Global Climate Change Obligations, promulgated by an international group of legal experts in 2015. Building from existing international and human rights law, the Principles asserted that "all States and enterprises have an immediate moral and legal duty to prevent the deleterious effects of climate change"—a duty based not on any "single source of law" but rather various background norms and universal rights like the right to life.[393] Preeminent among these duties is the "precautionary principle," the idea that you should err on the side of caution and assume that the worst can always happen.

Rights are relative. Just as the Supreme Court allows racial gerrymandering and mass incarceration despite the Fourteenth Amendment's guarantee of "equal protection under the laws,"[394] so courts may permit climate-destructive activity despite environmental constitutional guarantees to the contrary. For example, the Norwegian Supreme Court recently allowed the granting of oil exploration licenses in the Barents Sea despite the national constitution's guarantee of "the right to an environment that is conducive to health and to a natural environment whose productivity and diversity are maintained." While the court acknowledged that emissions from oil production might impede that right,

---

392 U.N. GA Res 37/7, Prin. 1 (1982).

393 Oslo Principles on Global Climate Change Obligations at 1, 3, available at https://globaljustice.yale.edu/oslo-principles-global-climate-change-obligations.

394 US Const., Amend. XIV § 1.

it found that the activity of exploration itself did not amount to a violation.[395]

But even if affirmative environmental rights do not of themselves guarantee better policies, constitutionalization is important because liberal political systems—the dominant form across the globe—tend to funnel all questions of social good into the framework of rights. In the United States, movements for racial, gender, and sexual justice have regularly packaged their demands in the language of the federal constitution, winning rights to non-discrimination in voting and hiring, the right to same-sex marriage, and many others. Indeed, many advocates think that the absence of social and cultural rights in our country—an exception to the international rule—is an index of our system's devotion to economic power. The fact that there is no federal right to housing or health care, while there is a right to corporate free speech, tells you much of what you need to know about our class society. A similar argument could be made regarding the U.S. Constitution's silence on the environment.

There is a lot to critique in this focus on rights, and we will get to that critique at the end of the chapter. But for now, it's worth thinking about how a constitutional framing might help to combat climate change.

The federal constitution's failure to provide environmental rights does not mean that the document is useless for climate advocates. In 2005, a group of homeowners and the government of

---

395 *Greenpeace Nordic Ass'n and Nature and Youth v. Ministry of Petroleum and Energy*, 18-060499ASD-BORG/03 (Supreme Court of Norway Dec. 22, 2020), available at http://climatecasechart.com/non-us-case/greenpeace-nordic-assn-and-nature-youth-v-norway-ministry-of-petroleum-and-energy/; Norwegian Constitution, Art. 112.

St. Bernard Parish, next to New Orleans, sued the federal government for contributing to the damage caused by Hurricane Katrina and other storms. Although the lawsuit did not address failures to combat climate change, it did model how property owners and local governments might frame liability claims related to sea-level rise: under the Fifth Amendment, the federal government cannot damage or destroy property without compensation (called a "taking"). The plaintiffs alleged that the government's failure to build adequate flood-control systems had resulted in precisely that. Thirteen years after the case was filed, the Eighth Circuit Court of Appeals ruled for the United States, finding that a takings claim cannot be based on government inaction.[396]

Unlike their federal counterpart, many state constitutions include provisions related to environmental rights. Montana's constitution, for example, mandates that "[t]he state and each person shall maintain and improve a clean and healthful environment in Montana for present and future generations" and that "[t] he legislature shall provide adequate remedies for the protection of the environmental life support system from degradation and provide adequate remedies to prevent unreasonable depletion and degradation of natural resources."[397] Illinois's constitution states that "[e]ach person has the right to a healthful environment. Each person may enforce this right against any party, governmental or private, through appropriate legal proceedings subject to reasonable limitation and regulation as the General Assembly may provide by law."[398]

---

396 *St. Bernard Par. v. United States*, 88 Fed. Cl. 528 (2009).

397 Mont. Const. Art. 9 § 1(i) and (iii).

398 Ill. Const. Art. 10 § 2.

Some of these environmental constitutional rights are substantive—straightforward guarantees of environmental health
or ecological balance—while others are procedural, requiring the
government to follow certain information-gathering or administrative steps when making decisions that impact the environment.[399]
A good example of the complexity of environmental rights can be
found in *Robinson Township v. Commonwealth*. In the wake of the
fracking boom in the Marcellus Shale, the Pennsylvania government
passed a law that overrode local zoning and city planning ordinances
and imposed a state-wide policy promoting fracking. The state's
supreme court ruled that a provision of the law that used drilling
royalties for purposes unrelated to maintaining the natural public
trust violated Pennsylvania's Environmental Rights Amendment,
which guaranteed citizens' "right to clean air, pure water, and to the
preservation of the natural, scenic, historic and esthetic values of the
environment." Though this decision did not prohibit fracking, it did
make clear that the government must respect environmental rights
when making development decisions, and allowed municipalities
some leeway in deciding how to protect the environment themselves. (This theme of local self-government, as well as the court's
endorsement of positive public trust obligations, are relevant to
some of the legal activism considered later in this chapter.)[400]

---

399 *See* James R. May and Erin Daly, *Judicial Handbook on Environmental Constitutionalism* (United Nations Environment Programme, 2017); Sam Kalen,
"An Essay: An Aspirational Right to a Healthy Environment?," *UCLA Journal
of Environmental Law and Policy* 34 no. 2 (2016), 156-195.

400 *Robinson Township v. Commonwealth*, 623 Pa. 564 (2013) (citing PA Const.
art. I, § 27). *Robinson* was a plurality opinion, meaning that its reasoning
lacked precedential force; in 2017, a majority of the state supreme court
endorsed *Robinson*'s holdings in *Pennsylvania Envtl. Def. Found. v. Commonwealth*, 640 Pa. 55, 86.

In other countries, environmental constitutionalism is the norm: one source counts "some kind of fundamental right to a quality environment" in the constitutions of 150 of 193 U.N. members.[401] Kenya's constitution declares that "[e]very person has the right to a clean and healthy environment."[402] Chile guarantees the "right to live in an environment free from contamination." [403] Many other countries have specific provisions related to water, sustainable livelihoods, or the environmental rights of groups like women, children, or Indigenous communities. The constitutions of the Dominican Republic and Tunisia even have specific provisions requiring the government to ensure environmental well-being in the face of climate change.[404]

Climate lawyers have begun using such provisions as a basis for litigation. In a remarkable case in Pakistan, a farmer named Asghar Leghari sued the national government for failing to implement its climate policies. The Lahore High Court found that this failure amounted to a violation of the right to life, the right to a healthy environment, and various principles of democracy and social justice, and ordered the creation of a national Climate Change Commission to respond to the crisis. Focused particularly on threats to water and agriculture, the Commission operated under the supervision of the court until 2018, when, having completed much of its work, it was wrapped up in favor of a broader

---

401 May and Daly, *Judicial Handbook on Environmental Constitutionalism*, 79.

402 Constitution of Kenya Ch. 42.

403 Constitution of Chile Art. 19 § 8.

404 "Constitution of the Dominican Republic, Art. 194; Constitution of Tunisia, Art. 45." (*then following footnotes will each be one number higher*)

climate policymaking approach, which will be regularly audited by the court.[405]

In the past several years, courts around the globe have entertained related questions, with varying degrees of responsiveness. Some highlights from this emergent climate rights front include:

- In 2005, a court ruled in Nigeria that the practice of gas flaring—whereby companies like Shell release excess gas from production sites—violates the rights to life and dignity under the country's constitution and the African Charter on Human and Peoples' Rights, in part because of its contribution to global warming.[406]

- In 2018, Switzerland's Federal Administrative Court ruled that a group of older women, who argued that they were at particular risk of harm due to the government's failure to enact adequate warming reductions, could not sufficiently distinguish themselves from the general public in order to sustain a claim under the Swiss Constitution and the European Convention on Human Rights.[407]

- In 2019, the General Court of the European Union ruled against a group of agricultural and tourism workers from

405 *Leghari v. Pakistan*, W.P. No. 25501/2015 (Lahore High Court, Pakistan Jan. 25, 2018), available at http://climatecasechart.com/non-us-case/ashgar-leghari-v-federation-of-pakistan/.

406 *Gbemre v. Shell Petroleum Development Company of Nigeria et al.*, FHC/B/CS/53/05 (Federal High Court of Nigeria, Benin Judicial Division Nov. 14, 2005), available at http://climatecasechart.com/non-us-case/gbemre-v-shell-petroleum-development-company-of-nigeria-ltd-et-al/.

407 *Verein KlimaSeniorinnen Schweizet al. v. Federal Department of the Environment, Transport, Energy and Communications (DETEC)*, Judgment A-2992/2017 (Federal Administrative Court of Switzerland Nov. 27, 2018) (unofficial translation prepared on behalf of KlimaSeniorinnen), available at http://climatecasechart.com/non-us-case/union-of-swiss-senior-women-for-climate-protection-v-swiss-federal-parliament/.

various European countries, Kenya, and Fiji, who argued that the European Union's plans for reducing emissions were insufficient and violated the Charter of Fundamental Rights of the European Union, including the rights to conduct a business, the rights to life, integrity of the person, property, and equal treatment, and the rights of children. Just as in Switzerland, the court found that the plaintiffs were indistinguishable from the general public and thus lacked standing.[408]

- In the Philippines, a consortium of environmental and social justice groups petitioned the national Commission on Human Rights—an investigatory body established under the constitution—to look into the potential liability of "carbon majors," the largest industrial producers of fossil fuels, for violations of human rights. After a three-year investigation, including hearings in Manila, London, and New York, the Commission concluded that corporate contributors to global warming had a "moral responsibility" to reduce their emissions, and that they could be held liable under various domestic and international legal principles for impeding efforts to move the global economy away from fossil fuels. While a definite advance in climate law, the Commission's conclusions were vague on how violations should be addressed, and even suggested that

---

408 *Carvalho et al. v. European Parliament and Council of the European Union*, No. T-330/18 (General Court of the European Union May 8, 2019), available at http://climatecasechart.com/non-us-case/armando-ferrao-carvalho-and-others-v-the-european-parliament-and-the-council/.

international human rights laws need to be updated in order to handle the problem.[409]

- In 2020, the Supreme Court of Ireland quashed the country's climate mitigation plan, finding that it was impermissibly vague in describing how to meet the national greenhouse gas reduction goals set in conjunction with the Paris Agreement. At the same time, the court found that a right to a healthy environment does not exist and that the environmental group bringing the challenge to the plan lacked standing to litigate the case.[410]

Other cases based on fundamental rights—usually the rights to life and dignity—have been filed in Canada,[411] France[412], Peru[413], and elsewhere. While nearly fifty years have passed since the Stockholm Declaration on environmental rights, we are still in the very early

---

409 Memorandum for the Petitioners, *In re Greenpeace Southeast Asia and Others*, CHR-NI-2016-0001 (Republic of the Philippines Commission on Human Rights Sep. 19, 2019), available at http://climatecasechart.com/non-us-case/in-re-greenpeace-southeast-asia-et-al/; Isabella Kaminski, "Carbon Majors Can Be Held Liable for Human Rights Violations, Philippines Commission Rules," *Climate Liability News* (Dec. 9, 2019), https://www.climateliabilitynews.org/2019/12/09/philippines-human-rights-climate-change-2/.

410 *Friends of the Irish Environment CLG v. Ireland*, Appeal No. 205/19 (Supreme Court of Ireland, July 31, 2020 (unapproved opinion), available at http://climatecasechart.com/non-us-case/friends-of-the-irish-environment-v-ireland/.

411 *Mathur et al. v. Ontario*, No. CV-19-00631627 (Ontario Superior Court of Justice, Canada Nov. 25, 2019), http://climatecasechart.com/non-us-case/mathur-et-al-v-her-majesty-the-queen-in-right-of-ontario/.

412 "'Affair du Siècle' (Case of the Century): Brief on the Legal Request Submitted to the Administrative Court of Paris," *Notre Affaire à Tous and Others v. France*, Administrative Tribunal of Paris, France (Mar. 14, 2019) (translation courtesy of Marine Yzquierdo and the Legal Strategy Team of Notre Affaire à Tous), available at http://climatecasechart.com/non-us-case/notre-affaire-a-tous-and-others-v-france/.

413 Petition (demanda de amparo ambiental), *Álvarez et al. v. Peru*, Superior Court of Justice, Lima, Peru (Dec. 16, 2019), available at http://climatecasechart.com/non-us-case/alvarez-et-al-v-peru/.

stages of climate rights law, with a proliferation of test cases and an uncertain judicial future.

If you want a hint of what the best in climate rights litigation might look like, though, there is one precedent that stands above them all: the *Urgenda* case from the Netherlands.

Urgenda

Urgenda is a Dutch environmental non-profit organization which, in 2013, joined hundreds of co-plaintiffs in a lawsuit against its national government. Their case took a familiar tack. According to the agreements that the Dutch state had signed under the United Nations Framework Convention on Climate Change, the country was bound to lower its emissions to 25 to 40 percent of 1990 levels by 2020, followed by much steeper reductions. The state was failing to do so, and it admitted as much. Although the international climate treaties weren't binding, and although there was no explicit right to a healthy environment under Dutch or European human rights law, Urgenda and its allies argued that a rights violation had occurred and demanded action.

To substantiate their claims, the plaintiffs turned to the European Convention of Human Rights and Fundamental Freedoms—specifically its protection of the rights to life and to respect for family and private life[414]—and the jurisprudence of the European Court of Human Rights. Just as the federal constitution, state laws, and court rulings from the national and local level work together to create government obligations in the United States, so

---

414 European Convention of Human Rights and Fundamental Freedoms, Arts. 2 and 8.

these various sources of law created a legal duty with respect to climate change for the Dutch government. Considering the obvious threat that warming poses to health, security, and survival—a threat that the government acknowledged—this duty now required action to reduce emissions.

You know enough climate law by now to guess the Dutch state's response. First: there's no affirmative right to a stable climate. Second: the Netherlands cannot stop global warming on its own. Third: even if we should do something, this is a political matter beyond the court's jurisdiction.

For once, these old touchstones of fossil law failed. Urgenda and its co-plaintiffs filed their case in 2013. In 2015, a district court agreed with them, followed by an appellate court in 2018. In December 2019, the Supreme Court of the Netherlands affirmed, ordering the Dutch government to reduce national emissions at least 25 percent by the end of 2020.

The decision is worth reading for its cogency and seriousness. On the question of rights, the court dismissed the state's prevarications, finding that fundamental rights were obviously implicated by global warming and that an obligation to protect the environment could be "derived" from existing law.[415] With respect to whether the country's negligible contribution to emissions constituted a justification for inaction—the argument made by Chief Justice Roberts in his *Massachusetts v. EPA* dissent[416]—the court gave the proposition the minimal attention it deserved, noting that such

415 *Urgenda v. Netherlands,* No. 19/00135, 23 (Supreme Court of the Netherlands Dec. 12, 2019), available at http://climatecasechart.com/non-us-case/urgenda-foundation-v-kingdom-of-the-netherlands/.

416 *Massachusetts v. EPA,* 549 U.S. 497, 545-546 (2007).

reasoning would make all international climate efforts futile. The court likewise dispensed with the "political question" problem in a pithy reminder of what courts do: "In the Dutch system of government, the decision-making on greenhouse gas emissions belongs to the government and parliament. They have a large degree of discretion to make the political considerations that are necessary in this regard. It is up to the courts to decide whether, in taking their decisions, the government and parliament have remained within the limits of the law by which they are bound."[417]

Just like that, climate justice advocates finally had the direct, common-sense court decision they had been seeking: a ruling that a government was violating its duty to protect its citizens and to uphold its international obligations, and a judicial order to immediately reduce emissions in order to fix the problem.

Urgenda is a definite source of inspiration, an example of how the law as it currently exists can be leveraged to address global warming—if courts do their job of keeping the state honest. Of course, everything hinges on that "if." Some jurists, like those at the Netherlands Supreme Court and the Philippines Commission on Human Rights, are acting responsibly, and doing what lawyers in their position have always done: adapting the law to the needs of the day. The jury is still out, so to speak, on what practical effect their rulings will have, but at least they're trying.

Other courts have exploited legal uncertainty to evade this judicial reckoning. They harp on the purported problem of political interference, the absence of clear environmental rights, and the issue of standing to punt the climate ball down the field—hoping,

417 *Urgenda* at 6.

perhaps, that a magical market solution, or maybe a revolution, will win the game for them. Legitimate as these concerns might be in isolation, they simply lack credibility when used to justify evasion of the state's moral responsibility to protect its citizens from global warming—a responsibility that every nation in the world has recognized.

It is too soon to pass judgment on rights-based climate legal activism. Many efforts have stalled or failed, but *Urgenda* represents probably the greatest achievement to date for climate justice in the courts. This result will have to be multiplied and magnified, and quickly. In the meantime, it's worth filling in the gaps of climate rights law by making concrete the sort of vague environmental rights described above—either through domestic legislation or international convention—and continuing to press the point that climate change is not just environmental: it's a social and political crisis, too.

Indigenous Rights, Rising Seas, and Refugees

On that front, climate justice advocates have turned to more specific provisions within human rights instruments, especially those that pertain to particularly vulnerable populations: Indigenous peoples, those in areas of high level rise, and refugees. We saw some of this in the litigation surrounding Standing Rock and the Bagua conflict, where lawyers cited treaty obligations and conventions on Indigenous rights, with mixed results. In 2005, the Inuit Circumpolar Conference submitted a petition on behalf of Inuit peoples in the Canadian and U.S. Arctic to the Inter-American Commission on Human Rights, a branch of the Organization of

American States which, like its Filipino counterpart, has the power to investigate human rights violations and to recommend government actions, though it lacks any enforcement power. The petition described how global warming melts sea ice and permafrost, affects the health of humans and prey species, and disrupts weather patterns; these injuries, the Inuit claimed, were caused largely by U.S. greenhouse gas emissions, in violation of the United States' obligation to protect rights to culture, land, property, life, and health under agreements like the American Declaration of the Rights and Duties of Man and the International Convention on Civil and Political Rights.[418] A year later, the Commission rejected the petition, saying simply: "the information provided does not enable us to determine whether the alleged facts would tend to characterize a violation of rights protected by the American Declaration."[419]

In a related decision, the Commission's judicial wing, the Inter-American Court of Human Rights—whose jurisdiction neither Canada nor the United States recognizes—responded to a 2017 request for an advisory opinion on whether states are bound to respect environmental rights. The request came from the government of Colombia, which was particularly concerned about

---

418 Petition to the Inter American Commission on Human Rights Seeking Relief from Violations Resulting from Global Warming Caused by Acts and Omissions of the United States, No. P-1413-05 (Inter-American Commission on Human Rights Dec. 7, 2005), available at http://climatecasechart.com/non-us-case/petition-to-the-inter-american-commission-on-human-rights-seeking-relief-from-violations-resulting-from-global-warming-caused-by-acts-and-omissions-of-the-united-states/.

419 Letter from Ariel E. Dulitzky to Paul Crowley Re: Sheila Watt-Cloutier et al., Petition No. P-1413-05, (Inter-American Commission on Human Rights Nov. 16, 2006), available at http://climatecasechart.com/non-us-case/petition-to-the-inter-american-commission-on-human-rights-seeking-relief-from-violations-resulting-from-global-warming-caused-by-acts-and-omissions-of-the-united-states/.

the impact of rising seas on the Caribbean region. In its response, the court recognized "the existence of an undeniable relationship between the protection of the environment and the realization of other human rights"[420]—basically, the same point made by the *Urgenda* decision and others that you cannot respect traditional human rights without taking into account the environment. But the court went a step further, declaring that there is an "autonomous" right to a healthy environment, which, "unlike other rights, protects the components of the environment, such as forests, rivers and seas, as legal interests in themselves, even in the absence of the certainty or evidence of a risk to individuals."[421] As this was an advisory opinion, it had no immediate effect beyond its potential use as persuasive precedent.

Building on some of the same principles, a group of Indigenous communities from Louisiana and Alaska—including the Native Village of Kivalina, which launched one of the first common-law climate lawsuits against the United States (see Chapter 1, note 51)—submitted a complaint to a group of U.N. special rapporteurs, who are responsible for investigating human rights violations. The communities alleged that the U.S. government was violating various international obligations by allowing their lands to be destroyed by sea-level rise and other climate injuries, and demanded recognition of their rights and assistance with relocation.[422] The petition is still under review.

420 Advisory Opinion OC-23/17, 21, Inter-American Court of Human Rights (Nov. 15, 2017), available at http://climatecasechart.com/non-us-case/request-advisory-opinion-inter-american-court-human-rights-concerning-interpretation-article-11-41-51-american-convention-human-rights/.

421 *Id.* at 28.

422 Complaint re: Rights of Indigenous People in Addressing Climate-Forced

Another obvious nexus between human rights law and climate change involves climate refugees. Particularly in the Pacific, many people are already being forced from their homes due to sea-level rise and increased storm activity. In 2014, New Zealand's Immigration and Protection Tribunal granted residence to a family from Tuvalu which had filed a humanitarian appeal based in part on the risk of displacement by climate change, although the tribunal withheld judgment on whether such claims would be entertained in the future.[423] In 2020, the United Nations Human Rights Committee ruled for the first time that deporting an asylum seeker back to an area threatened with imminent harm from global warming may amount to a violation of the Covenant on Civil and Political Rights. This was a significant legal finding, though it didn't do much for Ioane Teitiota, the petitioner from Kiribati seeking asylum in New Zealand, because the Committee found that he had failed to prove any immediate danger, that there was the possibility of remedial measures fixing the problem in Kiribati, and—in a version of the common refrain—that the risks he faced were not sufficiently particularized, as they applied to Kiribati as a whole and not just to Teitiota.[424]

Displacement, submitted to United Nations Special Rapporteurs," (Jan. 15, 2020), available at http://climatecasechart.com/non-us-case/rights-of-indigenous-people-in-addressing-climate-forced-displacement/.

423 *In re: AD (Tuvalu)*, [2014] NZIPT 501370-371, Immigration and Protection Tribunal of New Zealand (June 4, 2014), available at http://climatecasechart.com/non-us-case/in-re-ad-tuvalu/.

424 Views adopted by the Committee under article 5 (4) of the Optional Protocol, concerning communication No. 2728/2016 (advance unedited version) (United Nations International Covenant on Civil and Political Rights Human Rights Committee, Jan. 7, 2020), available at http://climatecasechart.com/non-us-case/ioane-teitiota-v-the-chief-executive-of-the-ministry-of-business-innovation-and-employment/.

The upshot of these efforts? Climate rights are proceeding, if in piecemeal fashion, and it seems likely that in the coming years international bodies and some domestic courts will turn more and more to international agreements and to regional and national human rights instruments to hold governments' feet to the fire. We have even seen some affirmative, environment- or climate-specific rights take shape, as in the ruling of the Inter-American Court of Human Rights.

But litigation in this area remains vulnerable to some of the conceptual pitfalls we have encountered in all aspects of climate law: the law-politics distinction, the emissions contribution conundrum, and the particularization problem. Is it possible to circumvent these barriers by adopting a different legal paradigm altogether?

Enter the public trust doctrine.

Who Owns Nature?

Legal protections for the environment have always run up against one major obstacle: property rights. Especially in the United States, the idea that people can do with their belongings as they see fit—and the idea that people, land, trees, and animals can be belongings—are, or have been, items of basic constitutional faith. As a result, environmental law has tended to operate from the disabling premise that any imposition on property is legally suspect.

Let's invert this presumption. Assume instead that non-human nature belongs to all of us in common. Any individual initiative to farm, hunt, mine, or dam requires communal assent, because the public good is prior to private carve-outs. Environmental protection is the rule rather than the exception. Polluting activity is inherently suspect.

This, in a nutshell, is the idea behind the public trust doctrine. Nature—let's call it "natural resources"—belong to the public. They are held in "trust" by the government, in the same way that you might hold an inheritance in trust for a granddaughter: you have to guard it against diminution or misuse. To get technical, natural resources are the trust *res*, Latin for "thing," and all of us are the beneficiaries. The state is the guardian, or trustee. The law's main relationship to the environment thus lies in preventing damage to the *res* rather than preventing infringement on property rights. Mutual flourishing ensues.

So far, there is nothing particularly controversial about this, at least from a legal standpoint. The public trust doctrine is universally recognized in U.S. jurisdictions, and it appears in some guise in almost every state-centered legal system. Public trust advocates claim that the idea has a direct lineage from Roman law through the English common law and into the U.S. legal system, although the picture is a bit murkier: the sovereign responsibility to protect natural resources like navigable waters has long been recognized, but so too has the right of the state to "alienate"—sell off—these resources in the interest of economic development.[425] But since the nineteenth century, U.S. states have acknowledged that the public

---

425 For the debate on the history of the public trust doctrine, see Joseph L. Sax, "The Public Trust Doctrine in Natural Resource Law: Effective Judicial Intervention," *Michigan Law Review* 68 (1970), 471-566, 473; James L. Huffman, "Speaking of Inconvenient Truths: A History of the Public Trust Doctrine," *Duke Environmental Law and Policy Forum* 18 (2007), 1-103, 30; and Wood, *Nature's Trust*.

trust at least requires their governments to think hard before handing trust assets over to private hands.

What *is* controversial is the precise extent of this public trust. Traditionally, it has been applied to water; *Black's Law Dictionary* defines the "public-trust doctrine" as "[t]he principle that navigable waters are preserved for public use, and that the state is responsible for protecting the public's right to the use."[426] This makes sense: we don't want people drawing boundary-lines around rivers, lakes, and oceans, and these are seldom included on the list of natural items that someone can claim as property. The public trust doctrine is the reason why you're allowed to walk along the beach in most states, even if a millionaire controls the access points. And it's the reason why the Supreme Court forbade the city of Chicago from selling off a large section of its Lake Michigan waterfront to a railroad company in 1892; the Court wrote that "[t]he state can no more abdicate its trust over property in which the whole people are interested, like navigable waters and soils under them . . . than it can abdicate its police powers in the administration of government and the preservation of the peace."[427]

Great. So now that we know that many natural features besides rivers and lakes are important for public health and well-being, we can just extend the public trust doctrine to the mountains, valleys, and air—right?

Some law professors think so. In 1970, Joseph Sax, an early luminary of environmental law, published an article urging judges to take hold of this age-old principle and employ it to protect

426 *Black's Law Dictionary*, Bryan A. Garner, ed. (St. Paul, MN: West, 2009).
427 *Ill. Cent. R.R. Co. v. Illinois*, 146 U.S. 387, 453 (1892).

against problems like pesticide use and strip mining.[428] In the early years of modern U.S. environmentalism, there were signs that Sax's approach was taking hold: in 1983, the California Supreme Court relied on the doctrine to order the state to revisit its decision allowing Los Angeles to divert water flowing into Mono Lake.[429] But you should know by now that there is always room for competing interests: even if a court agrees that the public trust extends to a city park, for example, it might still allow the construction of a school to serve the equally important goal of educating the nation's youth.[430]

Here's how Mary Wood, professor of environmental law at the University of Oregon, explains the need for an expanded public trust in her 2014 book, *Nature's Trust: Environmental Law for a New Ecological Age*:

> Aided by government, mega-corporations seize astonishing amounts of property belonging to the citizens in common. This looting creates razed forests, toxic watersheds, ocean dead zones, suburban sprawl, decapitated mountains, ocean oil geysers, vanished species, and climate crisis. While this wreaks havoc for countless citizens, it provokes only dim outcry from the public, because the political frame surrounding environmental law conceals the public property character of these resources and thus obscures the sovereign's obligation in managing them.[431]

---

428 Sax, "The Public Trust Doctrine in Natural Resource Law: Effective Judicial Intervention."

429 *Nat'l Audubon Soc'y v. Superior Court of Alpine Cty.*, 658 P.2d 709, 732 (Cal. 1983).

430 *Paepcke v. Pub. Bldg. Comm'n of Chicago.*, 263 N.E.2d 11, 21 (Ill. 1970).

431 Wood, *Nature's Trust*, 165.

As the climate crisis coalesced, and as the entropy of U.S. environmental law became evident, another candidate for public trust *res* appeared: the atmosphere. The atmospheric trust doctrine, elaborated by Professor Wood, is pretty much exactly what it sounds like. The atmosphere is something we all depend upon, so let's consider it the trust property of the state and enact measures to prevent its degradation. In this scheme, we would treat "all nations on Earth as co-tenant sovereign trustees of [the] atmosphere, bound together in a property-based framework of corollary and mutual responsibilities."[432]

In 2011, the Oregon-based nonprofit Our Children's Trust put this doctrine to the test, coordinating legal actions on behalf of youth plaintiffs in all fifty states. These actions ranged from lawsuits demanding comprehensive climate change policies to agency petitions asking for updated regulations; they all sought court orders to reduce carbon emissions at least 6 percent a year from 2013 onward.[433]

Many of these efforts failed early: for example, the Arizona Court of Appeals found that, even if the public trust includes the atmosphere, there was no constitutional provision that would allow it to remedy the state's inaction in protecting that trust.[434] Other cases made headway. In 2016, a Washington state trial court agreed that the public trust includes the atmosphere and that the state Department of Ecology had a trust duty to promulgate regulations reducing emissions. Although this decision was later

---

432 *Id.* at 221.

433 *Id.* at 227-9.

434 *Butler v. Brewer,* No. 1 CA-CV 12-0347 (Ariz. Ct. App., Mar. 14, 2013).

overturned on administrative law grounds, the atmospheric trust principle survived.[435] In New Mexico, an appellate court held that the state had a public trust duty to protect the atmosphere, but that the courts could not intervene to independently enforce it even though the state had just scrapped its greenhouse gas emission regulations.[436] Advocates have launched atmospheric trust suits in Uganda, Canada, Pakistan, and elsewhere; these are all awaiting court rulings.[437]

This first wave of youth-led climate litigation accomplished more in the terms of organizing and awareness than it did in doctrinal change. Although the atmospheric trust idea has started to win some judicial recognition, it has not yet really altered how governments address global warming. But this first step prepared the way for another suite of cases that has had more tangible impact. An Our Children's Trust case in Massachusetts, for example, won a ruling from the state's highest court ordering the Department of Environmental Protection to enact specific greenhouse gas emissions requirements, even though the agency argued that various programs like a cap and trade program were sufficient under the state's Global Warming Solutions Act.[438] Ongoing cases in Montana, Florida, Alaska, and other states seek similar rulings, often based not on the atmospheric trust doctrine per se but on related

---

435 *Foster v. Wash. Dept. of Ecology*, No. 75774-6-1 (Wash. Ct. App., Sep. 5, 2017).

436 *Sanders-Reed ex rel. Sanders-Reed v. Martinez*, 350 P.3d 1221 (N.M. Ct. App. 2015).

437 See "Public Trust: Suits against governments," *Sabin Center for Climate Change Law Non-U.S. Climate Litigation Database* (2020), http://climatecasechart.com/non-us-case-category/public-trust/.

438 *Kain v. Dep't of Envtl. Prot.*, 49 N.E.3d 1124 (2016).

arguments about governments' constitutional responsibility to protect the climate from degradation.

We have already seen versions of these arguments: the state has to protect life, liberty, and property, and it can only do so by preventing catastrophic global warming. Our Children's Trust has breathed new life into these notions by building on the atmospheric trust concept to formulate a constitutional right to a stable climate system. The main audition of this idea has come not in the state cases but in a single lawsuit directed at the federal government: *Juliana v. United States*.

By far the most prominent climate litigation effort to date in the United States, *Juliana* combines many of the ideas we've explored thus far: the inadequacy of existing environmental law, the role of courts in a crisis, and the existence of sovereign duties to address global warming. It is also a shock test for the legal system: if *this* case cannot win, what hope is there for incremental reform?

Let's see how the courts have handled the pressure.

The Climate Case of the Century

Eugene, Oregon—home to Douglas firs, Olympic runners, and tie-dyed Ken Kesey disciples—is the unofficial capital of environmental law, or at least its activist wing. This small college city served as the base for many involved in the Earth Liberation Front in the early 2000s; needing a good lawyer, they turned to the local Civil Liberties Defense Center, led by Lauren Regan, which has built on its work fighting against the Green Scare to become one of the leading activist defense organizations in the country (it also led the Valve Turner defense team). The University of Oregon, which is based in Eugene, is home to some of the world's best environmental law faculty, including Mary Wood. After hearing Wood speak about the public trust at the law school's Public Interest Environmental Law Conference, Julia Olson founded Our Children's Trust in town.

In 2015, the organization sued the federal government for inaction on climate change. The complaint described how global warming injured its large list of youth plaintiffs, many of whom called Eugene home and had been involved in other legal actions with the group: Kelsey Cascadia Rose Juliana, the lead plaintiff, spent her free time in the nearby forests, mountains, and oceans and ate local seafood and farm-grown food, all of which were at risk from things like reduced snowpack, wildfires, and increased algal blooms; she also alleged psychological and emotional harm from the awareness of what was happening to her home and her future. Xiuhtezcatl Tonatiuh M. of Colorado (a minor at the time of the filing, and thus listed without a last name), suffered harm to his "sacred indigenous spiritual and cultural practices to honor and protect the Earth."[439] The lawsuit also brought its claims on behalf of future generations, who were represented by climate scientist James Hansen as their guardian.

The complaint was blunt: the U.S. government was largely responsible for the climate crisis. As defendants, the suit named the United States of America, President Barack Obama, and a suite of department and agency heads, including the head of the EPA. "By their exercise of sovereign authority over our country's atmosphere and fossil fuel resources," the complaint read, "they permitted, encouraged, and otherwise enabled continued exploitation,

439 Complaint at 8, *Juliana v. United States*, 947 F.3d 1159 (9th Cir. 2020).

production, and combustion of fossil fuels, and so, by and through their aggregate actions and omissions, Defendants deliberately allowed atmospheric CO_2 concentrations to escalate to levels unprecedented in human history, resulting in a dangerous desta-bilizing climate system for our country and these Plaintiffs."[440]

The plaintiffs' legal theory included just about everything men-tioned in the preceding sections. The public trust is being damaged by climate change, and the U.S., as trustee, is liable for its failure to protect it. The Fifth Amendment guarantees the right to life, liberty, and property, but the government is violating these rights as it allows the climate crisis to spiral out of control. It is also vio-lating the Fourteenth Amendment's promise of equal protection under the law by allowing youth and future generations to bear the brunt of this harm. Finally, the "unenumerated rights" of the Ninth Amendment include "the right to be sustained by our country's vital natural systems, including our climate system," which is now at risk because of U.S. climate policy.[441]

The evidence backing these claims reads like a rap sheet of climate crime. The federal government has known since the 1960s that it needs to address anthropogenic climate change, and detailed predictions and plans for doing so have existed since 1990. Ignoring its own experts, the government has instead gone ahead with leasing federal lands for drilling, granting permits for oil and gas transmission, and providing huge tax breaks and subsidies to the fossil fuel industry—the legal infrastructure of the fossil fuel system seen in Chapters 1 and 2.

440 *Id.* at 2.
441 *Id.* at 92.

Notice how the *Juliana* approach sidesteps traditional environmental law. Although passing references are made to various statutory schemes that allow federal agencies to regulate carbon emissions or to fund overseas natural gas development, the crux of the matter is not what the federal government has or has not done with its environmental laws. The point is what it has done *despite* its environmental laws. At this level of constitutional generality, the only question is whether or not a right has been violated. If it has, then a remedy follows—or should.

Here's what the plaintiffs asked for: order the government to "prepare and implement an enforceable national remedial plan to phase out fossil fuel emissions and draw down excess atmospheric CO_2 so as to stabilize the climate system and protect the vital resources on which Plaintiffs now and in the future will depend."[442]

This was a long shot, to say the least. If the Supreme Court thought that the humble Clean Power Plan was excessively ambitious (see Chapter 1), what would judges do with a demand to overhaul the energy economy in the name of inviolable rights?

Well, they could take it seriously. And that's just what happened on November 10, 2016—two days after Donald Trump was elected—when Judge Ann Aiken of the Eugene Division of the federal District Court of Oregon ruled against the federal government's motion to dismiss the lawsuit. It was perhaps the most groundbreaking climate decision we've yet seen in this country.

A motion to dismiss simply that a lawsuit is fatally flawed, and that there is no need to go to trial before declaring a winner. A judge's role at this stage is to evaluate the legal substance of a

442 *Id.* at 4, 94.

plaintiff's claim, not to dig into the facts, which the court must assume are true as stated by the plaintiffs. For Judge Aiken, this meant deciding whether or not *Juliana*'s novel claims about climate rights held water.

In her ruling, Aiken accepted many of the basic premises that have proven hard for other courts in global warming cases to digest. The United States could be liable for climate harms, having caused a quarter of all historic greenhouse gas emissions. The plaintiffs had standing based on their specifically alleged harms, even if others suffered similarly. And the difficulty and unpredictability of fixing the problem was no reason not to try: "redressability does not require certainty."[443] Most crucially, Aiken refused to avoid dealing with the climate issue simply because it was "political": lots of rights questions are political, but this is not *carte blanche* for courts to ignore them.

On the public trust question, Aiken cleverly avoided answering whether the atmosphere is a trust *res* by noting that traditional trust resources, like the shoreline, are impacted by global warming: thus, there is a governmental trust obligation to protect against the harms of climate change. Although other courts had cast doubt on the federal government's public trust duties, Aiken assimilated the problem to the "fundamental rights" question of the plaintiffs' Fifth Amendment claim: is there a right to a stable climate?

For all the ink that has been spilled on this issue, Aiken's response was remarkably lucid and brief. "I have no doubt that the right to a climate system capable of sustaining human life is

---

443 *Juliana v. United States,* 217 F. Supp. 3d 1224, 1247 (D. Or. 2016), *rev'd and remanded,* 947 F.3d 1159 (9th Cir. 2020).

fundamental to a free and ordered society," she wrote. "To hold otherwise would be to say that the Constitution affords no protection against a government's knowing decision to poison the air its citizens breathe or the water its citizens drink. Plaintiffs have adequately alleged infringement of a fundamental right."[444]

In elaborating this idea, Aiken had some convenient precedent at hand. Just a year before, the Supreme Court had decided *Obergefell v. Hodges*, which recognized same-sex marriage as a "fundamental right." The Constitution obviously does not say this in so many words, but, as *Obergefell* described, courts have been expanding the list of rights—privacy, abortion, and even voting, none of which enjoy explicit constitutional protection—for centuries.[445] Courts may have a bizarre account of how this is done—judges can discover new principles in the "penumbra" of the Bill of Rights, for example—but the basic fact is that constitutional jurisprudence is as much about creating new law as it is about applying the old. Even assessing the constitutionality of government action—"judicial review"—is something invented by Justice Marshall, the fourth chief justice: nowhere does the Constitution grant judges this power.[446] If courts can decide that it's their job to "say what the law is," then surely it's reasonable for them to find a constitutional right to a "climate system capable of sustaining human life."

Aiken got this: at the end of her ruling, she noted that a "deep resistance to change runs through defendants' and intervenors' arguments for dismissal" and lamented the fact that "[f]ederal

444 *Id.* at 1250.

445 135 S.Ct. 2584 (2020).

446 *Marbury v. Madison*, 5 U.S.137 (1803).

courts too often have been cautious and overly deferential in the arena of environmental law, and the world has suffered for it."[447] The obvious solution? Step into the fray.

Alas, Aiken's boldness would be unique. If this first *Juliana* opinion signaled a potential sea-change in climate law, then what came next was a retreat of the tide: a re-assertion of the power of fossil law and a reversion to all the tired arguments we have heard from the mouths of its adherents.

Following Aiken's ruling, the youth plaintiffs and the United States began the discovery process, preparing and presenting expert reports on the scientific and legal questions contained in the complaint. In early 2017, in the waning weeks of the Obama administration, the government filed a required response to the allegations, admitting many of the facts about climate change but denying liability. But this government posture soon changed drastically: with Trump in office, the Justice Department put up stiffer resistance, jamming the court calendar with motions and cross-motions and questioning the admissibility of the plaintiffs' expert reports. Fossil fuel industry groups, who had asked to join the case in 2015, now jumped off, confident that the new administration would adequately represent their interests.

The government also asked a higher court to intervene in the proceedings, noting that Aiken's order was unprecedented. In October 2018, Chief Justice Roberts granted a stay on the eve of trial, a move reminiscent of the Supreme Court's intervention in the Clean Power Plan case. Although the Supreme Court later reversed this decision, the case now shifted to the Ninth Circuit,

447 *Juliana,* 217 F. Supp. 3d at 1262 (D. Or. 2016).

which sits between the district court and the Supreme Court and had received a clear signal from above that it should reconsider Aiken's decision on the motion to dismiss.[448]

The Ninth Circuit's opinion came in January 2020, and it bore all the hallmarks of a guilty judicial conscience. The court went out of its way to note the severity of climate change, and praised the plaintiffs' "compelling case that action is needed," which showed that "our elected officials have a moral responsibility to seek solutions."[449] Unfortunately, there was nothing that the court could do: "We reluctantly conclude . . . that the plaintiffs' case must be made to the political branches or to the electorate at large, the latter of which can change the composition of the political branches through the ballot box. That the other branches may have abdicated their responsibility to remediate the problem does not confer on Article III [federal] courts, no matter how well-intentioned, the ability to step into their shoes."[450]

The reasons for this evasion are familiar, but sketchy at best. The court described the implementation of a climate plan as "requir[ing] a host of complex policy decisions," which should be the purview of the other branches of government. It foresaw clashes with Congress over how to implement the plan, which would be improper. And it quoted a recent Supreme Court decision allowing racist gerrymandering

448 See "Juliana v. United States," *Sabin Center for Climate Change Law U.S. Litigation Database* (2020), http://climatecasechart.com/case/juliana-v-united-states/.

449 *Juliana*, 947 F.3d at 1175 (9th Cir. 2020).

450 *Id.* at 1175.

practices in North Carolina for the principle that federal courts should not get into the game of distributing political power.[451]

First response: this is a very skewed way of describing the plaintiffs' request for remedy and the proper role of the courts in "political" matters. Sure, fixing a rights violation involves policy decisions, but so does any intervention in matters of public import. To use the classic example, politics was squarely involved when the Supreme Court ordered the desegregation of public schools, and it's doubtful that the Ninth Circuit wants to overturn *Brown v. Board of Education*. Put simply, there is no clean distinction between law and politics. Deciding which you are doing—handling rights claims or meddling in policy—is a political decision in itself, and one so clearly affected by immediate pressures and personal preferences that the Ninth Circuit's pretense of neutrality is at best naïve and at worse an act of judicial bad faith.

Second response: this judicial deference to policymakers is suspect when policymaking is undemocratic. Nowhere in the Ninth Circuit's opinion is there acknowledgment of the fact that our executive and legislative branches are fundamentally compromised by their allegiance to the fossil fuel industry, which would seem to be a dispositive fact when discussing these branches' violation of constitutional rights. The grade-school civics class encomium to solve all our problems at the ballot box not only ignores the profound political role that courts have played since the founding of our country—think *Brown*, *Roe v. Wade*, or *Citizens United*—it also reinforces a fantasy of purely election-based social change that, in the government's corrupt response to the climate crisis, has

451 *Id.* at 1173, *citing Rucho v. Common Cause*, 139 S.Ct. 2484 (2019).

met its ultimate rebuttal. As the Supreme Court of the Netherlands noted in *Urgenda*, one of the fundamental duties of constitutional courts is to ensure that political branches do their job. To refuse this obligation out of a reluctance to act "politically" is to simply deny the function of judicial oversight altogether. (To the Ninth Circuit's credit, the opinion withheld judgement on whether a right to a stable climate system exists. By passing over this matter in silence, the court allowed for future actions based on the same theory.)

At least there was an impassioned dissent from Judge Josephine Staton. She chastised her colleagues for "throw[ing] up their hands" in the face of an eminently justiciable case, and unleashed a series of rebukes that capture in brief the main critiques of existing climate jurisprudence:

> As the last fifty years have made clear, telling plaintiffs that they must vindicate their right to a habitable United States through the political branches will rightfully be perceived as telling them they have no recourse . . . The majority laments that it cannot step into the shoes of the political branches, but appears ready to yield even if those branches walk the Nation over a cliff . . . Where is the hope in today's decision? Plaintiffs' claims are based on science, specifically, an impending point of no return. If plaintiffs' fears, backed by the government's *own studies,* prove true, history will not judge us kindly. When the seas envelop our coastal cities, fires and droughts haunt our interiors, and storms ravage everything between, those remaining will ask: Why did so many do so little?[452]

Judge Staton agreed with Judge Aiken that a climate right existed. But she took the idea a step further: she argued for a "perpetuity

452 *Id.* at 1159, 1175, 1181, 1183-4, 1191 (9th Cir. 2020) (Staton, J., dissenting).

principle" according to which the Constitution protects against government acts that imperil the survival of the Republic.[453] This idea has gotten some good press in the climate justice world,[454] but we need to be wary of its implications. What defines the perpetuity of the Republic? Does it mean that the Capitol still stands, or that capitalism remains our dominant economic system? What is a threat? Is it just climate change, or could it also be socialism? And who decides? Climate scientists? Economists?

For all these misgivings, it is still refreshing to see a federal judge going *too* far in articulating rights related to global warming. Aiken and Staton's opinions will go down as some of the first disturbances of the U.S. judiciary's ignoble climate abstention, and legal activists are sure to make use of them in the near future. Indeed, municipalities in Colorado and New Hampshire have already adopted Judge Aiken's language into ordinances that recognize the "right to a healthy climate," demonstrating how environmental constitutionalism can spread from the judiciary to the legislative arena[455] (more on such local rights-based climate activism in a bit). Of course, within the courts themselves, Aiken and Staton's decisions are losing opinions, and it's highly unlikely that our arch-conservative Supreme Court will reverse the Ninth Circuit's dismissal of *Juliana*.

453 *Id.* at 1178.

454 See Robinson Meyer, "A Climate-Lawsuit Dissent That Changed My Mind," *The Atlantic* (Jan. 22, 2020), https://www.theatlantic.com/science/archive/2020/01/read-fiery-dissent-childrens-climate-case/605296/; Mary Wood and Michael C. Blumm, "The dramatic dismissal of a landmark youth climate lawsuit might not close the book on that case," *The Conversation* (Jan. 23, 2020), http://theconversation.com/the-dramatic-dismissal-of-a-landmark-youth-climate-lawsuit-might-not-close-the-book-on-that-case-130162.

455 Dana Drugman, "N.H. Town Passes Law Recognizing Right to a Healthy Climate," *Climate Liability News* (March 14, 2019), https://www.climateliabilitynews.org/2019/03/14/exeter-new-hampshire-right-healthy-climate/.

So, for now, at least, despite the best effort of climate constitutionalism, the federal government has received judicial approval for its climate-wrecking activities.[456]

Expanding the Circle

That means it's time to think about legal strategies that go beyond even the constitutional framing of *Juliana*. Let's move another step up on the ladder of ambition and one step down into the fundaments of the law, and think about what it would mean to grant rights to nature itself.

Uniting the various climate law theories we've examined so far—from the expansion of the Clean Air Act to the Ninth Amendment's unenumerated rights—is the assumption that nature is an object of regulation. It has no voice in court—the court docket always depicts a conflict between one or more groups of humans—and its interests are merely those of the people it affects. Even under the public trust doctrine, nature remains a collection of property assets to be protected against misuse.

Common-sensical as the exclusion of nature from legal personhood may seem—when is the last time a tree took the stand?—it does not jibe with the philosophical reorientation that environmentalists are urgently pressing upon us. If we want to pull out of our ecological tail-spin, the story goes, we must surely find ways of relating to our natural surroundings that go beyond ownership, mastery, and perhaps even stewardship. Providential visions of a pastoral Earth happily subdued to human guidance have burned

456 For a fuller account of *Juliana* and the defendants and attorneys involved, *see* Lee van der Voo, *As the World Burns: The New Generation of Activists and the Landmark Legal Fight Against Climate Change* (New York: Workman, 2020).

away in the chaos of climate change, species extinction, and myriad other catastrophes. Shouldn't our legal system reflect something of this turn to ecocentric values?

The rights of nature movement answers in the affirmative. At once a campaign for legal reform and an ethical program dressed in judicial language, this movement seeks a short-cut around the thicket of environmental law by granting natural entities a much more central role in the legislation and litigation that concerns them. It aims, in short, to make nature a bearer of rights and a party with standing to sue.

There are two main intellectual sources for this campaign. First, the Western Enlightenment tradition has bestowed social value and political recognition through the granting of rights, slowly and imperfectly expanding its "circle of concern" to women, racial minorities, the poor, and children. In the United States, commitment to a natural law conception of rights—one in which rights are prior to, rather than dependent upon, the state—is especially strong, as evidenced by the persistent reliance on rights rhetoric by movements for social change.[457] For some, nature rights are an obvious next step as the environment enters political center stage and as we better understand the science of Earth systems. Though a minority tendency, respect for the autonomy and dignity of non-humans—seen in Pythagoras's belief in vegetal souls and Jeremy Bentham's campaign against animal cruelty—has always existed

---

457 Roderick Nash makes the most comprehensive case for the historical conti-
nuity between today's nature rights movement and the rights campaigns of
past liberation struggles in *The Rights of Nature: A History of Environmental
Ethics* (University of Wisconsin Press, 1989).

in Western culture alongside the more familiar theories of human dominion and inert nature.[458]

A subset of this tradition involves the spiritual commitment to the dignity of nonhumans, seen especially in the contributions of the U.S. Catholic priest and philosopher of religion Thomas Berry. As part of his theory of the "universe story"—in which the cosmos has been moving toward ever-greater subjectivity, diversity, and communion—Berry elaborated ten principles of "Earth jurisprudence." These include the propositions that "[t]he universe is composed of subjects to be communed with, not objects to be used. As a subject, each component of the universe is capable of having rights" and that "[a]ll rights are role-specific or species-specific, and limited. Rivers have river rights. Birds have bird rights. Insects have insect rights. Humans have human rights. Difference in rights is qualitative, not quantitative. The rights of an insect would be of no value to a tree or a fish."[459] In recent decades, Earth jurisprudence and the related movement for "Earth law" has been an important nexus for nature rights activism around the world.[460]

Unsurprisingly, this discussion of the rights of nature emerged in the Unites States in tandem with the birth of modern environmentalism and environmental law. As was the case with the political effort to control water and air pollution, ecological

458 For a good summary of this tendency as it relates to the rights of nature, see Oliver Houck, "Noah's Second Voyage: The Rights of Nature as Law," *Tulane Environmental Law Journal* 31 (2017-2018), 1-50.

459 Thomas Berry, *Evening Thoughts: Reflecting on Earth as Sacred Community*, Mary Evelyn Tucker, ed. (San Francisco: Sierra Club Books, 2006), 149-50.

460 See Judith E. Koons, "At the Tipping Point: Defining an Earth Jurisprudence for Social and Ecological Justice" *Loyola Law Review, New Orleans* 58, no. 2 (2012), 349-390.

science provided an impetus for nature rights. Conservationist Aldo Leopold, for example, built on the growing understanding of biodiversity to press for wildlife management policies, and in *A Sand County Almanac* defined what he called the "land ethic": "A thing is right when it tends to preserve the integrity, stability, and beauty of the biotic community. It is wrong when it tends other-wise."[461]

The key text for rights of nature advocates in the U.S. is law professor Christopher Stone's 1972 article "Should Trees Have Standing?: Toward Legal Rights for Natural Objects." In it, Stone notes the steady progression of rights recognition in the United States, and points out that the legal system already respects the rights of many inanimate objects such as corporations, trusts, municipalities, and ships. Such respect should be afforded the environment, too: without the ability to launch legal actions, suffer legal injuries, or win legal remedies, nature can only be indirectly represented by humans who happen to share its interests: "It is not inevitable, nor is it wise, that natural objects should have no rights to seek redress in their own behalf. It is no answer to say that streams and forests cannot have standing because streams and forests cannot speak. Corporations cannot speak either; nor can states, estates, infants, incompetents, municipalities or universities. Lawyers speak for them, as they customarily do for the ordinary citizen with legal problems." Stone also stressed the "psychic and socio-psychic aspect of rights": that is, the extra persuasive

---

461 Aldo Leopold, *A Sand County Almanac* (New York: Ballantine Books, 1970), 262.

charge that holding a right—as opposed to merely enjoying administrative protection—carries both in and outside the courtroom.[462]

Stone's case was compelling enough to convince Supreme Court Justice William O. Douglas, a dedicated outdoorsman, who called for granting the rights of nature in a dissenting opinion that same year.[463] The movement went dormant for some time—though occasionally attorneys would name an animal as a plaintiff in an Endangered Species Act case[464]—only to resurface in recent decades with the work of scholars like Klaus Bosselmann and Cormac Cullinan and in the legal activism described below. Relatedly, animal rights activists have in recent years pressed for legal protections for species like the chimpanzee.[465]

Just as important as the European and U.S. rights philosophies—and frequently underemphasized—is the contribution of non-Western legal systems, primarily those of Indigenous origin. Notice how the paragraphs above describe "our" legal system and "our" ideological shortcomings: this false universalism covers up the fact that, in many social and political traditions, something very much like the rights of nature already exists. While the terminology and the conceptual apparatus may be different, the fundamental notion—that nonhuman entities deserve equal respect and recognition—is the same. Tom Goldtooth, executive director of the

462 Christopher D. Stone, "Should Trees Have Standing?: Toward Legal Rights for Natural Objects," *Southern California Law Review* 45 (1972), 450-501, 464, 489.

463 *Sierra Club v. Morton*, 405 U.S. 727 (1972) (Douglas, J., dissenting).

464 *See, e.g., Citizens to End Animal Suffering & Exploitation, Inc. v. New England Aquarium*, 836 F. Supp. 45 (D. Ma. 1993); *Marine Mammal Protection Act); Hawaiian Crow v. Lujan*, 906 F. Supp. 549 (D. Haw. 1991).

465 *See* Steven M. Wise, *Rattling the Cage* (Cambridge, MA: Perseus Books, 2000).

Indigenous Environmental Network, cites North American examples like the concepts of Mitayuke Owasin (respect for all human and non-human relations) in the Dakota, Nakota, and Lakota traditions, Mino-bimaadiziiwin ("the good life") in Anishinaabe society, and the Good Mind philosophy of Iroquois nations.[466]

Most influential have been the South American Indigenous ideas usually translated into Spanish as "*buen vivir*" ("living well"): *sumak kawsay* in Quechua, *suma qamaña* in Aymara, and *ñandareko* in Guaraní. Broadly speaking, *buen vivir* refers to harmonious relations with the self, other humans, and the natural world, which is referred to as *Pacha Mama* in Quechua and Aymara. When it comes to questions of economic development and environmental protection, the framework of *buen vivir* usually pushes against exclusively extractivist strategies and in favor of regimes and policies that promote Indigenous self-governance over neocolonialism.[467]

---

466 Tom B.K. Goldtooth, "Indigenous Peoples Cosmovision, Conflicts of Conquest and Need For Humanity To Come Back To Mother Earth," in *Rights of Nature & Mother Earth: Rights-Based Law for Systemic Change*, Shannon Biggs, Tom Goldtooth, and Osprey Orielle Lake, eds., (Bemidji, MN: Movement Rights, Women's Earth & Climate Action Network, Indigenous Environmental Network, 2017), 15-19, available at https://www.ienearth.org/wp-content/uploads/2017/11/RONME-RightsBasedLaw-final-1.pdf. For the link between North American legal traditions and Stone's rights of nature, *see* Steve Pavlik, "Should Trees Have Standing in Indian Country?" *Wicazo Sa Review* 30, no. 1 (2015), 7-28.

467 See Eduardo Gudynas and Alberto Acosta, "El buen vivir o la disolución de la idea del progreso", in *La medición del progreso y del bienestar. Foro Consultivo Científico y Tecnológico, México*, Mariano Rojas, ed. (Mexico: Foro Consultivo Científico y Tecnológico, 2011) 103-110; Alberto Acosta and Esperanza Martínez. *Naturaleza Con Derechos: De La Filosofía a La Política* (Quito, Ecuador: Ediciones Abya-Yala, 2011); Antonio Luis Hidalgo-Capitán and Ana Patricia Cubillio-Guevara, "Deconstruction and Genealogy of Latin American Good Living (Buen Vivir). The (Triune) Good Living and Its Diverse Intellectual Wellsprings," in *Alternative Pathways to Sustainable Development: Lessons from Latin America*, Gilles Carbonnier, Humberto Campondónico, and Sergio Tezanos Vásquez, eds. (Boston: Brill, 2017), 23-50.

Indeed, the major advances in nature rights have occurred in the context of decolonial Indigenous politics in South America. In Ecuador, the left-leaning government of Rafael Correa convened an assembly to rewrite the nation's constitution. Although Correa himself frequently clashed with Indigenous groups and was opposed to the rights of nature project, the resulting 2008 constitution was the world's first to recognize such rights, as described in Articles 71 and 72:

> Article 71. Nature, or Pacha Mama, where life is reproduced and occurs, has the right to integral respect for its existence and for the maintenance and regeneration of its life cycles, structure, functions and evolutionary processes.
>
> All persons, communities, peoples and nations can call upon public authorities to enforce the rights of nature. To enforce and interpret these rights, the principles set forth in the Constitution shall be observed, as appropriate.
>
> The State shall give incentives to natural persons and legal entities and to communities to protect nature and to promote respect for all the elements comprising an ecosystem.
>
> Article 72. Nature has the right to be restored. This restoration shall be apart from the obligation of the State and natural persons or legal entities to compensate individuals and communities that depend on affected natural systems.
>
> In those cases of severe or permanent environmental impact, including those caused by the exploitation of nonrenewable natural resources, the State shall establish the most effective mechanisms to achieve the restoration and shall adopt adequate measures to eliminate or mitigate harmful environmental consequences.[468]

468 Republic of Ecuador, Constitution of 2008. Available at Georgetown University Edmund A. Walsh School of Foreign Service Center for Latin American

In referencing "Pacha Mama," Article 71 was clearly intended to constitutionalize a version of Andean reciprocal relations with natural entities. Note how in these provisions the state is empowered to enforce nature's rights—including the right to restoration—but that property owners are still entitled to compensation for takings. This clause, as well as others that recognize the right to economic development and the state's guardianship over nature, introduce countervailing values to any absolute nature right.

While much lauded as a significant advance in environmental protection, Ecuador's constitutionalization of nature rights has been controversial in application. Despite the existence of Articles 71 and 72, the Correa government proceeded with destructive extraction projects: the Yasuní-Ishpingo Tambococha Tiputini Initiative, for example, promised to ban oil drilling in the Yasuní National Park, home to many Indigenous communities, if foreign governments contributed half of the anticipated $7.2 billion drilling revenues the park offered. Ecuador received less than 1 percent of what it asked, and the government proceeded with extraction.[469] In Ecuadorian courts, judges have acknowledged the existence of nature rights, but have tended to balance them against other entitlements and have assessed government actions in much the same way as they did under the old environmental law paradigm: checking for compliance with assessment and consultation procedures.[470]

Studies Political Database of the Americas, http://pdba.georgetown.edu/ Constitutions/Ecuador/english08.html.

469 Louis J. Kotzé and Paola Villavicencio Calzadilla, "Somewhere between Rhetoric and Reality: Environmental Constitutionalism and the Rights of Nature in Ecuador," *Transnational Environmental Law* 6 no. 3 (2017), 401-433.

470 Craig M. Kauffman and Pamela L. Martin, "Testing Ecuador's Rights of Na-

In the view of some scholars, Ecuadorian judges need time to familiarize themselves with their new constitutional reality: although there is a lack of demonstrable advances in environmental protection in the country, increasing judicial references to Articles 71 and 72 suggest that the balance is shifting in favor of a nature-first approach.[471] Others argue that the main effect of Ecuador's rights of nature has been felt abroad, where they offer a concrete if ambiguous example of how legal systems might be reformed. In Ecuador itself, many Indigenous communities remain skeptical of the nature rights project. Although constitutionalization represents a positive step in integrating Indigenous values into the national sphere, these groups worry that bringing nature further into the ambit of the law might paradoxically subject their communities and environments to greater state control.[472]

In Bolivia, a pan-Indigenous Unity Pact helped to bring President Evo Morales and his Movement for Socialism to power in 2006. In 2009, a new Plurinational Constitution was adopted. It is worth looking at its preamble for an understanding of how nature

ture: Why Some Lawsuits Succeed and Others Fail." Paper Presented at the International Studies Association Annual Convention, Atlanta, GA, Mar. 18, 2016.

471 *Id.*; Hugo Echevarría, "Rights of Nature: The Ecuadorian Case," *Revista Esmat* 13 (2017), 77-85.

472 In 2018, the Amazonian Sarayaku people released the "*Kawsak Sacha*" ("Living Forest") declaration seeking recognition of the rights of the rainforest and the banning of extractive activities on their territory, in response to the Ecuadorian government's failure to prevent pollution in spite of the national constitution's recognition of the rights of nature. *See* Leila Salazar-López, "Sarayaku Launches Living Forest Proposal—*¡Viva Kawsak Sacha!*" (Amazon Watch, Aug. 10 2018), https://amazonwatch.org/news/2018/0810-sarayaku-launches-living-forest-proposal-viva-kawsak-sacha; *see also* E. Carolina Valladares and Rutgerd Boelens, "Extractivism and the rights of nature: governmentality, 'convenient communities' and epistemic pacts in Ecuador," *Environmental Politics* 26, no. 6 (2017), 1015-1034.

rights, at least in the Latin American context, are inextricably linked to Indigenous worldviews and decolonial struggle:

> In ancient times mountains arose, rivers moved, and lakes were formed. Our Amazonia, our swamps, our highlands, and our plains and valleys were covered with greenery and flowers. We populated this sacred Mother Earth with different faces, and since that time we have understood the plurality that exists in all things and in our diversity as human beings and cultures. Thus, our peoples were formed, and we never knew racism until we were subjected to it during the terrible times of colonialism . . .
>
> We take on the historic challenge of collectively constructing a Unified Social State of Pluri-National Communitarian law, which includes and articulates the goal of advancing toward a democratic, productive, peace-loving and peaceful Bolivia, committed to the full development and free determination of the peoples.

The constitution goes on to guarantee a suite of civil, political, and social rights, as well as the right to a healthy environment. At the same time, Articles 348 and 349 state that natural resources are the property of the people and are to be administered by the state.[473]

Nature rights do not appear in the Bolivian constitution itself; instead, the Unity Pact negotiated with the government to pass the 2010 Law of the Rights of Mother Earth, based on the Universal Declaration of Rights of Mother Earth that was adopted at an activist conference in Cochabamba, Bolivia earlier that year. The 2010 law charges the state with guaranteeing the "regeneration of Mother Earth," and mandates that "neither living systems nor

---

473 Bolivia (Plurinational State of)'s Constitution of 2009, available at https://www.constituteproject.org/constitution/Bolivia_2009.pdf.

processes that sustain them may be commercialized, nor serve anyone's private property." Article 5 states that "[f]or the purpose of protecting and enforcing its rights, Mother Earth takes on the character of collective public interest. Mother Earth and all its components, including human communities, are entitled to all the inherent rights recognized in this Law." Specifically, these are the rights to live, diversity of life, water, clean air, equilibrium, restoration, and pollution-free living. With regards to rights conflicts, the law says that the "exercise of individual rights is limited by the exercise of collective rights in the living systems of Mother Earth" and that the state must adopt the precautionary principle and develop policies for "balanced forms of production and patterns of consumption."[474]

In their specificity and scope, Bolivia's nature rights appear to surpass those of Ecuador, and, in 2012, the government passed an additional law to implement these rights. But what appeared to many international observers to be a more serious commitment to nature rights-based policymaking was complicated not only by the persistent and unavoidable problem of competing legal interests— for example, the 2012 law promoted "integral development,"[475] a vague goal that accommodated many exceptions to ecocentric planning—but also by fractures in the Indigenous movement that had brought Morales to power. Members of the Unity Pact withdrew from the nature rights legislative process over concerns that

---

474 Law 071 of the Plurinational State, Art. 2(3) and (5), Art. 5, Art. 7(1-7), Art. 6, Art. 8(2) (Dec. 21 (2010). Trans. Earth Law Center, available at http://f.cl.ly/items/212y0r1ROW2k2F1M021G/Mother_Earth_Law.pdf.

475 Law 300 of the Plurinational State (Ley Marco de la Madre Tierra y Desarrollo Integral para Vivir Bien), (Oct. 15, 2012), availabe at http://www.fao.org/fileadmin/user_upload/FAO-countries/Bolivia/docs/Ley_300.pdf.

environmental guarantees were being watered down. In short order, Morales embraced an economic strategy dependent on foreign sales of gas, and his government removed conservation protections in order to open up land for a massive highway construction project in the Amazon, angering many of his erstwhile allies.[476] The failure of nature rights to prevent these developments—similar to the early experience in Ecuador—lends credence to Indigenous and feminist critiques of a legal reform project still reliant upon the state's colonial and patriarchal legacies.[477] Morales' government was removed by a 2019 coup, only for his socialist movement to regain power in 2020 elections; debate over how best to implement the promise of nature rights will no doubt continue as the political situation develops.[478]

A brief pause before we move on. You'll have noticed that the emphasis in this section has shifted from judge-made law to popular constitutionalism, and that the key actors have been Indigenous political groups rather than environmental lawyers. Indeed, one

476 Louis J. Kotzé and Paola Villavicencio Calzadilla, "Living in Harmony with Nature? A Critical Appraisal of the Rights of Mother Earth in Bolivia." *Transnational Environmental Law* 7 no. 3 (Nov. 2018), 397-424. For a defense of the government's policies, see the essay by Álvaro García Linera, Morales's vice-president: "Geopolítica de la Amazonía: Poder hacendal-patrimonal y acumulación capitalista" (La Paz, Bolivia: Vicepresidencia del Estado Plurinacional, 2013), available at https://www.vicepresidencia.gob.bo/IMG/pdf/geopolitica_de_la_amazonia.pdf.

477 See, for example, Miriam Tola, "between Pachamama and Mother Earth: gender, political ontology and the rights of nature in contemporary Bolivia," *Feminist Review* 118 no. 1 (April 2018), 25-40 and Carmen Martínez Novo, "Ventriloquism, racism and the politics of decoloniality in Ecuador," *Cultural Studies* 32 (2018), 389-413.

478 *See* Rachel Ramirez, "How indigenous Bolivians lost faith in Evo Morales after the Amazon blaze," *Grist* (Nov. 27, 2019), https://grist.org/justice/how-indigenous-bolivians-lost-faith-in-evo-morales-after-the-amazon-blaze/; Ellen Taylor, "Evo Morales and the Rights of Mother Earth," *CounterPunch* (Nov. 29, 2019), https://www.counterpunch.org/2019/11/29/evo-morales-and-the-rights-of-mother-earth/.

theme throughout this book has been the global Indigenous movement's leading role in twenty-first century political ecology. Try as they might, colonial nations like the United States have generally been unable to assimilate Indigenous peoples into their constitutionally ordered polities, and these polities' poor response to ecological crisis has opened the door to new ways of thinking about sovereignty and environmental governance. Ecuador and Bolivia are the key examples; elsewhere, Indigenous mobilization has also been key to adjusting states' relation to nature.

"An Authentic Subject of Rights"

In New Zealand, for example, the legislature approved an agreement in 2017 with the Whanganui Iwi Maori people that recognized the rights of the Whanganui River, known as a living being under the name "Te Awa Tupua." The agreement, which had been signed years earlier, acknowledged that the river's ecosystem should be considered as an integrated whole—as opposed to a series of discrete locations subject to various property rules and restrictions—and that the Whanganui Iwi, who depend on the river, could act as guardians of the newly created "legal person."[479]

The formal adoption of the Te Awa Tupua agreement followed on the heels of a momentous decision from Colombia's Constitutional Court, which in 2016 recognized the legal personhood of the Atrato River. The Atrato flows through the Chocó department in the country's west, home to Afro-Colombians and various Indigenous groups. In recent years, mining and illegal

---

479 Te Awa Tupua (Whanganui River Claims Settlement) Bill, New Zealand Government Bill 129—2 (Mar. 20, 2017).

logging have contaminated the river and severely endangered residents' health and livelihoods, leading to claims of rights violations. In a 2016 decision, the court agreed, finding not only that the residents' fundamental rights to life, health, and well-being had been violated by the government, but that the Atrato itself was suffering injury as a legal subject. Noting that Colombia's constitution established a "social legal state" and not just a "legal state"—meaning that social, material, and cultural rights deserve as much respect as civil and political rights—the court found that this implied an "ecological constitution" in which biocentrism takes precedence over anthropocentrism. "According to this interpretation," the court wrote, "the human species is just one event in a long evolutionary chain that has lasted for billions of years, and is thus in no way the master of other species, biodiversity, natural resources, or the fate of the planet. Nature is thus an authentic subject of rights that must be recognized by the state." The Atrato, its watershed, and its tributaries were recognized as a "legal entity" entitled to protection and restoration, and the court ordered the creation of a guardianship panel for the river as well as plans to end illegal mining and restore the area's ecological health.[480]

In short order, Colombian courts recognized the rights of other rivers.[481] In 2018, the country's Supreme Court of Justice recognized the Colombian Amazon as a "subject of rights," finding that

480 Decision T-622, 22-3, 39-40, 41 (Constitutional Court of Colombia, 2016), available at https://www.corteconstitucional.gov.co/relatoria/2016/t-622-16.htm.

481 Elizabeth Macpherson and Julia Torres Ventura, "The Tour to Save the World: Colombia wins the Yellow Jersey for the Rights of Nature," *International Union for Conservation of Nature* (Sep. 3, 2019), https://www.iucn.org/news/world-commission-environmental-law/201909/tour-save-world-colombia-wins-yellow-jersey-rights-nature.

the "duty of human solidarity with nature" had been violated by deforestation, much of it linked to global warming and the state's failure to respect its commitments under the Paris Agreement and the interests of future generations.[482]

It should be noted that these remarkable opinions—which elegantly synthesize the Western Enlightenment rights tradition and the environmental concerns of the nation's Afro-Colombian and Indigenous peoples—are the product of a very progressive constitutional culture. In stark contrast to the hermetic and formalist style that characterizes the U.S.'s conservative federal judiciary, Colombian opinions often evince an engagement with a wide variety of international legal, historical, and anthropological source material, and pay close attention to the ways in which the law fails to accord with social and natural reality (the influence of this approach can be seen in the Bagua opinion issued by the Amazonas court of Peru, discussed in Chapter 3). A major advantage of Colombian constitutional law is the availability of direct pleadings, which permit injured parties to seek immediate constitutional relief without the arcane tests of standing and justiciability that have clotted our own system. If U.S. constitutional jurisprudence served as a model for Latin American countries in the nineteenth and early twentieth centuries, the political urgencies of the moment suggest that the vector of influence will now flow in the opposite direction.

Building on these decisions, international rights of nature are having their moment. Mexico City recognized them in its 2017

---

482 Decision STC4360-2018, 20, 45 (Supreme Court of Justice, Civil Division, Colombia, 2018), available at http://climatecasechart.com/non-us-case/future-generation-v-ministry-environment-others/.

constitution.[483] In India, a court recognized the legal personhood of the Ganges and Yamuna Rivers before being reversed by the country's Supreme Court.[484]

Although the U.S. Supreme Court is not about to follow the lead of its Colombian counterpart, there's nonetheless cause for hope in our country. Take the work of the Community Environmental Legal Defense Fund (CELDF). Based in Pennsylvania, CELDF has assisted in international efforts like the drafting of Ecuador's rights of nature provisions, and has worked with the Ho-Chunk Nation and the White Earth Band of the Chippewa to write legal personhood for nonhuman entities into their governing documents.[485] Its most significant contribution to the movement is its model of "community rights" legal activism, which seeks to combine direct democracy and the abolition of corporate personhood with the establishment of the rights of nature.

CELDF operates from an analysis very similar to the one justifying expansion of the public trust doctrine: our existing system of environmental law is broken, and we need more than technical fixes to address both political and ecological decline. Simply put, "sustainability is illegal under our system of law."[486] But in contrast to the public trust emphasis on state property stewardship, the community rights model vests hope for change in a doctrinal shift

483 Political Constitution of the City of Mexico, Art. 13(A)(3) (2017).

484 "India's Ganges and Yamuna rivers are 'not living entities,'" *BCC* (July 7, 2017), https://www.bbc.com/news/world-asia-india-40537701.

485 "Advancing Legal Rights of Nature: Timeline," *Community Environmental Legal Defense Fund* (2020), https://celdf.org/advancing-community-rights/rights-of-nature/rights-nature-timeline/.

486 Community Environmental Legal Defense Fund [CELDF], *On Community Civil Disobedience in the Name of Sustainability: The Community Rights Movement in the United States*, 1 (Oakland: PM Press, 2015).

away from the dominance of property rights and in a bottom-up model of constitutional reform that starts in municipalities.

CELDF's theory of change goes like this: "Democracy Schools" teach community organizers and residents about the ways in which the law promotes corporate profits and environmental harm. Municipalities then pass ordinances to target specific types of harmful business activity and to assert the priority of community and nature rights over the rights of corporations. In the past decade and a half, dozens of local governments have passed versions of these community rights bills, many of them including rights for nature. These ordinances usually contradict state and federal laws—thus the model of "collective municipal legislative civil disobedience"—and so the battles go to court. As in the legal activism of the Valve Turners and the movements studied in Chapter 3, this confrontation is deliberate: CELDF argues that legal change requires "frontally challenging long-settled legal doctrines as denials of the right to community self-government, and using eventual rulings as *proofs* of how the structure actually operates." This "nascent constitution-making" eventually moves up to the state and national levels, where CELDF envisions constitutionalizing nature rights and community self-government, restricting the personhood of corporations, and adding social and cultural rights to our eighteenth-century framework.[487]

Consider an ordinance that CELDF helped to pass in Tamaqua Borough in eastern Pennsylvania, where toxic sludge from coal mines has poisoned and killed residents. The ordinance notes

---

487 Id. at 28, 31. *See also* Thomas Linzey and Anneke Campbell, *We the People: Stories from the Community Rights Movement in the United States* (Oakland: PM Press, 2016).

that the Borough "has been rendered powerless by the state and federal government to prohibit the application of sewage sludge by persons that comply with all applicable laws and regulations," because, under our system of "preemption," municipalities generally can't outlaw commercial activity that a higher jurisdiction allows. Pennsylvania state law allows "persons" to dump toxic sludge. So Tamaqua Borough's ordinance declares that any corporation dumping sludge in the Borough will not be considered a legal person, effectively cutting off the problem at its legal source. Furthermore, corporations are barred from damaging the municipality's natural systems, and "Borough residents, natural communities, and ecosystems shall be considered 'persons' for the purposes of enforcement of the civil rights of those residents, natural communities, and ecosystems." All this is couched within the assertion of the right to self-government.[488]

Similar CELDF efforts have seen varying levels of success. The city of Pittsburgh recognized the rights of nature in 2010 in tandem with a ban on fracking.[489] Toledo recognized Lake Erie as a rights-bearing entity in 2019 to prevent toxic agriculture runoff.[490] As expected, the push-back to these moves was intense: the Ohio Chamber of Commerce and business interests organized a legal challenge to the Toledo ordinance, which a federal court struck down in 2020 because the lake's right to "exist, flourish,

---

488 Tamaqua Borough Sewage Sludge Ordinance, No. 612, Sec. 2, 3, 7.5, 7.6 (Sept. 19, 2006).

489 Pittsburgh Ord. No. 37-2010, § 1 (effective Dec. 1, 2010) codified at Pennsylvania Code of Ordinances, City of Pittsburgh, § 618.03(b).

490 "Breaking News: Toledo Voters Enact Lake Erie Bill of Rights," *Community Environmental Legal Defense Fund* (Feb. 26, 2019), https://celdf.org/2019/02/breaking-news-toledo-voters-enact-lake-erie-bill-of-rights/.

and naturally evolve" was deemed too vague under the Fourteenth Amendment (possible violators of the right would not know when they were violating) and because passing the law exceeded Toledo's authority as a municipality.[491] In Grant Township, Pennsylvania, a community rights ordinance that asserted the municipality's right to ban fracking was overturned in court, where a gas company pled violations of its own rights and was awarded over $100,000 in legal fees.[492] In early 2020, however, the state environmental protection agency reversed its earlier position and revoked the company's fracking well permit in light of the Township's ban.[493]

One of the most striking aspects of the Grant Township effort was the community's decision to legalize civil disobedience. In 2016, the local government passed an ordinance that allowed anyone to "enforce the rights and prohibitions of the charter through direct action" should the courts fail to uphold the Township's limitations on corporate power. This was a decidedly radical move: it asserted that the community's interest in a healthy environment trumped judge-made law. "If enforcement through nonviolent direct action is commenced," the ordinance read, "this law shall prohibit any private or public actor from bringing criminal charges

491 Order Invalidating Lake Erie Bill of Rights, No. 3:19-CV-434 at 5-6 (N.D. Ohio, Feb. 27, 2020). Toledo later dropped its challenge to the order. Sarah Donaldson, "Toledo drops LEBOR appeal," *Farm and Dairy* (May 12, 2020), https://www.farmanddairy.com/news/city-of-toledo-drops-lebor-appeal/612200.html.

492 Jon Hurdle, "Judge says Grant Township must pay $100,000 in legal bills after injection well dispute," *State Impact Pennsylvania* (Apr. 3, 2019), https://stateimpact.npr.org/pennsylvania/2019/04/03/judge-says-grant-township-must-pay-100000-in-legal-bills-after-injection-well-dispute/.

493 Letter from Scott Perry to Douglas Kuntz Re: "Yanity" Well Permit No. 37-063-31807-00-00, Pennsylvania Department of Environmental Protection (Mar. 19, 2018), available at https://celdf.org/wp-content/uploads/2020/03/Yanity-Letter-2.pdf.

or filing any civil or other criminal action against those participating in nonviolent direct action."[494]

The legalization of environmental civil disobedience represents the merger of court-based civil legal activism and the campaigns of people like the Valve Turners, who seek to make their ostensibly criminal actions in defense of the climate the new law of the land. Just like the necessity defense, Grant Township's approval of direct action in defense of environmental rights rebukes fossil law with a dose of progressive grassroots democracy.

What can we make of the rights of nature movement thus far? As is always the case in environmental law, there tends to be a sharp fall-off from imagination to implementation, and the examples of Ecuador and Bolivia call for a healthy skepticism. Nature rights are not a panacea. No constitutional or judicial declaration of ecological justice and ontological equity can solve the ecological crisis on its own, and organized industry resistance—aided by governmental bad faith—will continue to be a formidable problem. For example, voters in Orange County, Florida overwhelmingly approved a November 2020 ballot measure that grants legal standing to the Wekiva River and local watersheds, but in the same year the Florida legislature passed a law banning any local nature

494 Grant Township Ordinance No. ____-2016, Establishing a Right to Be Free from Prosecution for Nonviolent Direct Action Carried Out to Enforce the Grant Township Home Rule Charter's Rights and Prohibitions; Legalizing Nonviolent Civil Disobedience to Activities Authorized by Illegitimate State and Federal Laws and Court Rulings That Violate the Rights and Prohibitions of the Grant Township Home Rule Charter (2006), https://d3n8a8pro7vhmx.cloudfront.net/timdechristopher/pages/189/attachments/original/1462369094/Grant_DA_Ordinance_Final.pdf?1462369094; *see* Kate Stringer, "Faced With a Fracking Giant, This Small Town Legalized Civil Disobedience," *Yes!* (May 13, 2016), https://www.yesmagazine.org/environment/2016/05/13/faced-with-a-fracking-giant-this-small-town-just-legalized-civil-disobedience/.

rights provisions — a conflict that will have to be worked out in the courts and in the statehouse.[495] Political pressure is the only way to enforce new rights.

Still, the sheer creative power of nature rights is a definite asset for the climate justice movement. People tend to be inspired by the idea that we can expand our circle of ethical concern and our ideas of political belonging. More so than other types of legal activism, the rights of nature are in tune with the big-picture questions of morality and philosophy that motivate calls for things like energy democracy and the Green New Deal. If human-nonhuman relations are in need of a drastic fix, then nature rights are probably the law's best solution to date. The fact that they are a consistent plank in platforms for decolonial and Indigenous justice also demonstrates the way in which they are better-equipped than other, narrow environmental law ideas to bridge the gap between environmental policy and social equity.

A consistent critique of nature rights questions their feasibility. How are we supposed to know what nature wants? Who gets to speak for the trees? And will rivers now have the right to flood poor people's homes? While it's true that there are important procedural questions to be resolved, these concerns are not really all that troublesome. By and large, we have a good idea of what makes ecosystems flourish and what makes them suffer; human health is often a good index of this. Guardianship and citizen-suit provisions in the constitutions and court cases above, which allow either designated

---

495 Joseph Bonasia, "Rights of nature bolstered by Orange charter vote," *Orlando Sentinel* (Nov. 12, 2020), https://www.orlandosentinel.com/opinion/guest-commentary/os-op-orange-rights-of-nature-invading-sea-20201112-jyr36yqpgvdunptsnasvdhcnvm-story.html.

parties or any person with a sufficiently close interest in the health of a natural entity to plead that entity's case, take care of the standing and speaking problems (we've also had centuries of experience representing the interests of voiceless minors and corporations in court). As for competing interests, there will always be lots to be worked out in practice. We already adjudicate conflicts between humans and nonhumans. The point of nature rights is simply to even the score a bit. And as the climate crisis shows, the environmentally-friendly path is often the human-friendly path as well.

Another objection to nature rights has to do with a resistance to legalism in general. We saw a version of this in Indigenous Ecuadorians' concern over expanding the reach of the state through Articles 71 and 72. In specific situations, there may well be reason to question the assertion of the power to adjudicate new areas of socio-environmental interaction. But overall, nature rights are not as much about expanding the reach of the law as they are about reducing the legal privileges of private and public actors who harm the environment. As the activism of CELDF demonstrates, this legal change can, and should, dovetail with campaigns for other forms of social justice. We may well bemoan the prevalence of rights reasoning in our society, but the fact remains that, for now, law is the water in which we swim. We need better law even if we want to build toward a future in which law is no longer needed. As the philosopher Christine Korsgaard puts it in a discussion of animal rights: "the way that we organize ourselves is by making laws, which set the terms of our interactions and so unite us into an effective whole. If the law says it is permissible for a person to inflict torments on an animal in order to test a product, for instance, then there is nothing anyone can do to protect that animal. So it is one of those cases—and there are certainly others—in which the only thing that can afford protection against the power of the law is the law itself."[496]

The varieties of legal activism studied in this chapter operate from the same premise. Without naively accepting the ideological framework of the status quo, they seek to use the legal tools we have at hand to change humanity's relation to the environment. The climate crisis makes these campaigns ever more pressing. The fact that most of these efforts are too young to be properly evaluated for their efficacy is both a cause for regret—we could have used nature rights before we passed 350 parts per million of atmospheric carbon—and a reason to dedicate ourselves to their realization.

What the efforts to use private law, human rights, the public trust, and nature rights demonstrate is that we cannot rely upon traditional environmental law to topple fossil law. Instead, we need claims and concepts that more fundamentally recognize the ecological aspect of our politics and the impact of our politics on our ecology. At its best, climate legal activism both acknowledges this dependence and seeks to improve it—from a relationship of dominance and degradation to one of mutual dignity and well-being.

---

496 Christine M. Korsgaard, "Animals, Personhood, and the Law," *Think: Philosophy for Everyone*, 12 no. 34 (2013), 25-32.

Conclusion

Climate change imposes an uncomfortable power on the living. Quotidian activities—charging a phone, eating an orange—entail ramifying ecological effects on future generations, human and nonhuman. The degree of our acquiescence or resistance to the fossil fuel system affects tomorrow's society more than it does ours, as every delay in the transition to renewable energy produces growing suffering and loss in the years and centuries ahead. The injustices of our present world order—one aspect of which, fossil law, this book has explored—distribute this future-shaping power unevenly, magnifying the moral import of every present violation of right and dignity.

When seeking a standpoint from which to assess our society's response to global warming, then, it's useful to imagine how we would be judged by those unborn beings over whom we exercise such terrible control. And let it be noted that this "we" is not a universal subject, not a species-being in which all differences are effaced: it's shorthand for a global system of economic activity and political control, in which a minority commit the greatest depredations. Those passively or unwillingly part of this system, and those who contribute only a fraction of its injuries, have little to fear in the historical reckoning.

Taking the general view, what will today's law of climate change look like from the vantage of 2100, or 2300, or even 2500, when the emissions produced in the production and consumption of this book will still circulate in the atmosphere?

For one thing, our jurors of the future will look at 2021 and find the continued, unjustifiable, and irrational dominance of fossil law. At a time when there is no doubt that drastic measures must be taken to eliminate the use of fossil fuels as quickly as possible, our laws and structures of authority still by and large promote the production and use of oil, gas, and coal over healthier alternatives. This is the case both in the legal system's most fundamental doctrinal commitments, such as the protection of private property and the naïve faith in legislative action to address warming, and in its enforcement of the existing state of affairs through the criminal legal apparatus.

This indictment of fossil law may acknowledge the piecemeal progress of a countervailing force, modern environmental law. Great progress has been made in curbing the worst industrial abuses of human and natural health, and two generations of committed lawyers have won significant protections for water systems, clean air, and endangered species. But, more than fifty years after the field's birth—an era that curiously coincides with the appearance of the climate emergency in science and politics—it cannot be said to have lived up to its initial promise. Rather than tackling the root of the problem—capitalist growth—environmental law has endeavored to mitigate its worst effects. It must now transform itself into a practice that deals not with an ostensibly external nature but with the complicated relations of social and natural systems—a transformation that will likely erode its status as a sub-discipline. All law is now environmental, and the environment is not outside us.

Noting this shift, the future's judgment will also acknowledge that, for all its denial and delay, our era had started to pull the scales from its eyes. Decades of organizing, education, and resistance by activists and affected communities has finally started to produce state policies to reduce warming. The Paris Agreement, the Clean Power Plan, the national and state-level commitments to carbon-free economies: these at least signal that a change in direction is required, and quickly. We don't know yet how successful these policies will be. Our future jurors will likely find them inadequate. But there's hope that much more aggressive reductions will be built on these tentative advances.

Most of the content of this next wave of policymaking has already been laid out in detail. We know how to move our energy production entirely away from fossil fuels, and we know that we can do so within a few decades.[497] We know that climate justice involves much more than the substitution of fuel sources, as plans like the Green New Deal thoroughly describe how to design a social system that prioritizes low-carbon labor such as care work, meets the needs of the poor and sexual and racial minorities through

497 *See, e.g.*, Mark Z. Jacobson, Mark A. Delucchi, Mary A. Cameron, Stephen J. Coughlin, Catherine A. Hay, Indu Priya Manogaran, Yanbo Shu, and Anna-Katharina von Krauland, "Impacts of Green New Deal Energy Plans on Grid Stability, Costs, Jobs, Health, and Climate in 143 Countries, *One Earth* 1, no. 4 (Dec. 20, 2019), 449-463 (noting that 80 percent of fossil fuel use can be eliminated by 2030).

programs like reparations and community ecological resilience projects, and democratizes the economy through measures such as the partial public ownership of corporations.[498] The specificities of such proposals must be decided through political conflict. But we do not lack the imagination for the fight.

More pertinent to the themes of this book, our descendants will find in our time the seeds of a legal system to replace fossil law. Inchoate as many of these strategies and ideas might be, they already provide a rigorous grounding of utopian aspirations in existing legal forms. Chief among them are:

- The expansion of tort law, including scientifically reasonable theories of causation and attribution, an amplified conception of joint liability, and more just standards of standing and redressability;

- The public trust doctrine and the corollary atmospheric trust doctrine, involving the vigorous exercise of state power to preserve and improve natural resources on which all humans depend;

- Environmental rights, building off of existing human and constitutional rights to protect the interests in livelihood, health, culture, and property that are threatened by global warming and the construction of fossil fuel infrastructure;

- The rights of nature, providing the highest level of legal status for nonhumans and ecosystems and moving the legal system away from its anthropocentric bias, as well as

---

498 *See, e.g.*, Kate Aronoff, Alyssa Battistoni, Daniel Aldana Cohen, and Thea Riofrancos, *A Planet to Win*; Jacob Fawcett, "The Global Green New Deal," *People's Policy Project* (2019), https://www.peoplespolicyproject.org/wp-content/uploads/2019/06/GlobalGreenNewDeal.pdf.

acknowledging community rights against corporate and
state oppression;

- The climate necessity defense and its related theories
of justification, offering activists and Earth defenders a
means by which to seek social sanction for their direct
enactment of the principles above.

The preceding chapters have provided numerous examples of this
prefigurative law in action. The legal activists of tomorrow will
be able to build on the state and municipal lawsuits against fossil fuel producers in the United States, the success of the Dutch
Urgenda public trust and constitutional rights case, and the incipient acknowledgment of nature rights in Latin America and U.S.
communities.

Similarly, the story of the Valve Turners shows how extra-legal action is crucial to any project of legal reform. Revolutions in
rights do not originate in courthouses. The rapid growth of the climate necessity defense provides a case study of how direct action
translates radical ideas into legal doctrine, a process that must be
repeated over and over again as the ideals of climate justice move
from the margins of global power to its center.

One of the essential facts of the Valve Turner cases is that
the defendants acted in solidarity with the Water Protectors at
Standing Rock. As has been shown time and again in the book,
Indigenous movements represent the vanguard of climate justice,
and this is especially the case in the legal arena. Many of the most
important fossil fuel conflicts arise on Indigenous territory, and
these conflicts produce progressive jurisprudence like the Bagua
decision in Peru and constitutional advances like the Bolivian Law

of the Rights of Mother Earth. Our future jurors will note the irony that peoples and traditions recently condemned to the dustbin of Western history will prove to be some of the most important architects of a new society.

One question that remains unresolved in this focus on legal progress is what the precise role of the law should be in the transition from fossil fuels. Enthusiasm for courtroom victories can too easily dovetail with support for an expanded and increasingly unaccountable regulatory state, or for a model of technocratic global governance that would sever the (already tenuous) connection between popular power and climate politics.[499] Should we really invest our hope for change in judicial opinions and constitutional amendments?

Not exclusively, of course. As this book's focus on social movements and direct action demonstrates, such legal instruments never generate reform or revolution: they formalize it. So the emphasis on legal activism is an acknowledgment of the importance of a midway point between grassroots resistance and political victory. The judicial recognition of the climate necessity defense, for example, comes after years of civil disobedience and likely years before any comprehensive national climate policy. It's always worth fighting for this type of recognition in order to move the process of concrete change along.

There is also the problem of democratic accountability in the courts. Too often, judges act for the powerful and against the powerless and use their relative insularity from the legislative

---

499 This is the specter warned of in Jeff Wainwright and Geoff Man, *Climate Leviathan.*

and executive branches to promote elite interests. But this is not always the case: one need only recall the advanced Supreme Court decisions of the Civil Rights era, or the judge-made protections for dissident free speech, to see how the judicial branch can act as an agent of progressive democratic values. Climate change demands a similar intervention, as legislatures, executives, and regulatory agencies have time and again proven their obedience to the fossil fuel industry. Courts are one of the best avenues we have to make climate justice a policy of the state.

There should be a democratic consensus justifying such judicial intervention. If opinion polls are to be believed, this consensus already exists.[500] So establishing new environmental rights doesn't just provide a practical means of addressing the climate crisis; it also memorializes a popular judgment of which values and interests deserve protection. Hybrid forms of grassroots activism and legal reform, such as the Grant Township ordinances described in Chapter 4 that recognize nature rights, ban fracking, and legalize civil disobedience in defense of these laws, are one way to keep this judicial climate law project honest.[501]

500 Anthony Leiserowitz, Edward Maibach, Seth Rosenthal, John Kotcher, Parrish Bergquist, Abel Gustafson, Matthew Ballew, and Matthew Goldberg, *Politics & Global Warming, November 2019* (New Haven: Yale University, George Mason University, and Yale Program on Climate Change Communication, 2019), https://climatecommunication.yale.edu/wp-content/uploads/2020/01/politics-global-warming-november-2019b.pdf (finding, for example, that 69 percent of registered voters support a revenue-neutral carbon tax; 75 percent support regulating carbon dioxide as a pollutant; 62 percent support the president declaring a climate emergency in the event of congressional inaction; and 76 percent support U.S. participation in the Paris Agreement).

501 Jeremy Brecher offers a version of this argument—popular constitutionalism as a means of advancing climate justice—in *Climate Insurgency: A Strategy for Survival* (Boulder, CO: Paradigm Publishers, 2015).

But does reforming the rule of law necessarily extend rule *by* the law? This book has mostly been concerned with Western legal systems and their conception of the law as a universally applicable, rule-bound instrument of state power whose mandates are backed by the threat of violence. An emancipatory politics would seek to move past the coercion inherent in such a scheme, and, again, Indigenous traditions and legal thinkers have been central to efforts to realize a more consensual form of social order.[502] Describing such an order is beyond the scope of this book, but many of the pre-figurative legal projects described above—particularly those that remove natural systems from regimes of property and state control and grant them legal subjecthood while recognizing decentralized community decision-making as the means of protection—move incrementally from a model of unitary sovereign power to a vision of less formal governance.

For those working at the intersection of the legal system and climate change, the immediate task is to transform the law from an instrument of fossil-based capital to a tool of climate justice. Even as this new climate law may be used to reimagine the sovereign terrain on which it is deployed, it must, for the time being, engage its opponents there. Those suffering the worst effects of global warming need legal remedies now. Future generations require their interests to be represented in court. Nonhumans and ecosystems must have their voices heard, and, as the law is a human endeavor, that hearing will occur in the human language of rights.

---

502 For a good survey of these efforts, *see* Aaron Mills, "The Lifeworlds of Law: On Revitalizing Indigenous Legal Orders Today," *McGill Law Journal* 61, no. 4 (2016), 847-884.

We face a long age of climate instability. We are being judged by the future. To acquit ourselves, we will need to prove not only that we imagined the new law of climate change, not only that we advocated for it, but that we enforced it, too, in the courts and in the streets.

Author's Note

The dual role of author and advocate is an uneasy one. In this book, I've done my best to provide an objective survey of the law and legal concepts surrounding climate change—albeit with a bias toward my home country, the United States—while at the same time taking an affirmative position on the side of those resisting the fossil fuel system and articulating progressive alternatives to our existing legal regime. Readers can best judge my negotiation of those two commitments.

As a lawyer, I served on the legal teams of each of the Valve Turners. The particular description of these cases, as well as the analysis and judgments I provide, are mine alone, and should not be attributed to any of the clients or the other attorneys involved. The narrative contains no disclosures of events, personal details, or legal strategy that would violate the confidentiality of the attorney-client relationship, and, prior to publication, I gave each client the opportunity to review the manuscript and to offer any objections or critiques. All the information I provide on the cases can be found in publicly available documents.

Some acknowledgments are in order. I owe a debt of gratitude to the Valve Turners—Michael Foster, Leonard Higgins, Emily Johnston, Annette Klapstein, and Ken Ward—and their co-defendant supporters and journalists—Lindsey Grayzel, Reed Ingalls, Sam Jessup, Ben Joldersma, and Steve Liptay—not only for their courageous action, but for the opportunity to tell their story. The local counsel involved in the four Valve Turner trials—in Minnesota, Tim Phillips; in North Dakota, Mike Hoffmann and William Kirschner; in Montana, Herman Watson IV; in Washington, Ralph Hurvitz—brought tremendous courtroom skill to the cases, and, often short on time and without pay, devoted themselves to an effort that looked like a loser from the start. I'm glad we surprised some people.

Immense credit is due to Lauren Regan of the Civil Liberties Defense Center, who led and coordinated the Valve Turner legal team along with her associate Cooper Brinson. Lauren was my first movement lawyer mentor in law school: during the transformational summer I spent working for her in Eugene, I learned that there need not be a contradiction between a life of practice and a life of political and ethical commitment. The planet and its people are lucky to have her.

I am a staff attorney at Climate Defense Project, along with my co-founders Alex Marquardt and Kelsey Skaggs. We started our little legal non-profit just after graduating from law school, where we sued our university over its investments in fossil fuels and got a taste for climate movement lawyering. Their friendship, solidarity, and dedication has changed my life, and working with them has helped—to modify a phrase of Cornel West's—to feel a little less well adjusted to injustice. I cannot thank them enough for this gift.

In the climate justice movement, the efforts of organizers with Climate Direct Action and the Climate Disobedience Center have made the climate necessity defense a viable part of the fossil fuel resisters' toolkit. No advance in the law occurs without the sacrifice of people like them. The legacy of those who stood their ground at Standing Rock and at Bagua—not to mention at the countless other battles against fossil fuels, from L'eau Est la Vie to Burnaby Mountain—will be central to the future history of climate justice. They fight for all of us.

I could not have written this book without the perspicacious critiques and generous attention of some excellent readers: Alyssa Battistoni, Thomas Linzey, and Melissa Scanlan. Thank you.

I wouldn't have the freedom and privilege to do this work without my mother and father. Your loving care and support through all the years of my life has made all the difference. And to my sister: thank you for keeping me honest. I love you all.

Finally, I want to offer my deepest love and gratitude to Apollonya. You've made me who I am. I don't think every love affair also involves critical editorial assistance, so I count myself uniquely fortunate. You're my model of how to marry the love of learning with the love of the natural world. And to the boy from Atlantis: hang in there, little man. We're trying to make your world a better place.

All author proceeds from this book will be donated to Grassroots Global Justice Alliance, a group of climate justice organizations based in the United States that promote a just transition to a feminist economy.

About the Author

Ted Hamilton is a climate movement attorney, writer, and literary scholar. After law school, he co-founded Climate Defense Project, which provides legal assistance to climate justice activists. He lives in Worcester, Massachusetts.